Warlord Politics in China
1916-1928

HSI-SHENG CH'I

Warlord Politics in China
1916-1928

STANFORD UNIVERSITY PRESS
Stanford, California   1976

The research on which this book is based was
supported by the Center for Chinese Studies
of the University of Michigan

Stanford University Press
Stanford, California
© 1976 by the Board of Trustees of the
Leland Stanford Junior University
Printed in the United States of America
ISBN 0-8047-0894-0   LC 75-7482

Published with the assistance of
The Andrew W. Mellon Foundation

To my parents

Acknowledgments

In the preparation of this manuscript, I have benefited from the comments of many friends and colleagues on different sections: Andrew Nathan of Columbia University, James Sheridan of Northwestern University, and Jeffrey Obler and Joel Schwartz of the University of North Carolina. I am particularly indebted to Professor Tang Tsou of the University of Chicago, and Professors Albert Feuerwerker, Allen Whiting, and Ernest Young of the University of Michigan, for reading the manuscript in its entirety. All offered incisive criticisms that helped me to improve the quality of the final product.

I also wish to express my appreciation for the financial assistance I received. While a graduate student at the University of Chicago, I was given a Ford Foundation fellowship to work under Professor Morton A. Kaplan, who broadened my vista to include the potentiality of applying international political theories to the analysis of domestic politics. In 1969, an NSF grant allowed me to do research in New York for one summer. In 1970–71, I spent a year as a research associate at the Center for Chinese Studies, University of Michigan. I not only was given free rein with my time and provided with generous secretarial assistance, but was placed in the company of some of the most exciting and accomplished China specialists in this country. This intellectual atmosphere was all that a person could wish for in undertaking research of this kind.

Finally, I want to thank my wife, Ssu-wei, who never failed to provide moral support even during the bleakest of times. Without her cheerfulness, resourcefulness, and untiring encouragement, this study would never have been completed.

Contents

1. Introduction — 1
2. The Emergence of the Military Factions — 10
3. The Composition of the Military Factions — 36
4. Military Capabilities: Recruitment — 77
5. Military Capabilities: Training — 91
6. Military Capabilities: Weaponry and Tactics — 116
7. Economic Capabilities — 150
8. Normative Aspects of Military Politics — 179
9. The Chinese Political System — 196

    Appendixes
    A. Political and Military Leaders, 1916–1928 — 243
    B. Chronology — 246

    Notes 251   *Bibliography* 267   *Index* 277

Maps and Figures

MAPS

Provinces of China, 1916–1928	*facing p.* 1
Distribution of factional power in China, 1920, prior to the Chihli-Anhwei War	210
Distribution of factional power in China, 1922, on the eve of the First Chihli-Fengtien War	212
Distribution of factional power in China, 1924, at the conclusion of the Second Chihli-Fengtien War	216
Northern Expedition, 1926–1928	228

FIGURES

1. The Krech-Crutchfield-Ballachey sociometric model	62
2. Sociometric diagram of the Anhwei faction	69
3. Sociometric diagram of the Chihli faction	70
4. Sociometric diagram of the Fengtien faction	71

Tables

1. Educational Background of Division Commanders, 1916 and 1924 — 103
2. Educational Background of Highest Provincial Military Authorities, 1916–1928 — 104
3. Educational Background of Fengtien Militarists, 1924 — 105
4. Monthly Output of Armaments, China and Manchuria, 1923 and 1928 — 119
5. Highway Mileage in China, 1928 — 129
6. Mileage of Government-owned Railways, 1930 — 130
7. Number of Troops Mobilized for Major Wars, 1916–1928 — 137
8. Size of Major War Zones, 1916–1928 — 137
9. Casualties in Major Wars, 1916–1928 — 138
10. Distribution of Salt Gabelle Revenues, 1918–1928 — 155
11. Foreign Loans to China, 1916–1927 — 158
12. Revenue Received from Government Bonds, 1912–1926 — 159
13. Volume and Value of Feng-p'iao, 1916–1927 — 163
14. Opium Revenues Paid to Militarists in Eleven Provinces, 1924 and 1927 — 164

Warlord Politics in China
1916-1928

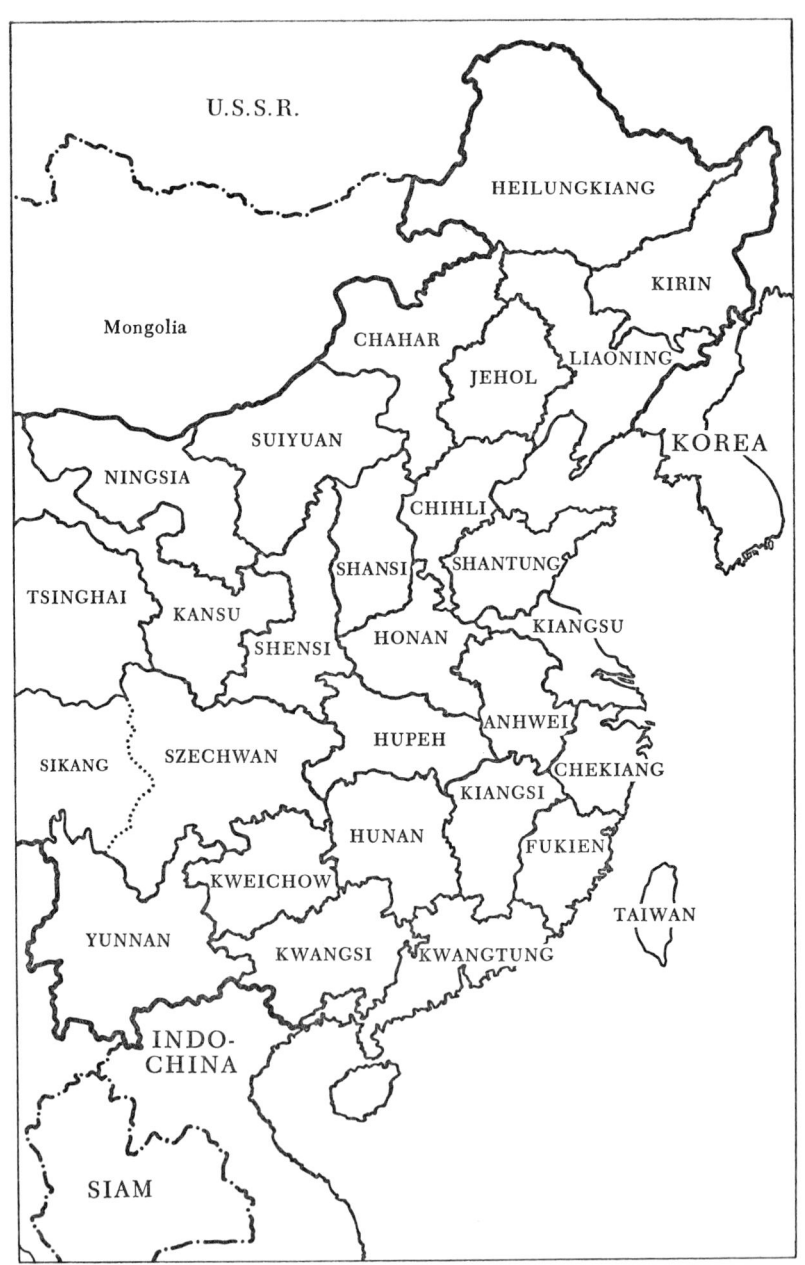

Provinces of China, 1916–1928

CHAPTER 1

Introduction

ANYONE who is even faintly familiar with modern Chinese history knows two things about the 1916–28 period: first, it was the "warlord" period, and second, it was a confused and destructive period.

The general interpretative works of modern Chinese political history usually accord very scant coverage to this period, usually in the form of an introduction to the Nationalist and Communist movements that followed. Even the more specialized studies usually fail to give a full and accurate account of the role of the "warlords." One suspects that the chief reason for this gap in the literature is the complexity and confusion that shroud the behavior of the political actors of this period, compounded by the difficulty of finding the appropriate conceptual tools to deal with them. The result is that "warlordism," or more appropriately militarism, remains the least understood phenomenon in modern Chinese history.*

---

* Throughout this book, the term "militarists" will be used to refer to individual political actors. Although "warlord" is a commonly used term, and is so used in the title of this book to denote a period of modern Chinese history, it is loaded with pejorative connotations. Even during the 1920's, there were always disagreements about who was a "warlord" and who was not and, more basically, about what the attributes of a "warlord" were. An admired military leader was never called a "warlord"; the term was reserved for a bad military leader. C. Martin Wilbur defines militarism as "a system of organizing political power in which force is the normal arbiter in the distribution of power and in the establishment of policy" ("Military Separatism and the Process of Reunification under the Nationalist Regime, 1922–1937," in Ho Ping-ti and Tsou Tang, *China in Crisis*, 1: 203). The following text similarly eschews value judgments; a "militarist is simply one who exercises power in such a system.

Some scholars have examined this period within a traditional legal-institutional matrix. While they acknowledge the existence of powerful military figures in politics, they nevertheless view China as a single political entity with the central government as the hub of political activities. This view naturally leads to the identification of the constitution, the presidency, the cabinet, and the parliament as the major components of the Chinese political system.

If China had had a stable political system, this kind of study could give us a penetrating understanding of the basic structure and processes of the Republic. The trouble is, however, that in the thirteen years after the founding of the Republic, China had at least four different constitutions, and all of them became dead letters as soon as they were promulgated. Other laws and regulations also shed little light on the nature and functions of the regime.[1] Most political institutions were also in a state of flux; the form of government alternated among monarchy, republic, regency, etc., a number of times during this brief period. In addition to the major institutional changes, the head of state changed nine times in less than twelve years between 1916 and 1928 in the north alone; the average tenure was less than sixteen months. In the south the same "musical chairs" phenomenon was occurring in the rival KMT government with equal abandon.

Confusion and instability also prevailed in the cabinet. Altogether, there were 24 cabinet reshuffles, and 26 persons held the position of prime minister during the 1916–28 period.[2] The longest tenure was seventeen months, the shortest was two days; the average tenure ranged from three to five months. The cabinet did not hold office long enough to lay down long-range policies. Furthermore, the cabinet was not an independent decision-making body functioning according to the fundamental laws of the Republic; rather, it was the most pliable administrative tool used by the militarists to impose their will upon the Chinese people.*

---

* If the cabinet had indeed been an institution to reckon with in national (northern) politics, one would expect the northerners to have kept this political power among their own fellow provincials. The opposite, however, was true. Of the 26 prime ministers and 95 cabinet ministers, the southerners outnumbered the northerners by almost two to one. (For biographical sketches of these ministers, see Ch'en Hsi-chang, *Pei-yang* 2: 517–40.) In view of the emphasis on interpersonal relations and local ties in political circles during this period,

Introduction 3

Little needs to be said about the parliament, which was even more discredited in the public eye than either the presidency or the cabinet. It followed a tortuous course of survival and was put out of business several times. It became an utterly corrupt, incompetent, and parasitic organization filled with petty politicians. During the 1920's it was split into the pro-Peking and pro-KMT factions, and it later simply withered away in the midst of public contempt. The acceptance of bribes by many members of parliament in 1923 to help Ts'ao K'un get elected president earned them the nickname of "swine-representatives." It is difficult to treat these people as serious political factors.

This brief discussion should suffice to show that the traditional legal-institutional approach to explaining Chinese politics suffers from severe limitations. For there never was an independent central government during this period, if we understand this to mean a government that stood at the apex of the power structure, with the various militarists subordinate to it within that structure. When the political actors acted, they seldom felt constrained to conform to any kind of institutional criteria. The most important decisions were made not by the government in Peking but by the local governments independently.

There is a variation of the legal-institutional approach, which might be called the bipolar approach. This approach does emphasize the political disintegration of the country. Furthermore, it recognizes the militarists as the most potent political forces in the north. However, in dealing with the situation in the south, most scholars of this persuasion try to impute to it a high degree of political awareness and cohesion under the leadership of the KMT. In talking about the "north" and the "south," they convey the impression that China was somewhat analogous to a bipolar situation, i.e. a direct confrontation between two political-geographical areas.[3] This approach presents a gross distortion, because it greatly inflates the significance of the role played by the south and lumps all northern politico-military forces into one undifferentiated category. It also tends to attribute to the south certain structural characteristics that it did not actually possess during much of this

---

the only plausible explanation of this anomaly is that cabinet posts did not carry much power. In fact, cabinet members were often mere errand boys for the powerful militarists and could be appointed or dismissed at their pleasure.

period. In addition, the ideological position that most scholars using this approach take also causes them to drag in many issues —such as constitutionalism and legitimacy—which were at best of marginal relevance to most other political actors.

The bipolar approach is unsatisfactory for four further reasons. First, the so-called "northern bloc" was far from being a homogeneous and consolidated group. During most of the period, serious struggles went on among supposed members of this group. Second, the south was equally troubled by incessant internal strife and was also far from being a united bloc. Third, there were frequent cross-boundary alliances among important elements from both of the two "blocs." Finally, the KMT did not actually gain a stronghold in the south until the later part of the period. Its earlier existence was nominal and inconsequential. During those years, political activities revolved around certain key northern militarists, and the existence (or nonexistence) of the KMT made little impression upon the northern militarists. At best, then, this approach offers a victor's interpretation of history, but it hardly does justice to the northern militarists who dominated the political scene long before the KMT started playing an active role.

It is only recently that some scholars have begun to show concern over the glaring gap that exists in our knowledge of early Chinese Republican history. Either explicitly or implicitly, they have shifted the intellectual focus and have sought new horizons and new factors in interpreting Chinese politics. Some have concluded that the most important political phenomenon was neither the defunct government in Peking nor the north-south struggle, but the role of the military in politics. Ralph Powell and F. F. Liu have contributed significant studies of this phenomenon.[4] There are also at least two published monographs on individual militarists (Feng Yü-hsiang, and Yen Hsi-shan) and a number of unpublished Ph.D. dissertations on other individual militarists.[5] The literature is still relatively scarce, however, and the years 1916–28 remain to be explored.

One way to narrow the gap in our knowledge would be to produce more biographical monographs of prominent military figures of this period. In general, these monographs share the view that there was no national politics at the time, that Chinese politics can best be understood in terms of the various regional or local governments dominated by powerful militarists. When a large number of case studies have been accumulated, the theory goes, the findings will enable us to arrive at generalizations valid for the whole of China through the inductive process. Put differently, it is hoped that the multiplication of studies on individual militarists or their regimes will eventually enable us to piece them together into a mosaic and to generate a body of propositions, hypotheses, and even perhaps systematic knowledge about Chinese politics in its entirety.

This scheme, however, must remain unfulfilled until many more case studies, covering most of the important local regimes in the country, have been undertaken. The studies now available, though highly stimulating in themselves, cannot claim to have approached that goal. Furthermore, the few militarists who have been studied were anything but typical of their ordinary contemporaries. We cannot draw a generalized picture of China under military rule by inferring from the conduct of these exceptional members of the group. We need to know more about the majority of militarists who controlled the rest—and by far the most important parts —of China. That knowledge, however, is not likely to be available for a long time to come.[6]

While the study of individual militarists as a way of understanding Chinese politics is certainly a sound strategy, it is not the only strategy, nor is it necessarily the best one. For even when we have obtained detailed knowledge about all the individual militarists and their local regimes, much will remain to be learned. One of the dangers of concentrating exclusively on individual militarists or regimes is the tendency to be too deeply involved in the details and to produce a set of disjointed and fragmented pictures of Chinese politics. Because there are inevitable divergences and similarities among the numerous militarist regimes, we will still have to go through a distilling process to sort them out and put them in appropriate categories in order to draw an accurate total picture.

If this view is valid—and I believe that it is—then we need not be too distressed by the dearth of information about most major militarist regimes. For an understanding of the "national" politics of China, the pattern of *interaction* among the militarists is probably more relevant than the particular aspects of their internal rule. Any political system is what it is partially because the participants conduct their political behavior according to their own will, and partially because they have to act under certain systemic constraints beyond their control. In other words, while we do not deny that political actors (or, for that matter, human beings) are generally action-oriented or goal-oriented, there are certain environmental factors that constrain their behavior in important ways. The examination of these factors may reveal certain crucial aspects of the militarists' behavior that might be neglected if only internal conditions of militarist regimes were studied. In this book, then, we want to shift the focus away from discrete political phenomena *within* the individual militarist regimes and toward the relationships *among* them in our search for an overview of the Chinese political process during the 1916–28 period. What we aspire to construct is a coarse-screen macroscopic view rather than a fine-screen microscopic study of the period.[7]

Our analysis differs from the microscopic studies in some essential ways. A typical microscopic study deals with a single militarist or his regime and is usually eclectic in organizing the data. While the author may focus on certain aspects of the man or his regime, he usually does not spell out the underlying theories that guide his research interests, nor does he articulate the relationships among the diverse aspects he has chosen to study. He selects and processes the facts according to his own implicit criteria. Each of the few existing microscopic studies of early twentieth-century militarism is marked by a different approach and focuses on different aspects. Thus it is rather difficult to draw generalizations about militarism from them.

In contrast, this work is guided by the criteria of systems theory. While microscopic studies organize historical materials to describe discrete and unique events concerning a militarist or his regime, the systems approach tries to organize historical materials into separate but related categories. Through the selection of a set of variables, systems theory attempts to establish a pattern of behavior that characterizes the system and separates it from the environment. The data are selected and examined in a systematic way, in accordance with certain explicit criteria.

This study is based on the premise that certain variables are more crucial to the understanding of militarism than others, and their relevance will be shown in the course of the book. Thus, while the end-product is a macroscopic analysis of Chinese militarism, the bulk of the book will deal with what we consider to be the system's crucial aspects—organization, weapons technology, military training, financial resources, and value systems. Each in its own way affected the system of behavior among the militarists. Although some of the following chapters may look rather detailed, the primary intention is not to tell the reader which militarist did what, but to describe how such behavior may provide clues to how the system operated. That is, our purpose is to provide a fresh perspective toward understanding Chinese politics in a systematic way.

The reader will soon realize that this work is primarily concerned with the general attributes of the politics of militarism. Our underlying assumption is that political disintegration and fragmentation in China had gone so far as to make it inadmissible to treat the country as having a single political regime. There is some evidence to support this assumption. First, the Peking government was formally challenged at all times by one or several rival "governments" during this period. Jurisdictional confusion and disputes constituted a major portion of political activities, and durable and stable "national" organization was nowhere in sight. Second, the relationships among political actors were not well defined by either institutional norms or stable expectations and were constantly changing. The decision-making process was decentralized and informal. Most militarists resorted to diplomacy, implicit coordination, alliance, and eventually war to establish their positions. Political decisions often could determine whether a political unit would survive or perish. Third, in contrast to the shifting power configuration on the national level, there were a number of militarist factions whose internal organizations were of a higher order of integration, better defined and more stable. The sense of community was stronger within these organizations than among them, and it was sanctioned and reinforced by a large number of psychological as well as physical forces. They were therefore able to play a continuing role in the political arena, though their political fortunes might change from one year to the next.

If these observations are accurate (they will receive further elaboration in subsequent chapters), then a new conceptualization of the problems and a new set of analytical tools are required for an understanding of this period. For these aspects of Chinese politics during the 1916–28 period seem more to resemble an international than a domestic situation. Certainly, the issues of war and peace, of bargaining and negotiation, of alliance and counteralliance can be better understood by drawing upon related knowledge from the discipline of international relations. Hence, in the course of our inquiry we will use concepts, hypotheses, and theories developed in international relations whenever they seem to apply.

Now that I have described the conceptual framework guiding the study, let me briefly outline what I aspire to accomplish in this book. Broadly speaking, I have set for myself three tasks. The first task is to identify and to define the militarists, the actors in the political system, in terms of their personal and social characteristics. The socioeconomic backgrounds and the attitudes of men can have a profound impact on the way they perceive and analyze their political environment, which in turn gives shape and meaning to the norms and rules that guide their political activities. Therefore, we need to answer these questions: Who were these militarists? How and why did they join the military profession? What forces brought them into different political groups? What were the basic ingredients of their value system and how were these values manifested in their outward political behavior?

The second task is to describe the environment surrounding them. To talk about environmental limits is to talk about capabilities. Here the most important questions are: What kinds and amounts of economic resources did the militarists have at their command? How efficiently were they mobilized, distributed, and utilized? In what ways did technology affect the political decisions of the militarists? With respect to the more intangible capabilities: What was the quality of education received by the militarists? How cohesive were their organizational ties? What kind of politico-military organizations did they create? How skilled were they in diplomacy, and what kind of political and military leadership did they exert? In order to bring the study within reasonable bounds, it is necessary to classify the actors, especially when there were a large number of them, according to their capabilities. The more powerful actors will necessarily receive more attention, and the less powerful little or no coverage. There are pitfalls in comparing

Introduction 9

actors on the basis of their capabilities, but comparison is inevitable. Although we cannot devise a scientific method of measurement, we can try to rank the actors on a scale, thus sidestepping the more serious problem of translating the power elements of the actors into numerical terms.

The third and final task is to describe and analyze how the actors behaved. We will demonstrate that politics in the 1916–28 period is not nearly as hopelessly confusing as has been generally assumed. The militarists were quite shrewd and calculating, and they followed rules in dealing with each other. Once their rules and norms are deciphered, it is easier to comprehend their political behavior. In the final chapter, the dynamics of politics will be analyzed. Many of the findings in the earlier chapters will be synthesized, and we will then be able to suggest some plausible explanations of why the militarists thrived in the 1910's and 1920's, and how their influence waned in the late 1920's.*

* That this study stops at 1928 should in no way be taken to mean that the Northern Expedition of the KMT successfully eliminated militarism in China. Rather, in this year a particular pattern of interaction among the political actors was terminated. As a matter of fact, the conditions and forces that brought about this termination are crucial to an understanding of the politics of the subsequent Nationalist era.

CHAPTER 2

The Emergence of the Military Factions

IN THEIR discussions of the early Republican period, all writers employ the terms "faction" or "clique" to describe the broad lines of conflict among politico-military groups. But their definitions are often vague: misidentifications are made, and misconceptions go unchallenged. Clearly, a term or concept is not very useful unless its full meaning has been explored. Since a political analysis of the early Republican period must rely heavily upon an analysis of factional struggle, common sense requires that we seek information in four basic areas: First, we should provide a chronological interpretation of the origin of the major factions. Second, we should examine the immediate causes prompting militarists to form factions, and how they actually did it. Third, we should identify as accurately as possible the constituent membership of major factions. Fourth, we should identify the basic sources of cohesion of the factions or their lack thereof.

A detailed historical review of the period becomes necessary in order to provide the factual basis for a better understanding of the issues raised in the first two areas. The composition and cohesiveness of the factions will be analyzed in subsequent chapters.

The purpose of this chapter is to lay the ground for a more detailed analysis of the strength and weakness of the military factions in early Republican China. The first part of the chapter traces some of the developments of the role of the military under the Ch'ing dynasty that might have precipitated the rise of military power in the Chinese polity. The second part examines the events from 1911 to 1920 that led to the emergence of military factions.

In the story told here we shall see that while Yüan Shih-k'ai was alive, the Peiyang Army remained a highly cohesive force, even though some rivalry might have existed among his chief lieutenants. After Yüan's sudden departure from the scene in 1916, there was no one military leader capable of inheriting his mantle. In the search for a formula that could both preserve the power of the Peiyang Army and subdue the southern rebels, a schism gradually developed between Tuan Ch'i-jui and Feng Kuo-chang which in time involved most of the leading Peiyang members. Thus, ironically, what began as an effort to restore Peiyang's political paramountcy ended in its hopeless division into opposing factions.

Historical Background

In order to understand the historical as well as the social and political factors that produced modern Chinese militarism, it is necessary first to review briefly the origin and structure of the military in the Ch'ing dynasty.

The forerunner of the Ch'ing military was the Banner armies created by Nurhaci in 1601. Another type of military forces, the Green Standards, so called because they used green-colored flags, came into being somewhat later. From the beginning of the Ch'ing empire until the 1850's, these two forces constituted the bulwark of imperial defense, and together they were called the *chin chih ping*, or national army. But by the early nineteenth century both forces had outlived their usefulness. The hereditary system of the Banner forces, which was created to monopolize military power in the hands of a small elite and to make its members feel that their personal interests were intertwined with those of the empire, in the long run contributed significantly to the Banners' undoing. Their exclusiveness gave them a distorted sense of importance and complacency. They became reluctant to innovate and were slow to respond to new challenges. Since the job usually came as a birthright, there was no particular incentive to work hard for advancement. The creeping influence of a civilian style of life in the barracks also led to a more relaxed atmosphere and made it all but impossible to enforce military discipline.

For the Green Standards, corruption became a major problem. It became a usual practice for officers to conceal vacancies in their units in order to pocket salaries for nonexistent soldiers. The situation deteriorated so much that by the middle of the century it was not uncommon for units to have only half or even a sixth of the authorized manpower, while drawing full pay from the empire.[1]

Furthermore, both the Banners and the Green Standards suffered from the lack of competent officers. In the Green Standards, a person could obtain a position by simply making a financial contribution to the empire. The Green Standards and a large portion of the Banners were stretched thin throughout the empire. This dispersion made the units less responsive to rapid mobilization to cope with a large-scale threat. In addition, it made centralized supervision more difficult. Irregular practices were easily concealed from the authorities in Peking.

The T'ai-p'ing Rebellion of 1850 provided an acid test of the strength of the Ch'ing military establishment, and both these forces proved to be totally unequal to the task. Within a short time they were routed, and they nearly caused the empire to crumble with them.

In this crisis there emerged a new breed of military forces, chiefly the Hsiang-chün created by Tseng Kuo-fang in 1853, the Ch'u-chün of Tso Tsung-t'ang (1860), and the Huai-chün of Li Hung-chang (1862).[2] Together, these armies defeated the T'ai-p'ings and gave the Manchu regime a new lease on life. However, the rise of these armies also radically changed the distribution of political and military power within the empire and laid the foundation for the subsequent development of militarism. For these were regional armies organized by local gentry and scholars. When they first came into being, they were actually looked at with suspicion by the Imperial Court. Only after they had conclusively demonstrated their ability to deal with the rebels did the Ch'ing government begin to give them limited financial support. These factors made it difficult for the Ch'ing government to exercise stringent control over them after the defeat of the rebels in 1866. The victory enabled these ethnically Han Chinese forces to supersede the Manchus and become the major military power. This fundamental alteration of the imperial military power structure also had far-reaching political ramifications: after the beginning of the T'ai-p'ing Rebellion, there began to be a marked increase in Chinese, particularly those who had distinguished themselves as military commanders, occupying key imperial positions.[3]

In time, however, these regional armies, referred to collectively

The Emergence of the Military Factions 13

as Braves (*yung*), also began to deteriorate, once the T'ai-p'ings had been suppressed. Despite attempts to modernize them, the Braves continued to suffer one defeat after another in a series of engagements with foreign armies, and they were roundly beaten in the first Sino-Japanese war of 1894-95.

The defeat and humiliation of 1895 finally caused the Manchu Court to embark on a sweeping reform of the military establishment. Immediately after the war, Chang Chih-tung, then Viceroy of Liang-chiang, began to advocate the training of a new army, and proceeded to form a Self-Strengthening Army of about three thousand men. He adopted the German army model, engaged German officers as instructors, and used Chinese graduates of military schools as assistants. In October 1895, the Imperial government formally declared the inauguration of a new pilot training program for the army. Hsiao-chan, a town southeast of Tientsin, was selected as the training base, and the original size of the army was set at ten battalions, about four thousand men. Within a few months, a 37-year-old official by the name of Yüan Shih-k'ai was placed in charge of the entire program, and the force was redesignated the Newly Established Army. Under Yüan's vigorous management, the program offered instruction in infantry, cavalry, artillery, and scouting under the supervision of German officers. Foreign equipment was used. Soon the force was expanded to seven thousand officers and men, many of whom were to play prominent roles in Chinese politics in the next two or three decades.

In the meantime, the Imperial government also tried to create a new type of provincial force called the *Hsün-fang-ying* and encouraged provincial governors to train their own new armies. Because the Hsiao-chan program was under the supervision of the Minister of Peiyang, and because Yüan himself later served in that capacity, the armies that were in one way or another related to Hsiao-chan or to Yüan personally came to be known as the Peiyang Army. In the south, the provincial army training program following the lead of Chang Chih-tung also produced a number of provincial armies, which sometimes were referred to as the Nanyang Army. Actually, the latter was less than an army, because these southern programs were not integrated under a single command system as the northern armies were.

While little progress was made in the south, in the north the

Newly Established Army made serious efforts to use the talents of foreign instructors, to introduce modern weapons, to improve the provisions and living conditions of the soldiers, and to upgrade their combat skills and discipline. When the Manchu prince, Jung Lu, inspected Hsiao-chan in February 1899, he was enormously impressed and reported back to the Empress most enthusiastically about Yüan's undertaking. Soon afterward, a larger army, the *Wuwei-chün*, was formed by imperial decree, and Yüan became the commander of one of its four armies, each with about nine thousand officers and men. Although all the armies were organized and trained according to the example set by Yüan, the other three armies were slow in responding to the new regulations and the new spirit, and the reorganization proceeded rather lethargically. During the Boxer Rebellion, the majority of this new force was either broken up or completely decimated, with the exception of Yüan's army, which did not participate in the campaign.

In January 1901, the Yangtze viceroys petitioned the emperor to create a modern army. This brought forth an imperial decree ordering reorganization of the army. Yüan's army, now called the Peiyang Standing Army, was ordered back once again to Hsiao-chan for training. Not long afterward, Li Hung-chang died, and Yüan succeeded him as viceroy of Chihli as well as Minister of Peiyang.

At Hsiao-chan, in addition to further reorganization and intensification of training, Yüan established the Peiyang Military Academy, and he created a short-course military school at Paoting in 1903. Now, his domination of military power in the north was enhanced, for he not only had the best trained force in the north, but also educated his own corps of officers to lead them. By 1905 the Peiyang force had grown to six divisions (*cheng*), each with 12,500 men. At least five of them were under the command of Yüan's trusted subordinates.

Such overwhelming power inevitably caused alarm. In 1905, the Imperial government announced a scheme to create 36 divisions of a new army. Each province was to set up its own training office for new armies. In 1907, the Ministry of War, which had been established the previous year to oversee military affairs for the whole country, promulgated regulations governing the completion of the training programs for the 36 divisions. In that same year, Yüan lost the viceroyship of Chihli, and at the end of 1908 he was forced into semi-retirement. But by then, Yüan had already established a considerable military following. On the eve of the 1911 revolution, there were some sixteen divisions and sixteen mixed brigades in the country. Of these, about seven divisions and four mixed brigades were considered to be loyal to Yüan personally. The rest were scattered in the empire under separate provincial commands.

The Role of the Military, 1911–1917

The establishment of the new Republican political order bears testimony to the power of the militarists, because its success can be directly attributed to the machinations of Yüan Shih-k'ai in collaboration with the top-ranking line commanders of the Newly Established Army, especially those who petitioned for the abdication of the infant emperor on January 26, 1912. During Yüan's presidency, the Peiyang military faction began to assert itself more aggressively and to intrude increasingly into the political arena. Peiyang officers received favored treatment in appointments, promotions, and financial rewards. As the Peiyang structure became more expansive and powerful, however, internal strains and conflicts slowly emerged.

In the first five years of the Republic, Yüan's personal prestige and status within the Peiyang Army, together with his presidential powers, served as a temporary restraint upon the ambitions of the militarists. But even Yüan was not always successful in curbing their constant interference in national and local affairs, partly because Yüan himself was never reluctant to use military support as his trump card in dealing with other political groups. In reaction, the political opposition also resorted to force to resist Yüan's pressure, as evidenced by the Second Revolution of 1912–13. The propensity to use force to resolve political conflict brought about a phenomenal increase in the number of men under arms and a resurgence of regional armies. It also whetted the militarists' appetite for a more active role in national politics.

So long as Yüan was alive and his Peiyang machine was the dominant military power, a semblance of national unity was preserved. When Yüan died in 1916, the restraining hand was removed. Almost instantly the militarists plunged into the vortex of national politics. Militarists of various statures began to contend for territories as well as resources. The central government, under the presidency of General Li Yüan-hung, who was not a Peiyang man, rapidly lost its grip on the country.

On the national political level, the cleavage between the Peking government and the KMT opposition was sharpened by differing opinions over which of the constitutions should be honored. The disputes over the president's tenure and the advisability of convening the old parliament further complicated the situation. Within the Peking government, there was also the rivalry between President Li and Premier Tuan Ch'i-jui because of differences in personality and differences over whether China should declare war against Germany. Consequently, the political system was thrown into utter confusion.

It was during this interval that great destructive forces began to work on the provincial and local levels to accelerate the tendencies toward disintegration. The country was divided into many separate, independent or semi-independent areas, each with a militarist as the supreme power. Increasingly, national politics lost its impact upon the people, and the national government receded into the background while the militarists thrust themselves to the fore in various areas.

In the absence of a new commonly accepted leader, the first reaction of the Peiyang militarists was to try to preserve the solidarity of the group by collective effort. Nobody could dictate order as Yüan had. Commanders now enjoyed greater autonomy in their own units; at the same time they tried to introduce a new form of collective leadership in lieu of a single dictator within the established Peiyang system. They remained loyal to the Peiyang group and they regarded the group's interests as paramount, but the decision-making power became more diffused among the local militarists. The foremost of the local militarists were, of course, the provincial military governors. They jealously guarded their newly acquired political autonomy, and they also attempted active intervention in national politics with increasing boldness.

The most prominent intermilitarist decision-making body at this time was the Association of the Provincial (Military) Governors (*sheng-ch'ü lien-ho-hui*), formed in Sepember 1916. More and more, important political issues were discussed and decided in the periodic conferences of this association rather than in Peking. The most famous of these conferences were those called by General Chang Hsün at Hsüchow. The first Hsüchow conference, held only four days after Yüan's death on June 9, 1916, was attended by representatives from seven northern provinces. Because of the trauma of Yüan's passing and the resulting uncertainty about the future of Peiyang, the conference was called to solidify the group and map a strategy for political survival.[4]

Only three months elapsed before the second Hsüchow conference was called on September 20, 1916. It was expanded to include the military governors or their representatives from twelve provinces, as well as many division commanders and district defense commissioners. The most important accomplishment of this conference was the emergence of the concept of a "grand alliance." In addition to electing Chan Hsün the "Great Leader" of this alliance, the participants also declared their readiness to use force collectively against anyone attempting to disrupt national unity or making unreasonable political demands. The language employed was so sweeping that it could be interpreted to apply not only against the parliament, the KMT, and the southwest, but also against elements in the Peking government, since the alliance now claimed the power to decide what was good for the central government.[5] And in fact, on September 25, a circular telegram was signed by 34 militarists (including practically all the important military governors, civil governors, and division and brigade commanders), opposing the central government's appointment of the new foreign minister, T'ang Shao-yi. As a result, T'ang was forced to resign.[6]

The third Hsüchow conference was held in January 1917. Now the participants felt ready to thrust themselves into politics; their specific demands included the dismissal of undesirable members of the president's personal staff, restrictions on parliament, and the dismissal of unworthy cabinet ministers.[7] As the feud between President Li Yüan-hung and Premier Tuan Ch'i-jui escalated, Tuan invited a number of militarists to congregate at Peking on April 25, 1917, to lend support to his advocacy of war against Germany. When they were rebuffed by Li, they went to Tientsin and precipitated the crisis that produced the monarchical fiasco engineered by Chang Hsün.

In addition to the Hsüchow conferences, there were a number

of smaller and more frequent conferences held by the militarists to discuss points of common interests. Together these conferences represented a provisional arrangement for making decisions at a time when the militarists were groping for a new alignment of power.

It is worth noting that the provincial military governors seldom exercised complete control over their domains. There were many other lesser local militarists, division commanders, district defense commissioners, or even brigade commanders who were anxious to grab a piece of territory. With or without formal declarations, these lesser militarists became practically independent of both the central government and the provincial government. Thus, in 1916–17, national policies could not be made without the concurrence of the provincial militarists, and provincial decisions could not be made without the cooperation of the local militarists.

This state of affairs was apparently intolerable to the militarists in general. While the majority of them had no objection to having autonomy themselves, they opposed the exercise of autonomy by others, especially those under their nominal control. Order had to be reestablished. Whereas everybody hoped to improve his own position against the others, nevertheless he would agree that unity should be restored and authority reestablished.

The Emergence of Military Factions, 1917–1920

As we have seen, the primary concern of the Peiyang group during 1916–17 was undoubtedly to stay together as a group and to continue its dominance in national politics. No militarist in the Peiyang group objected to the perpetuation of the group's influence, but differences of opinion existed on how the group could best preserve that influence. The main barrier to Peiyang's search for hegemony was the dissident movement in the southwestern provinces, which established its own rival military government in September 1917, thus presenting the Peking government with a constitutional challenge.

Early in July, in anticipation of trouble in the south, Tuan had made his first move to extend Peiyang control by dispatching a northern division into Hunan. Tuan's selection of Hunan as his first target was by no means accidental. The best route to attack the south was the Peking-Hankow railway, which reached Kwangtung through Hunan. Most of this line ran through provinces con-

The Emergence of the Military Factions

trolled by military governors who were either friendly to Tuan or could be won over. In addition, Hunan was weak militarily and was outside the Peiyang group. An attack on Hunan would not jeopardize the interests of any Peiyang members. A final advantage was that Hunan was adjacent to the province of Szechwan, which had been troubled by the presence of Yunnan and Kweichow troops. The conquest of Hunan would thus enable Tuan to send troops directly from Peking to the border of Kwangtung and also to send another expedition into Szechwan and invade the southwestern provinces from the rear.

With these considerations in mind, Tuan's cabinet announced on August 6, 1917, the appointments of Fu Liang-tso to replace T'an Yen-k'ai as the military governor of Hunan and Wu Kuanghsin as the commander in chief of the Upper Yangtze Valley as well as commissioner of Szechwan. Fu was a native of Hunan, although he had spent most of his adult life in the north and had closer connections with the Peiyang militarists than with his native provincials, including a marital relationship with Tuan's family. (The other appointee, Wu, was Tuan's fellow provincial and brother-in-law.) Tuan's choice of Fu, a man with a Hunan background, showed his desire to placate the Hunanese and to conceal the significance of this move. As a further gesture of assurance to the Hunanese militarists, Fu announced that he would not bring with him any northern troops and that he did not intend to change the internal military structure of Hunan.[8] However, once he assumed office, the northern troops that had been concentrated on the border immediately began to pour into the province.

In the meantime, the Hunanese had not been idle. When Fu's appointment was announced, the incumbent governor, T'an Yen-k'ai, showed no sign of resistance, and he even sent a personal representative to Peking to welcome the new governor. However, he lost no time in secretly deploying troops within the province for a showdown. When the necessary arrangements had been completed, two Hunanese militarists declared independenc on August 16, and fighting broke out right away. Thus unfolded the first major war of the militarists, during which the Peiyang group came apart. Various militarists reacted to this war with different perceptions and definitions of self-interest and group interest, and these differences slowly replaced old identities with new ones.

Available evidence indicates that Tuan's expedition failed to receive President Feng Kuo-chang's cooperation from its very inception. According to Ts'ao Ju-lin, the leader of the Communications Clique and a close associate of Tuan, when the fighting in Hunan broke out, Feng refused to issue the proclamation for a punitive expedition and encouraged the military governors of the three Yangtze provinces—Li Shun of Kiangsu, Ch'en Kuang-yüan of Kiangsi, and Wang Chan-yüan of Hupeh—to voice their opposition by circular telegrams.[9] It is also reported that he revealed his displeasure at the war to the commanders of the 8th and 20th divisions, causing them to use slowdown techniques in their fighting.[10]

Feng's opposition to the Hunan campaign was undoubtedly motivated partly by personal rivalry and jealousy.* If Tuan succeeded in subduing Hunan and the south by military force, he would inevitably overshadow Feng and become the new leader of the Peiyang group. It is also possible that Feng's opposition was based partly on a genuine difference in views. Feng had been in the Yangtze area for a few years; he knew more about the regional sentiments and the leaders of the southern provinces; he had some firsthand knowledge of the problems of regional administration. Thus he probably was more tolerant toward demands for local autonomy and believed that the national political authority did not have to assert itself dictatorially. There might even have been some truth in the charge (leveled by Tuan's men in 1918) that Feng was prepared to see a country divided between the north and south. Tuan, on the other hand, had been involved in politics on the national level for years and had witnessed at close range the political evils of the division of the country. He tended to value unity and authority more than anything else and would not hesitate to crush any obstacles standing in the way.

In any event, Feng's noncooperation, and sometimes obstruction,

* Their difference on the Hunan question was but part of a larger conflict of personality that had developed over the years. This conflict was first reflected during the controversy over the declaration of war against Germany. Feng declined to join the militarists who demonstrated against President Li in support of Tuan, nor did he sign the declaration of independence sponsored by the military governors. *North-China Herald* (hereafter referred to as *NCH*) May–June, 1917. When Feng found himself in line for the presidency after President Li's flight, he would not leave his Kiangsu base until he appointed Li Shun to succeed him in Kiangsu, and Ch'en Kuang-yüan to be governor of Kiangsi. Li Chien-nung, 2: 501.

The Emergence of the Military Factions

soon caused Tuan's campaign a lot of trouble. His victory in the first few weeks of the campaign in October 1917 proved to be short-lived. By early November, the northern troops had suffered several losses, and the commander of the 8th (northern) division, Wang Ju-hsien, boldly petitioned the central government to proclaim a cease-fire. Wang's refusal to fight forced Governor Fu Liang-tso to flee from the provincial capital. In the meantime, Ts'ao K'un (military governor of Chihli) and the military governors of Kiangsu, Kiangsi, and Hupeh also declared themselves in favor of seeking a peaceful solution. To compound Tuan's predicament, the expeditionary force he had dispatched under the command of General Wu Kuang-hsin to expel the Yunnan-Kweichow troops from Szechwan also suffered a series of reverses.[11] Facing the prospect of the total bankruptcy of his first major military adventure and personal bid for Peiyang leadership, Tuan resigned from the premiership on November 15, accusing President Feng of double-dealing.[12]

Tuan's resignation did not mean he had abandoned the Hunan campaign, however; it was only a tactical retreat to prepare for a renewed offensive from a different base. In December, Tuan moved to head the newly established Bureau of War Participation, ostensibly to supervise preparations for China's eventual participation in the European war against Germany. Barely three months later, Tuan was back in the premier's office (March 23, 1918). During this interval, Tuan engineered a number of maneuvers that completely changed the political atmosphere that had been unfavorable to his military policy. A brief account of the events during this interval shows his strategy.

Among the military governors presumably inclined toward a peaceful solution of the Hunan question, only Li Shun and Ch'en Kuang-yüan fervently shared Feng Kuo-chang's antipathy and were hostile to Tuan from the very beginning.[13] The others were not nearly as committed to a position. On December 1, 1917, two Hupeh militarists declared their independence from the provincial government and raised the prospect that they might march east and occupy sections of the Peking-Hankow railway, thus severing General Wang Chan-yüan's line of communication with the north and making his position in the province untenable. Although Wang had previously spoken for peace in Hunan, the northern reverses in Hunan had caused him to reassess the whole situation. The southern allied forces entered Hunan not only to help the local people drive out the northerners, but also to push as far north as they could. Besides, even within Hupeh, many local units nominally under Wang's command had shown signs of unrest, and some had actually gone over to the Hunanese side. If these challenges were not dealt with sternly, the Hunanese and the Hupeh militarists might enter into an alliance to drive him out altogether. Confronted with this new situation, Wang modified his previous stand and urged the Peking government to send reinforcements to Hupeh.[14] During the period December 1917–January 1918, Wang moved closer to the war party, as fighting in Hunan was renewed and intensified after a brief respite following Tuan's resignation. By the end of January 1918, Yüehchow (Hunan) was recovered by the allied Hunan-Kwangsi forces, and the rebellious Hupeh militarists were fighting northern troops in western Hupeh to a standstill.

The Hupeh rebellions and the reopening of hostilities in Hunan alerted other Peiyang militarists to the possibility that these joint southern efforts might cut off the Peking-Hankow railway and leave the northern troops stranded in Hunan. To counter this threat, the northern militarists called a conference at Tientsin on December 3, 1917. The conference was sponsored by Ni Tz'u-ch'ung of Anhwei, Chang Huai-chih of Shantung, and Ts'ao K'un of Chihli and was attended by representatives from ten other provinces. The most important result of the conference was that Ts'ao K'un abandoned his peace policy and became an ardent war advocate.*

The participants resolved to continue the Hunan campaign, to pledge a number of troops from each province, and to request Feng Kuo-chang to issue a presidential mandate for a punitive expedition. Apparently the conference was a victory for Tuan, for on December 22, Ts'ao K'un started sending a detachment of troops to reinforce Wang Chan-yüan in Hupeh. President Feng, however, still tried to stand by his peace policy. On December 25, he issued

---

* This conversion might have been facilitated by some political horse-trading between Ts'ao and Tuan. Possibly Ts'ao was promised the consolidation of his position in Chihli and his election to the vice-presidency in the next election. See *Hsü Shu-cheng tien kao* (hereafter referred to as *HSCTK*), no. 135; Ts'ao Ju-lin, pp. 172–73.

a presidential mandate reaffirming the need for peace and urging a general cease-fire and reconciliation. The next day, the three military governors of the Yangtze provinces responded with a circular telegram supporting the president and indicating that they had indeed been seeking diligently to arrange a settlement with the south.¹⁵ That Wang Chan-yüan also signed the telegram seems strange in light of what had happened to him. The only plausible explanation is that he was trying to use both sides to maintain his own position.* The attitude of Li Shun and Ch'en Kuang-yüan, however, was consistently intransigent. Thus, for instance, at the end of December, when Shantung planned to transport some contingents south to Hupeh, both Li and Ch'en denied them transit rights.¹⁶

Both these attempts to frustrate the new war fever proved futile once Ts'ao K'un added his weight to the war party. After mid-December 1917, Tuan began to enlist the military governors of Fengtien, Shansi, Shensi, Chekiang, Anhwei, and Kansu to put pressure on Feng to appoint Ts'ao K'un to head the expedition. On January 30, 1918, after his alternatives were exhausted, including an alleged attempt to escape from Peking and return to his Yangtze base, Feng bowed to reality and appointed Ts'ao K'un, Chang Huai-chih, and Chang Ching-yao commanders of the expeditionary forces with orders to proceed to the south. On the same day, Ts'ao was also made Pacification Commissioner of Hunan and Hupeh and civil governor of Chihli. The first assignment gave Ts'ao full power to direct the campaign at the front, while the second one further strengthened his hold within Chihli, where he had already been the military governor.

Ts'ao's conversion to the war party accomplished only one of the three major tasks that Tuan had set for himself. The presence

* The opportunism and fence-sitting of Wang Chan-yüan is best illustrated by the following report made by Hsü Shu-cheng. In late January 1918, Li Shun of Kiangsu approached Wang Chan-yüan and Ch'en Kuang-yüan with a proposal for joint action. Specifically, the three provinces would (1) resolutely refuse right-of-way to any northern troops through Pukow or Hankow, (2) adopt coordinated action in an emergency, and (3) institute joint defense measures. Wang put his signature to the document. At the same time, he also dispatched a secret report to Hsü Shu-cheng about the whole episode and affected to be very upset at Li Shun's audacity. If Hsü's report is true, as it seems to be, then Wang Chan-yüan was obviously engaged in a lot of double-dealing. *HSCTK*, no. 21, Feb. 3, 1918.

of Li Shun in Kiangsu and Ch'en Kuang-yüan in Kiangsi and their collusion with Feng meant that his policy might still be sabotaged. In addition, the control of the cabinet by Wang Shih-chen, who was sympathetic to a peaceful solution, was viewed by Tuan with suspicion. Therefore, in order to carry out his policy smoothly, Tuan had to eliminate the Kiangsu-Kiangsi axis as well as to take over the cabinet from Wang.[17] Since Tuan at this time did not command sufficient force of his own to force his opponents' removal, he had to rely on other militarists. Ts'ao K'un's force was already assigned to the Hunan front; the only other nearby source of support was Chang Tso-lin of Fengtien. When Tuan learned that Li Shun was contemplating a more formal alliance with Kiangsi and Hupeh to act in coordination against Tuan and to refuse Tuan's troops passage through their respective territories, a deal was quickly worked out between Tuan and Chang.*

On February 25, 1918, Chang Tso-lin ordered Fengtien troops into Chihli to take up strategic positions around the capital. In the meantime, he presented President Feng with four demands and implied that his continued loyalty to the president would depend on their acceptance. In essence, Chang asked for the dismissal of the three military governors in the Yangtze area, the reconstruction of a new cabinet under Tuan, the appointment of himself as inspector general of Manchuria, and the training and equipping of an additional Fengtien division to be underwritten by the central government.[18]

Tuan was, to say the least, greatly elated by the timely Fengtien help. Even before the Fengtien troops moved in, Tuan began reprisals against Kiangsu and Kiangsi. On February 5, Ch'en Kuang-yüan of Kiangsi was stripped of his military rank by official order. On February 21, Chang Huai-chih was appointed high commissioner for Hunan and Kiangsi (*chien-yüeh-shih*) and was directed to divert a part of the expeditionary army into Kiangsi to prepare for Ch'en's ouster. Nor had Tuan forgotten the other thorn in his side—Li Shun. However, Chang Tso-lin's intervention in February shifted the political balance so much in Tuan's favor that it was

* On January 28, 1918, Tuan caused the information to leak to Chang Tso-lin that a shipment of Japanese arms would arrive at Ch'ing-huang-tao on February 3. With Tuan's connivance, Chang intercepted the arms and expropriated them. See *HSCTK*, nos. 15, 19, 21, 41, 58, 60, 64.

The Emergence of the Military Factions

no longer considered necessary to remove Li before the Wang cabinet could be toppled.[19] The presence of Fengtien troops in the backyard of the central government apparently made the difference, and on March 6, premier Wang retired from his office.

Meanwhile, the expeditionary force was making headway in Hunan and had regained much lost ground. In mid-March, the bond between Tuan and Chang Tso-lin was further strengthened when Chang appointed Hsü Shu-cheng, Tuan's righthand man, as his deputy commander of all Fengtien forces inside the Great Wall. On March 22, representatives of northern militarists gathered at Tientsin for another conference and decided to ask Feng to reappoint Tuan as premier and to recapture Ch'angsha, the capital of Hunan, before offering peace again.[20] The next day Tuan was reinstated as premier. Tuan had now fulfilled all three tasks and could turn his full attention to the prosecution of his policy of unifying China by military power.

Four days after assuming office, Tuan named Chang Ching-yao to be the new military governor of Hunan in anticipation of a total victory. This in the long run proved to be a costly political blunder. For the brunt of the fighting in Hunan had been borne essentially by Ts'ao K'un's 3d Division, under the leadership of Wu P'ei-fu as its acting commander. Since Wu had almost singlehandedly saved the northern troops from disaster and defeated the Hunanese in battle after battle, it was natural for him to expect to be rewarded. In contrast, Chang Ching-yao was an incompetent leader who had suffered many humiliating defeats, but he had seniority in Peiyang and a closer personal relationship with Tuan.[21]

There were other aspects of Tuan's policies that might have created the doubts and anxieties in the minds of his military allies that brought about a gradual erosion of the united front. The most important case was the gradual alienation of Ts'ao K'un from the war party.[22]

Ts'ao K'un's alienation was brought about by a number of factors. The first factor was his anxiety about his long absence from his home base, Chihli. In late March and early April, 1918, there were newspaper reports that Tuan was about to give Wu full charge of directing the Hunan campaign, keep the 3d Division in Hunan, appoint Ts'ao K'un the high commissioner of Hunan and Hupeh, and appoint Hsü Shu-cheng to succeed Ts'ao as military governor of Chihli. This would mean that Ts'ao would lose direct control of the 3d Division and his base in Chihli, while assuming a seemingly prestigious new position with little political power. Although Hsü Shu-cheng strenuously denied these rumors, Ts'ao's mind was apparently quite unsettled.[23]

On June 15, 1918, an incident of enormous political implications took place that must have had a strong impact on Ts'ao's attitude toward Tuan's party. This was the assassination of Lu Chien-chang. General Lu was a senior member of the Peiyang group. He was also an uncle of Feng Yü-hsiang, then commander of the 16th Mixed Brigade. According to Ts'ao Ju-lin's testimony, Lu, who was anti-Tuan, had prevailed upon Feng to stall in his march against the south and to plan instead a surprise attack against Ni Tz'u-ch'ung, Tuan's most ardent supporter.[24] As Lu was traveling in the north promoting anti-war sentiment among the troops, he was lured to Hsü Shu-cheng's residence in Tientsin and summarily executed. Lu's execution touched off a wave of indignation in military circles. Ts'ao was reported to be particularly enraged that a Peiyang comrade of such long standing was so cruelly dealt with and that this criminal act took place in territory under his jurisdiction.[25]

Last but not least, Ts'ao's attitude was affected by his apprehension of the rapid growth of Tuan's military and political power. It must be remembered that the Hunan campaign was not an ultimate objective in itself, but a prelude to the conquest of the southern provinces leading to eventual national reunification. But Tuan's experience had clearly taught him that the northern militarists could be just as defiant as the southerners. He could not forget that the cooperation of the northern militarists in the Hunan campaign had been secured at considerable financial and political cost. Therefore, in Tuan's view, the hope for national unification by force lay not in continued cooperation with other militarists but in establishing a separate army that would be absolutely loyal to Tuan personally. Chang Tso-lin, Ts'ao K'un, and others were only temporary allies who might turn into enemies in the future. As Tuan himself once put it, a unified country meant that all local centers of power would have to be circumscribed, and military power would definitely have to be eliminated from politics.[26] Therefore, at the same time that Tuan cooperated with the various

The Emergence of the Military Factions

militarists in the Hunan campaign, he also laid the groundwork for the creation of an independent military force.

Less than two months after Tuan was reinstated as premier, the Sino-Japanese Mutual Defense Pact was signed. According to its provisions, Japan was to help furnish instructors and equipment to China for the establishment and training of three divisions and four brigades. According to a contemporary report, the Chinese General Staff and the Ministry of War would each send ten students to the highest military college in Japan and appoint them to important duties after their return; the Chinese arsenals would manufacture all rifles and ammunition upon Japanese models and all arms currently required would be supplied by Japan.[27] Although Tuan and his associates insisted that the purpose of these new forces was to prepare for China's participation in the First World War, President Feng and other knowledgeable militarists must have known that this was only a smoke screen; the government had never seriously planned active participation in the European war on such a gigantic scale.* It was obvious to them that such a large force was being raised with the suppression of internal enemies in mind. Tuan guarded this force jealously, appointing his most trusted lieutenants as commanders, and gave it preferential treatment.

In order to carry out his policy of forceful unification, Tuan also needed money, but most of the local sources of revenue had slipped under the control of local militarists. Here, again, Tuan found the Japanese willing lenders. According to Li Chien-nung, in the seven months after he assumed office (March–October, 1918), Tuan negotiated at least six different loans with Japan totaling 120 million Chinese yüan. A few other loans were reportedly negotiated at the same time, but their exact amount cannot be ascertained.[28]

With the war chest filled and a huge army under training, Tuan made his next move to control the machinery of the central government. The Anfu Club was the political arm created for this purpose in May 1918. The nominal leaders of the Anfu Club were Wang I-t'ang, Liu En-ko, and Tseng Yun-p'ei, but the real power behind the scenes was the ubiquitous Hsü Shu-cheng. Its base of operation was the parliament. When the new parliament convened

---

* Foreign diplomats were told that China planned to send between 500,000 and one million men to Europe. Reinsch, *An American Diplomat in China.*

in August 1918, the Communications Faction (including both the Liang Shih-yi wing and the Ts'ao Ju-lin wing) won about 100 seats and the Research Faction only 20 seats, while Anfu Club members gathered nearly 330 seats.[29] Tuan clearly intended to use this parliamentary majority to dictate the coming presidential election and to dominate the central government.

These ominous signs of the rapid growth of Tuan's personal power were not lost upon his enemies and allies. After the 3d Division had captured Ch'angsha and seen the fruits of victory snatched away by Chang Ching-yao, Ts'ao and Wu began to show their apathy to the war. In mid-April, Ts'ao had protested to Tuan that the 3d Division was too exhausted to fight on and should be sent back to the north for rest and training. He also complained that he was ill and asked to be given a leave of absence. On April 18, the 3d Division occupied Hengchow, which gave it a stronghold away from the shadow of Chang Ching-yao. There it halted operations against the Hunanese. Ts'ao's differences with Tuan had obviously developed to serious dimensions, for Tuan made a hasty visit to the front to assure Ts'ao that sufficient provisions had been made for the prosecution of the war and to urge him to take the complete victory that was in sight. Ts'ao was unmoved.[30]

Soon afterward, Wu began negotiating with the Hunanese generals for an informal truce. By May 30, Ts'ao had lost all interest in the war, and he went back to Chihli for its duration.

Having failed to entice Ts'ao's continued support with honey, Tuan's party tried to subvert Ts'ao's following. At the cabinet meeting of June 4, Hsü Shu-cheng reportedly proposed that if Ts'ao and Chang Ching-yao did not attend to their duties immediately, Wu P'ei-fu should be made commander in chief of the whole expeditionary force against the south.[31] He also reportedly told Wu that he could expect rapid promotion, since the senior Peiyang members were getting old.[32] To Tuan's exasperation, however, Wu remained loyal to Ts'ao. The upshot of all the manipulations was that Chang Huai-chih, who now had little military power, was ousted from the military governorship of Shantung, an incident that further confirmed Ts'ao's belief that Tuan was too treacherous to be trusted. The departure of Ts'ao and Wu from the war party was dramatized on August 21, when Wu led his commanders to issue a circular telegram openly advocating an immedi-

The Emergence of the Military Factions

ate cessation of all civil war. The southern military government in Canton promptly endorsed Wu's proposal. A month later, the commanding generals of all the northern and southern units at the Hunan front issued a joint statement calling for a general cessation of hostilities and the convening of a peace conference.

During the same period, Ts'ao received still more evidence of Tuan's lack of good faith. One of Tuan's primary purposes in forming the Anfu Club was to use the parliament to replace President Feng when his term expired. The animosity between Feng and Tuan became more acute as the September election drew near. There was, however, no indication that Ts'ao would fight for Feng's cause. On the contrary, he, Chang Tso-lin, and Hsü Shu-cheng had met at Tientsin at the end of July and agreed that Hsü Shih-ch'ang should be nominated for the presidency. The Tientsin conference also reaffirmed Tuan's previous pledge that Ts'ao would be elected vice-president. The Anfu-controlled parliament elected Hsü Shih-ch'ang president on September 1 on the first ballot with an overwhelming majority. Yet the same parliament, which earlier had also given the speakership and vice-speakership of both houses to Anfu leaders, could not muster even a simple quorum to vote on the vice-presidency, and the office was left unfilled. Under these circumstances, it was natural for Ts'ao to suspect that Tuan was deliberately reneging on his promise. Thus Ts'ao's withdrawal of support from Tuan became irrevocable.

Deprived of Ts'ao's fighting instrument and faced with a universal demand for peace, Tuan found the political atmosphere impossible, and he resigned as premier on October 10, 1918. As soon as Tuan left the cabinet, the peace forces gathered momentum. By November preparations were under way for a peace conference between the north and the south. Under the urging of Ts'ao K'un and the military governors of the three Yangtze provinces, it was finally convened in Shanghai on February 20, 1919. No sooner had the conference begun, however, than it bogged down over a number of differences between the two sides. But the basic stumbling block was Tuan's determined opposition to any conciliation with the southern rebels.

It is very likely that up to this time Ts'ao and Wu were merely trying to force Tuan out of office so that the southern campaign would die a natural death. There is no evidence to suggest that they were contemplating at this point the elimination of Tuan as a political force. But they soon discovered their error. For Tuan stayed on as the director of the War Participation Bureau, by virtue of which he kept his hold on the new forces being trained with Japanese assistance. Even after the conclusion of the First World War in November 1918, Tuan managed to preserve the War Participation Army, by changing its name (first to National Defense Army and then to Northwestern Frontier Army) and by making Hsü Shu-cheng its commander on June 24, 1919. In order to continue Japan's participation in the army training program after the world war, Tuan and Japan also signed, in February 1919, an agreement extending the Mutual Defense Pact until both China and Japan had signed the Peace Treaty with both Germany and Austria and until all Allied forces were evacuated from Chinese territory.[33]

Tuan's action was in clear defiance of the peace effort, and the expansion of his military power was obviously aimed at the south when the time was ripe. Consequently, on May 14, the southern delegate to the peace conference presented eight demands, which among other things demanded the repudiation of all secret agreements between China and Japan and the punishment of the officials responsible for such agreements.[34] The northern delegate refused to accept the demands, and both delegates then resigned. Since the northern chief delegate now refused to serve, Tuan seized this opportunity and pressured the prime minister into appointing the leader of his Anfu Club, Wang I-t'ang, as the new chief delegate on August 11. This was interpreted quite correctly by the south as a thinly veiled attempt either to dominate or to sabotage the peace movement. Consequently, the southern delegate refused to meet with him, and the peace conference came to a standstill.

The failure of the peace conference undoubtedly antagonized Ts'ao and Wu and made them realize that Tuan's resignation from the premiership had not ended their troubles. It also made them move closer to Li Shun and Ch'en Kuang-yüan in a concerted effort to check the influence of Tuan. Thus it was about this time that Ts'ao, Wu, and the military governors of the Yangtze provinces found an identity of interests in opposing Tuan, and the term Chihli faction, which had been loosely used for some time, began

The Emergence of the Military Factions

to have a more definite meaning. After Feng's death on December 29, 1919, Ts'ao's forces became the backbone of the Chihli faction.

At the same time, Tuan's relationship with his other ally, Chang Tso-lin, had also turned sour. The Tuan-Chang alliance had been a marriage of convenience from the beginning. Altogether, Chang sent some six thousand men to the capital and some additional brigades to Anhwei to check Kiangsu, in order to boost Tuan's position.[35] On the other hand, Tuan paid high prices in both arms and money, which enabled Chang Tso-lin to consolidate his rule within Manchuria and to improve his army.[36] By the summer of 1918 Chang was already looking for new territorial gains. As Chang's position became more secure, his need for Tuan declined correspondingly. His relations with Hsü Shu-cheng deteriorated, and he removed Hsü from the Fengtien army in mid-August, charging him with embezzlement. A new dimension was added to the friction when Hsü was appointed in June 1919 to command the Northwestern Frontier Army. The inclusion of the vast territories of Inner Mongolia under the jurisdiction of a new administrative organ, the Office of the Supervision of the Frontier Affairs, posed a roadblock to Chang's expansionist scheme, and he viewed the presence of the Northwestern Frontier Army in Fengtien's vicinity with great apprehension. These events pulled Chang progressively away from Tuan and toward the emerging Chihli faction.

Throughout the autumn and winter of 1919, Wu P'ei-fu kept up an intensified barrage of circular telegrams against Tuan and his political cohorts and their policies. The warm public responses caused Wu to become bolder in his telegraphic warfare, and in January 1920, he formally requested the Peking government to permit the return of the 3d Division from the Hunan front. After his requests had been repeatedly ignored or rejected, Wu began to evacuate the families of his officers.[37]

At the same time, the alliance against Tuan was boosted by the entry of Honan. During the month of February, reports were circulated to the effect that Tuan was about to remove the military governor of Honan, General Chao T'i, and replace him with Wu Kuang-hsin. Chao and his brother reacted by mobilizing their forces, and they declared that they would fight rather than quit. It was reportedly due to the intercession of Ts'ao K'un that the Peking government agreed to keep Chao as military governor, and only replaced his civil governor.[38] As a result of this episode, Chao, who had previously been friendly with Tuan, decided to join hands with the militarists of the Chihli faction.

By the spring of 1920, an alliance between the Fengtien and Chihli factions was being forged against Tuan's Anhwei faction. On April 9, 1920, a conference was called at Paoting, the provincial capital of Chihli, where an eight-province alliance was entered into by Chihli, Kiangsu, Kiangsi, Hupeh, Honan, and the three Manchurian provinces. By this time the pattern of opposition was clearly set, and a war seemed inevitable unless Tuan gave in. Specifically, Tuan's opponents demanded (1) the reorganization of the cabinet to rid it of Anfu domination; (2) the appointment of a more satisfactory delegate and the reopening of the peace conference; (3) the abolition of the Northwestern Frontier Bureau; and (4) the transfer of the command of the Northwestern Frontier Army from the Northwestern Frontier Bureau to the Ministry of War.[39]

These demands, of course, were totally unacceptable to Tuan. Thereupon, on May 20, 1920, Wu began to evacuate from Hunan, which was promptly taken over by local forces, resulting in the flight of Chang Ching-yao from the provincial capital. Wu marched along the Peking-Hankow railway toward Paoting. In June, after discussions with President Hsü and with Tuan, Chang Tso-lin went to Paoting, where he conferred with Ts'ao K'un, Wu P'ei-fu, and a delegate of Li Shun. Presumably, Chang delivered the ultimatum to Tuan and tried to dissuade him from pursuing his policy, while at the same time he made some final arrangements with Ts'ao in case Tuan was recalcitrant. Tuan stood his ground. On July 4, Hsü Shu-cheng was relieved by presidential order of his position as chief of the Northwestern Frontier Bureau and commander of the Northwestern Frontier Army. The army was to be placed under the command of the Ministry of War. In defiance of this order, the Northwestern Frontier Army was mobilized on July 6 and declared war against Ts'ao. The opposing armies came into contact on July 14, and by the 19th all hostilities had ceased. Tuan was roundly beaten, and took refuge in the Japanese concession in Tientsin.

Conclusions

Our historical review suggests that the atomization of the country after Yüan Shih-k'ai's death caused general alarm among the Peiyang militarists, who had been accustomed to privileged positions and enormous power. In contrast to the wave of independence movements that swept southern China, the northern militarists at first stayed together and tried to preserve their political influence. As an interim device, during 1916–18 they resorted to collective leadership exercised through the intermilitarist conferences. While political decision-making power was being shared by a larger number of people, however, everyone was aware that power must be recentralized and the rebellious areas taken back into the fold. Over the question of how this could best be achieved, the rivalry between Feng Kuo-chang and Tuan Ch'i-jui emerged; Feng was in favor of the peaceful resolution of conflict, while Tuan was in favor of uniting the country by force. At this stage, the rivalry provided merely the skeleton of factional struggle but not yet the factions proper, because many of the main actors were yet to enter the stage.

Tuan was the more forceful of the two main antagonists, and he built up a powerful personal following. On the political front, he created the Anfu Club. With a plentiful supply of arms and money from Japan, he succeeded in creating a relatively cohesive group or faction. Tuan's opponents, on the other hand, were not nearly as energetic or powerful. At best, Feng could rely on the support of Kiangsu and Kiangsi, and the qualified support of some divisional commanders, notably from the 8th and 20th divisions. From the evidence, Wang Chan-yüan of Hupeh looks very much like an opportunist, ready to shift sides with the political wind. Throughout the four years between 1916 and 1920, his stand on war or peace remained vague and contradictory, probably intentionally so. As far as I know, he never openly rebuked Tuan or his lieutenants, nor did Tuan ever display any significant anger against Wang. In the 1920 war, he played a passive role. Thus, although most writers describe all three military governors of the Yangtze Valley as forming the backbone of Feng's faction, I believe that Wang's adherence is extremely doubtful. The best evidence of Wang's detachment from the Chihli faction is the fact that the faction gave him no spoils in the aftermath of the Anhwei-Chihli war and stood by when Wang was driven from Hupeh by local militarists.

Our review further demonstrates that it is inaccurate to identify Ts'ao K'un and Wu P'ei-fu with the Chihli faction from the very beginning, as some writers have done.[40] If we take a close look at history, we find that Ts'ao took a personal position on the war issue, not a factional position. Ts'ao probably was still thinking in Peiyang terms: he did not want to see Tuan's power as Peiyang power challenged by the southern rebels; he did not want to see Wang Chang-yüan's position in Hupeh endangered. At the same time, he also did not want to see Li Shun penalized for his opposition to the war, and he certainly was disgusted by Lu Chien-chang's "execution." A plausible explanation for this seemingly contradictory behavior is that Ts'ao was more concerned with the solidarity of the Peiyang group against external challenge and internal division than with factional gains or losses. Thus we see Ts'ao exerting full energy to help Tuan win the Hunan war, but also repeatedly expressing concern that Li Shun be treated magnanimously lest the Peiyang group break up.[41]

The Chihli faction did not become a genuine faction until Ts'ao K'un sealed his friendship with the followers of Feng Kuo-chang and ushered in a pattern of permanent opposition against Anhwei. The followers of Feng Kuo-chang had provided the skeleton of an opposition, but it was a very muted opposition. After Ts'ao's break with Tuan, which clarified the issues, events began to gather momentum and the political forces were moving toward a confrontation. Ts'ao brought to the faction military muscle and aggressive leadership. It was Ts'ao's forces who dared Anhwei to a test of strength and dealt it a shattering blow from which Anhwei was never to fully recover.

In the end, it was Tuan's arrogance that precipitated the crystallization of the Chihli faction. Tuan believed that the Peiyang lineage of authority could be reasserted only with organization and force. However, the Peiyang Army was in fact decentralized like the rest of the country. In order to resurrect Peiyang, Tuan was even willing to create a faction within Peiyang with separate political and military arms (the Anfu Club and the Northwestern Frontier Army), which later came to be identified as the Anhwei faction, and to silence Peiyang dissidents by dismissal, isolation, or execution. But Peiyang members were not accustomed to high-handed treatment; even Yüan had employed more diplomatic methods when discipline was necessary. Members of Peiyang tended to regard it as a family. The head of a Chinese family was supposed to be stern and magnanimous at the same time; he must not be acrimonious or vengeful. Above all, the Chinese family valued harmony and frowned upon open divisions. It was incumbent upon Tuan, as a claimant to the Peiyang leadership, to fulfill these requirements. When it became evident that Tuan intended to persist in his high-handed style, others began to join forces for self-preservation. Thus, what started as an attempt to restore Peiyang's harmony and hegemony ended by splitting it hopelessly asunder.

CHAPTER 3

The Composition of the Military Factions

OUR TASK in this chapter is to examine the membership and sources of cohesion of the military factions. Unfortunately, the available literature provides us with little systematic analysis of this subject. We need to examine the plausible motivations and underlying causes that affected the militarists' choice of political behavior if we are to discover how strong and enduring these factions were in terms of the nature and composition of their internal organization.

It is my contention that while the membership of each faction displayed considerable fluidity over the twelve-year period, the basic factors affecting an individual's choice of faction remained relatively stable. An exploration of these factors constitutes the first step toward a more systematic study of early Republican military politics in China.

It is possible to classify these factors into three major categories: personal associations, calculations of self-interest, and ideological ties.

Personal Associations

The militarists' personal associations that are relevant for our analysis included both the primary ties of blood and marriage and secondary ties, such as teacher-student ties, institutional relationships, old school ties, or geographical origins.

The first and most important of all personal ties were those within the family. In China's tradition-bound society, the family was the major building block of the social universe. It constituted the primary social unit within which most human interactions took place. It also provided the context within which most individual rights and obligations were defined. In this society, it was morally imperative for a man to take care of his offspring or next of kin to the best of his ability.[1]

In the military factions, we have ample evidence that this tradition was honored. For example, Chang Tso-lin of Fengtien gave his son important assignments at a very young age to prepare him for eventual leadership in the faction.[2] In Chihli, after the victory over Anhwei in 1920, Ts'ao K'un made one brother (Ts'ao Jui) the civil governor of Chihli province, another (Ts'ao Yin) the commander of the 26th Division, and a nephew (Ts'ao Shih-chieh) the commander of his bodyguard brigade. In Yunnan, T'ang Chi-yao's two brothers also held important positions; T'ang Chi-yü was the acting civil governor and director of military training, and T'ang Chi-lin was a division commander in the 1920's. It was quite common for a man to help other members of his family or clan to join the same faction so that they could rely on each other. This practice was universal, with little appreciable difference either between the north and the south or among the provinces.

The role of family and clan ties in the military factions differed significantly from that prevailing under Imperial bureaucratic practices. In the traditional bureaucracy, entry into officialdom was regulated to a large extent by the uniform examination system, which quite effectively barred nepotism. Thus traditional nepotism usually took the form of granting to family members sinecure positions over which the official had control. When politics was a vocation with limited and expectable payoffs and risks, most people were satisfied with giving their relatives and kinsmen relatively unimportant (though well-paid) positions and entrusting serious administrative business to talented people. But when political activities became strategic in nature—that is, when one's political future no longer depended on adherence to definite institutional criteria, but on the ability to survive in a hostile environment where rules of behavior were ill-defined—the family and clan, as the most cohesive social group, tended to assume a larger political role.

Furthermore, the abolition of the regular recruitment channels in 1905 and the decline of traditional political morality removed the institutional and moral restraints upon nepotism. Consequently, in the military factions, nepotism became widely practiced. Relatives and clan members were given key positions far more often than their competence warranted. Family ties constituted the most useful instrument for moving directly into high political circles.

Intrafamily relationships generally facilitated centralization. A man's status as the father in a family or the head of a clan helped stabilize his official leadership position. The fact that he was the undisputed source of social and moral authority strengthened his political authority. By delegating power to members of the family, he was able not only to live up to the image of a patriarch dispensing favors but also to transplant the social cohesion and personal loyalty of the Chinese family structure into the political arena and achieve a high degree of political solidarity with these same people. When the diffuse and affective relationships governing family members were directly transferred to the political arena, the consequence was an even higher measure of congruence between the family and political patterns of authority. This was most conducive to political integration within the factions, at a time of great political uncertainty.

This does not mean that the two quite different relationships of commander-subordinate and father-son would automatically coincide. But the family relationship always took precedence over the commander-subordinate relationship and remained the final reference of proper conduct, political or otherwise. In this sense, role conflict was not likely to occur, because all other roles were subordinate to a man's family role, especially when a father-son relationship was involved.

Marriage provided another important means of creating political ties. An existing marriage tie might be used to cement factional ties, or a marriage might be concluded explicitly for such a purpose.

Of course, marriage had long been used as a diplomatic instrument in China, where parents had complete authority over the choice of their children's spouses. In the early days of the Republic, Yüan Shih-k'ai employed it with remarkable finesse. He gave Tuan Ch'i-jui his adopted daughter and Feng Kuo-chang his family governess in marriage to strengthen his personal connections with these two most powerful figures in the Peiyang Army. He also married one of his sons to Vice-President Li Yüan-hung's daughter. In 1920, Ts'ao K'un and Chang Tso-lin became in-laws by a marriage between their children, paving the way for closer cooperation. In the south, marriage ties also linked important militarists.[3] In numerous cases, marriages were instrumental in fostering a sense of common interest and a closer political relationship between otherwise independent parties. If one party to a marriage was decisively stronger than the other, the result was usually co-optation rather than alliance. This kind of marriage was common; a militarist who wanted to show special favor to a promising subordinate, for example, might offer his daughter or other female relative as a way of cementing a lasting political bond. Yüan Shih-k'ai's relationships with his generals fall into this category. The wider the social gap between the parties concerned, the stronger the political bond, since the inferior party would feel more grateful to the superior party. The most effective method of co-optation was to marry off one's daughter to a young junior officer from a very humble background who would otherwise have difficulty in advancing professionally. In these cases, the relationship could approach one between father and son.

While this kind of marriage was quite common between superior and inferior within the same military unit, it did not occur frequently between members of different units who already had different political loyalties, because the difference in loyalties might not be removed by the marriage ties. When marriages were made between different political camps, the parties usually were of approximately equal strength so that the use of coercion would be unprofitable. Under these circumstances, marriage might bring the parties into a temporary alliance or a permanent coalition. When marriages of this type played a role in the formation of factions, the outcome was usually a pluralistic rather than a unitary and integrated organization.

In Chinese society, the most significant nonfamilial association was doubtless that between a teacher and a student. Sometimes the teacher-student relationship surpassed the husband-wife relationship or even brotherhood in importance, as evidenced in the common saying, "a teacher for one day is a father for a lifetime." Whenever such a teacher-student relationship existed, it was used to good political advantage.

In early Republican China, this tie was used as one of the cornerstones in faction building. Some militarists deliberately cultivated this relationship in order to bind their followers to them permanently. A purely political relationship might change in accordance with issues or relative power positions, but a teacher-student relationship, by virtue of its nonpolitical nature, could never be altered. Yüan Shih-k'ai realized this and developed a teacher-student relationship with his subordinates.[4] Chiang Kai-shek later adopted the same approach with even greater success. As the Whampoa graduates, who formed the backbone of the KMT's military structure, advanced in rank and achieved fame and high official positions, they still referred to Chiang as a teacher regardless of his current title.

Another widespread secondary tie stemmed from the institutional ties that many militarists had acquired. One was a superior-subordinate relationship in a particular military unit. Although the institutional tie between superior and subordinate was often likened to that between father and son or teacher and student in hierarchical terms, its political effect was not nearly as enduring. For one thing, the generational difference was not always clear. A superior might be no older than his subordinate, and thus not enjoy the prestige that traditionally was bestowed upon age. He might also be unable to claim seniority in service; his subordinate might have joined the unit earlier but advanced more slowly. More important, a superior-subordinate tie in its purest and simplest form was a contractual tie, a result of the chance meeting of two persons on different rungs of the bureaucratic ladder. An institutional superior-subordinate tie did have stronger political implication if the superior was older, clearly belonged to a senior generation in professional terms, and had held the superior position in the institution with the same subordinates for a prolonged period of time.

Thus, the superior-subordinate relationship as such contributed little to cementing political bonds. This point needs to be emphasized, because many writers seem to see any previous institutional tie between two persons as an adequate explanation for the political relationship that existed between them at a later stage. Their view, however, fails to explain why some institutional superior-subordinate ties did not bring about closer political rela-

The Composition of the Military Factions

tionships. For example, a common explanation of Ts'ao K'un's hold on the 3d Division and Wu P'ei-fu is that Ts'ao, as the commander of the 3d Division, had a superior-subordinate tie with the men of this division. But this explanation fails to take into account the fact that Tuan Ch'i-jui had created the 3d Division and had also been its commander on at least two occasions. And Wu P'ei-fu actually joined the division when Tuan, not Ts'ao, was the commander.[5]

These observations led us to realize the political importance of patronage ties, which usually developed coincidentally with superior-subordinate institutional ties but sometimes were quite independent of them. Historically, Chinese bureaucrats often played the role of patron to some promising young subordinate as a way of building up their own political power. Since the acts of patronage were performed as personal favors beyond the patron's official calling, the protégés were expected to reciprocate in a nonofficial capacity. What was demanded from the protégé was unswerving loyalty.

The relationship between Ts'ao and Wu is a good example of the strength of the combination of patronage ties and superior-subordinate relationship of long standing. When Wu was a junior officer, Ts'ao rewarded his talents with rapid promotion. By 1918, when Ts'ao made Wu the acting commander of the 3d Division, everybody, including Wu himself, regarded Wu as Ts'ao's protégé. Wu, being deeply imbued with traditional morality, reciprocated by giving Ts'ao his unquestioning loyalty. After 1920, and especially after 1922, as Ts'ao removed himself from active military duties to go into politics, Wu became the most powerful military commander of his time. Despite the fact that Ts'ao had obviously become a political liability, Wu continued to tolerate the machinations of Ts'ao's underlings to the extent of suffering political defeats and sometimes even public humiliation for the sake of maintaining his personal relationship with Ts'ao.[6] When Ts'ao's political life was threatened in 1924, Wu did not hesitate to come to his aid, even at the risk of his own eclipse.

Militarists were often drawn into the same faction because they had attended the same military school. The few national military schools for advanced learning and a host of provincial military schools constituted the major suppliers of officers. (Military education will be discussed in detail in Chapter 4.) While the provincial schools trained cadets mainly for local use, the national schools inevitably attracted ambitious young men from all over the country. These schools thus provided a chance for students to broaden their social horizons and acquaintances. After graduation, they usually returned to their native provinces for service in local units, but the lasting friendships they had made during the school years and their membership in a particular graduating class bore a special meaning for them, as had always been the case in traditional China. When a militarist was faced with a choice of joining one faction or another, everything being equal, he would join the faction where he had schoolmates whom he had previously befriended and trusted.

Nationally, the military schools created by the Peiyang Army were certainly the most influential. The Peiyang Military Academy founded by Li Hung-chang in 1885 was the precursor of all the Peiyang military academies. Wang Shih-chen, Tuan Ch'i-jui, and Feng Kuo-chang were all graduates of this school and were recruited by Yüan Shih-k'ai to train the new army.[7] Later, Yüan expanded his own training program at Hsiao-chan by establishing more military schools and by giving enlisted men in-barracks instruction. The people involved in various aspects of the Hsiao-chan program, together with the graduates of the Academy recruited by Yüan, came to be known as the hard core of the Peiyang group. By all standards, this was the most important single group in Chinese politics during 1916–28. A partial listing of those graduated from the Peiyang Military Academy and the highest position they held prior to 1920 shows their importance:

Chang Huai-chih	Military governor of Shantung
Ch'en Kuang-yüan	Military governor of Kiangsi
Ch'i Hsieh-yüan	Division commander
Chiang Yen-hsin	Military governor of Süiyuan
Chin Yün-p'eng	Prime minister
Feng Kuo-chang	President
Ho Tsung-lien	Military governor of Chahar
Ho Feng-lin	Defense commissioner of Shanghai
Li Ch'ang-t'ai	Division commander
Li Hou-chi	Military governor of Fukien
Li Shun	Military governor of Kiangsu
Lu Yung-hsiang	Military governor of Chekiang
Pao Kuei-ch'ing	Military governor of Kirin

The Composition of the Military Factions

T'ien Chung-yü	Military governor of Shantung
Ts'ai Ch'eng-hsün	Military governor of Suiyüan
Ts'ao K'un	Military governor of Chihli
Tuan Ch'i-jui	Prime minister
Tuan Chih-kuei	Military governor of Fengtien
Wang Chan-yüan	Military governor of Hupeh
Wang Chin-ching	Division commander
Wang Huai-ch'ing	Commander in chief of metropolitan gendarmerie
Wang Ju-hsien	Division commander
Wang Shih-chen	Prime minister
Wang T'ing-cheng	Military governor of Chahar
Yang Shan-teh	Military governor of Chekiang

The successor of the Peiyang Military Academy was the Paoting Military Academy. It also produced a corps of well-known officers, including Chang Ching-yao, Wu P'ei-fu, Ch'en Shu-fan, Liu Wen-hui, and T'ang Sheng-chih. A smaller but more select group of students received military training in the Japanese military academy, Shikan Gakko, or its affiliated preparatory schools. Unfortunately, because of the large number of graduates of these schools and the paucity of information about them, we are unable to trace their career patterns with a high degree of accuracy. It is also extremely difficult to document the extent to which militarists from these schools were drawn together exclusively by virtue of being schoolmates. However, commentators on modern Chinese history often employ such expressions as "the Paoting clique" or "the Shikan Gakko clique" in the armies. The heavy recruitment of Paoting graduates into the KMT military structure was partly due to the fact that Chiang Kai-shek himself had attended the Army Short-Course School—the predecessor of Paoting—in 1907–8. Wang Po-lin, the academic dean of Whampoa Military Academy, once estimated that Paoting graduates usually occupied posts at the intermediate level of the Whampoa faculty and constituted about 20 percent of the entire faculty. The lower stratum of Whampoa's faculty was composed largely of graduates from the Yunnan Military Academy, who constituted 60 percent of the faculty. (There too, we may be witnessing personal and school ties at work, for Chu P'ei-teh, who was undoubtedly one of the most powerful of the KMT militarists, was a graduate of the Yunnan school.) On the highest level, the principal members of the Chinese faculty were trained in the Shikan Gakko. These included Chiang Kai-shek, Ho Yin-ch'in, Wang Po-lin, and Ch'ien Ta-chün. Three of the four department heads at Whampoa were trained in Japan.

In fact, the Whampoa Military Academy itself offers an excellent case of how a school tried to imbue its cadets with a sense of identity with the school and to create an effective bond among themselves that would remain strong long after they left. The Whampoa Academy was extremely successful in inculcating an esprit de corps among its graduates, almost to the point of being clannish. As modern Chinese history amply proves, there was no other institution that succeeded in serving as the focal point of the political loyalty of its members as well as Whampoa did.

Geographical ties had always been a powerful force for drawing people into social and political groupings throughout Chinese history. Partly this can be explained by the lack of physical mobility in agrarian China. Although the same written script had been in use for nearly two thousand years, different localities still preserved their own very different folklores and dialects. These differences naturally fostered a strong local identity among the residents.*

The factional politics of the 1916–28 period also reflected geographical ties. The militarists preferred to recruit people from their own provinces or districts whenever possible. Regional armies were common. In addition to historical and cultural reasons, militarists usually avoided recruiting from remote places for two practical reasons: the soldiers might desert and return to their homeland, or worse, they might rebel or defect, especially when ordered to fight against their own provincials. A slightly less important reason was that an army of mixed geographical origins would have serious administrative problems, caused by different dialects, eating habits, and general styles of life.† By and large, the Peiyang militarists at least tried to recruit only north-

---

* There are other historical factors that gave the concept of locality a particular political importance. As Ho Ping-ti (*Chung-kuo hui kuan shih lun*) points out, the concept of locality was drilled into the minds of the politically conscious members of the traditional society through a number of institutions and regulations.

† For instance, when Feng Yü-hsiang was in Szechwan in 1915–16, he recruited some local soldiers. When he left the province, however, he released the Szechwan soldiers because he felt they would have difficulty adjusting to the life outside. Liu Ju-ming, "I ko hang wu chün jen ti hui i," *Chuan chi wen hsüeh* (hereafter referred to as *CCWH*), 5, no. 4 (Oct. 1964): 21–22.

erners, even when they possessed territories south of the Yangtze River.

The militarists' propensity to stay close to their fellow provincials was exhibited not only in recruiting policies but also in the search for political allies. They preferred other militarists who came from the same or neighboring areas. In both the Chihli and the Fengtien factions, a large proportion of the initial membership came from a few provinces. While the geographical distribution of members of the Anhwei faction was more dispersed, Tuan seemed to be closest to the people from Anhwei. Having said this, let me hasten to add that the conventional explanation of the factions is misleading, because it focuses on geographical origin alone as the organizing principle of the factions. If a member's geographical origin was not the same as the leader's, it is considered a deviation. This is too simplistic. Our analysis will show that geographical origin was but one variable influencing a militarist's choice of factions, and it was not always the most important one.

Local ties differed in the extent of their emotional content. Their intensity was in inverse relationship to the size of the geographical referents: the smaller the area, the stronger the identity. The tie was more intense when the community had a common language and was more isolated from the outside world. And, of course, individuals differed in the intensity of their sense of affinity with others from the same area. And last, all these factors were affected by the scope of the faction's operations. When a faction operated over a large geographical area, then a person's home province had significant meaning. When a faction operated over a small geographical area such as a single province, then a county or district tended to be a more important point of identification.

Occasionally, a number of people from a few counties or districts achieved a particularly high level of solidarity for historical reasons. In the factional politics of the early Republican period, for example, Anhwei's Ho-fei county stood out as a very significant locality, mostly because an antecedent of the Peiyang Army, the Huai-chün, had been founded by a Ho-fei man, Li Hung-chang. At least six Ho-fei men (Tuan Ch'i-jui, Tuan Chih-kuei, Chia Te-yao, Wu Kuang-hsin, Wu Ping-hsiang, and Nieh Hsien-fan) played very conspicuous roles in the Anhwei faction.

Usually, however, the province was taken to be the basic unit in identifying people's geographical origin. Although there is little comparative study of the varying strengths of provincial sentiments, my impression is that northerners were less identified with their provinces when they dealt with other northerners. Southerners were more conscious of their provincial differences even when they dealt with other southerners. Looking at the composition of various military factions, we find that southerners seldom crossed provincial boundaries to join the army of another province, while northerners from the provinces of Chihli, Shantung, and Honan often were found in the same faction but almost never in a southern faction.

Thus we label the factions Anhwei, Chihli, or Fengtien only for convenience. The nature of the faction as a political organization cannot be wholly understood in such restricted geographical terms.

Our analysis of the political functions of interpersonal relationships cannot be complete without a discussion of some other relationships that had been important in traditional Chinese bureaucratic circles. One is the so-called "shih-chiao," or friendship between two families that extended over more than one generation. Once a close political relationship had developed between bureaucrats, there was a great likelihood that their descendants would preserve and exploit it. Among families with a long tradition of academic and bureaucratic success, such ties could be very enduring and self-reinforcing. The militarists of the early Republican period, however, usually came from nonbureaucratic backgrounds with few preexisting political ties. Most of them were first-generation successes themselves. Therefore, the "shih-chiao" ties did not play a noticeable role in attracting people into the same military faction.

Another traditional tie was friendship. Historically, the idealized notion of friendship and sworn brotherhood had provided the dominant organizational ethos for many political groups, especially the secret societies. Although it was at times a stronger political force than many other personal ties, the political significance of friendship is more difficult to define. Friendship as an affective tie pure and simple was totally subjective. Unless two persons were locked into a sworn brotherhood, we have little basis for judging whether their political relationship was an extension

The Composition of the Military Factions

of their friendship. The task is made harder by the fact that friendship usually did not exist in isolation, but developed alongside other ties, such as classmate or colleague ties. Thus, while recognizing the profound importance of friendship in influencing political behavior, I can think of no way to measure it.

Calculations of Self-Interest

We are occasionally confronted with cases in which none of the personal ties described above was present in any significant degree. One plausible explanation in these cases is that the militarist's alignment policy was shaped by his perception and definition of self-interest. In order to analyze the utility of self-interest as a guide to understanding the faction-building process, we must differentiate several types of militarists with divergent configurations of interests.

First of all, there were those who had very little or no control of territory. This situation was most common at the beginning of the period, when boundary lines between militarists were ill-defined or unstable; between 1916 and 1920 there were many itinerant militarists.* There were great discrepancies in the strength of the militarists in this category. One might command a division with close to fifteen thousand men, another a battalion with a couple of hundred. Sooner or later these militarists would be forced to try to align themselves with a strong militarist with a territory, in exchange for recognition—and thereby some guarantee—of their status. A militarist who conducted these negotiations well and then judiciously employed force to capitalize on his diplomatic gains might even obtain great power and position within a very short time.

The rise of the new Kwangsi army is a vivid illustration of how an upstart army found a way to survive and prosper. According to Huang Shao-hung, a Kwangsi general who rose to great fame

---

* Wu P'ei-fu and Feng Yü-hsiang are two good examples. Before 1920, Wu's 3d Division was in Hunan and had to depend on Tuan Ch'i-jui for financial support as well as military supplies. Wu also had to depend on local funds contributed by chambers of commerce channeled through Chang Ching-yao. At times, Chang detained the funds, causing Wu considerable hardship. *HSCTK*, no. 1019. Feng's 16th Mixed Brigade was equally shiftless during those years. He also had to depend on the Peking government and the local governments for a living. For a detailed chronology of Feng's movements, see Sheridan, *Feng Yü-hsiang*.

in the Nationalist era, when Lu Jung-t'ing was driven out of Kwangtung in 1921, his rule over Kwangsi also started to crumble and Shen Hung-ying became a new military power in Kwangsi. At this time Huang himself and Li Tsung-jen commanded very meager forces and were barely able to survive, often moving from place to place. In 1922, Huang and Li, who had been classmates at the Kwangsi military school years before, decided to join forces. Their combined strength was still only about three thousand men and two thousand rifles. Of course, they could not expect this new force to be tolerated by Shen Hung-ying. Therefore, Huang approached Shen and offered to be his subordinate. As a result of the negotiations, Huang accepted Shen's commission as a brigade commander, and Shen supplied Huang's brigade with arms, ammunition, and funds. In this manner, the Huang-Li combination not only kept a piece of territory without harassment, but also received supplies and protection from a stronger power, all at the cost of being a nominal subordinate to Shen. In 1923, when Shen attacked Kwangtung, he left his rear undefended. After Shen was rebuffed in Kwangtung, Huang and Li disarmed the defeated soldiers and took away a large quantity of matériel, which greatly strengthened their forces. Turning again to diplomacy, they then persuaded Shen to bury the hatchet and join forces with them to attack Lu Jung-t'ing's remaining forces. In the autumn of 1924, these allied forces defeated Lu and drove him out of Kwangsi. Almost immediately Huang and Li turned around to attack Shen Hung-ying and totally defeated him. By the summer of 1924, when they repulsed an invasion of the Yunnan militarists, they had become the only military power in Kwangsi. Thus, through a judicious combination of force and diplomacy, a nomadic force of a couple of thousand men were able to expand to forty thousand men and to conquer an entire province.[8]

The Kwangsi force was outstanding for its phenomenal success, but its approach was not unique. Some militarists, satisfied with finding shelter and a regular source of income, remained subordinate to a stronger force; others went all the way for greater power and larger territory. In any event, they sought a territorial base, because the disadvantages of being without a territory were great. In the first place, defense posed enormous problems. Without a home base, the militarist was unable to develop a defense plan in advance. He had to fight on unfamiliar terrain and to improvise his defense from battle to battle. In the second place, a militarist who had to wage wars constantly without an assured source of human and material resources could not expect to survive for long. He needed at least enough men to replace battle casualties. He needed arms, preferably from his own arsenal, and food. He also needed money to pay his expenses and to enrich himself. Furthermore, he needed civilian labor to perform such chores as transporting supplies and digging trenches. All these needs could be met only when a territorial base was secured.

Thus, strategic considerations and sheer survival sooner or later compelled all such forces to seek a territorial base, through alliance or conquest, or both. Even as large and strong a force as Feng Yü-hsiang's found it expedient to join the Chihli faction, if only to bail itself out of a financial predicament. For these reasons, the militarists without territory were only a transient group. Those who realized where their self-interest lay attached themselves to a faction. Those who failed to do so simply vanished from the political landscape.

A second category of militarists included those who had some definite territorial base. Again, their strength varied. Although in theory the military governor was the sole authority in his province, in practice he did not always possess such authority. In some cases, other officials, with such titles as "Defense Commissioner of the Upper Yangtze Valley," or "Commander of Bandit Suppression Army," might claim authority over several provinces or parts of provinces. The overlapping structures of authority tended to produce clashes of interest between these officials and the provincial military governors.*

The military governor's authority could also be undermined from within. Usually the local militarists within a province had their own smaller spheres of influence, over which the military governor had only intermittent or poor control, if any.† They

---

* One dispute involved the strategically and commercially important city of Hsüchow. Although located in Kiangsu province, it was occupied by Chang Hsün after 1913 as the site of his Office of the Inspector General for the Yangtze Valley. This caused a lot of hard feeling between Chang and Feng Kuo-chang, the military governor of Kiangsu. *Biographical Dictionary of Republican China*, 1: 70; and *NCH*, Sept. 2, 1916; Oct. 14, 1916.

† Typically, the military structure of a province was very confused. First, there were units of the national army—divisions, brigades, regiments, etc.—many of which were independent or semi-independent of both the central and

collaborated with the military governors only to the extent that their own interests were not jeopardized. Since the majority of militarists during the early stages controlled only parts of a province, their main task was to reintegrate the politico-military forces and reassert their authority within their own provinces.

While internally the provincial governors spared no effort to suppress autonomous tendencies, externally they tried to follow a policy of neutrality or noninvolvement. This was especially true when they were sandwiched between strong neighbors. Under these circumstances, they would scrupulously follow the dictum of being "friendly to all but ally of none," and they often played one neighbor against another in the hope of retaining their independence. Shansi achieved admirable results by following this policy. Hunan also tried to stand aloof from the north-south constitutional dispute, but its chances of success were severely compromised by its geographical position.

When militarists were compelled to take sides in order to protect their own interests, their best policy was to join the militarists who posed the least potential or actual threat to their security, against those who posed the greatest threat. Here, the geographical constraint played a key role in their decisions. Since the most immediate threat usually came from one's closest neighbors, it would be wise to enter an alliance or a faction with a distant militarist who felt the same threat. This would reduce friction between partners and increase mutual security by confronting the opponent with a two-front problem. In this light, it seems perfectly logical that Chekiang, in order to keep Shanghai, entered into a closer relationship with Anhwei, which also had territorial problems with Kiangsu. Both, in turn, wanted to ally themselves with a stronger power

---

the provincial governments. Next, there were the strictly provincial units (*hsün-fang-tui*), which were raised, funded, and controlled by the powerful men in the province for garrison duties. Occasionally remnants of the Manchu Green Standards continued to exist under their old commanders and stood outside the provincial military structure. Further, there were a variety of military units under special administrative agencies, such as the water police, anti-smuggling forces, the salt gabelle troops, transportation protection forces, reserves or temporary forces, and numerous other emergency troops, constabularies of one kind or another, and personal guards. And last, there were numerous local militia organized on a voluntary basis, either by local gentry or by prominent merchants. For a discussion of these forces, see *The China Year Book, 1921–1922* (henceforth referred to as *CYB*), p. 536.

The Composition of the Military Factions

to counterbalance the potential threat of Kiangsu's allies, and they found Tuan eager to help. This pattern, which was followed with considerable consistency, probably helps to explain the territorial fragmentation of some factions.

The third and final category of militarists included the really powerful ones. Their great capabilities enabled them to pursue flexible external policies toward weaker militarists, through either peaceful incorporation or armed aggression. Generally, the powerful militarists were quite willing to forgo total integration in exchange for nominal allegiance and to postpone consolidation. At times, however, they also used physical force to bring recalcitrant militarists into the faction. The many wars fought in the early period and the drastic revisions in the constellation of each faction attest to the fact that physical conquest always remained as an ultimate means of faction building.

The presence of some very powerful militarists was catalytic to the division of militarists along factional lines. In general, weak and medium-strength militarists decided to enter permanent factions only after the other militarists had clearly demonstrated their superior political, military, and economic capabilities. An added incentive for joining a faction was provided if a militarist would thereby greatly increase his capabilities in comparison either with his own past or with neighboring territories.

Surveying the political landscape of China between 1916 and 1920, we see that the militarists who later became the rallying points of factional struggle had already distinguished themselves in many ways. In Manchuria, Chang Tso-lin was definitely the fastest rising star in the military hierarchy. He was a dynamic and aggressive leader, was widely popular, and possessed great political acumen. In 1916, Chang, who commanded one of the two Fengtien divisions (the 27th), forced the military governor of Fengtien to resign his post and then succeeded him. By 1917, he had outmaneuvered his rival, Feng Teh-lin, the commander of the 28th Division, and absorbed his force. The other militarists in Manchuria, such as Pi Kuei-fang, Hsü Lan-chou, and Meng En-yüan, were too old or weak, had rather colorless personalities, and had very little ambition. All were from Chihli province, rather than natives of Manchuria, which gave Chang an added advantage in the political struggle. Pi Kuei-fang knew nothing about military affairs, while the other two commanded only small forces. Under these circumstances, it became quite natural for other militarists in Manchuria to flock around Chang.[9]

Tuan Ch'i-jui was another dynamic leader and a militarist of great stature. He played an important role from the beginning of the Newly Established Army program at Hsiao-chan and developed a close relationship with Yüan Shih-k'ai. As the Peiyang Army expanded, Tuan assumed command of a number of its new units, including the 3d, 4th, and 6th imperial divisions. In these capacities, he acquired a wide range of institutional connections with most of the important militarists who rose from the Hsiao-chan background. Furthermore, as the primary architect of the Peiyang training programs, Tuan developed a lasting teacher-student relationship with many second-generation Peiyang officers. Shortly after the Republic was founded, Tuan became Yüan's minister of war; in 1913 he served briefly as acting premier. In later years, especially after Yüan's death, both posts were to become Tuan's primary bases of political operations. In three years (1916-19), Tuan not only had the power to oversee the organization and training of his own army (the Northwestern Frontier Army), but also had more opportunity than any other militarist to affect the transfer, promotion, and appointment of officers of other military units loyal to the Peking government, which enabled him to play the role of patron to a large number of young militarists. Last, by virtue of his control over the finances of the Peking government, he had a decisive voice in the distribution of funds, arms, and ammunition. Even the non-Peiyang militarists had to ingratiate themselves with Tuan in order to maintain a viable political life. Thus, Tuan was in a unique position to build a political following and to develop his own military power (the War Participation Army).[10]

In central China, we find another formidable figure in the person of General Feng Kuo-chang. Feng's major military activities during the Hsiao-chan period were in the area of military education, through which he came into contact with a large number of Peiyang soldiers and officers; with some of them he developed a direct teacher-student relationship. Moreover, Feng had served as the commander of different Peiyang units, and he later led the First and Second Imperial Armies in the suppression of the revolu-

The Composition of the Military Factions 53

tionaries. After the second revolution of 1913, Feng succeeded Chang Hsün as the military governor of Kiangsu, a post that he held for four years. During this period he expanded his personal military power to two divisions and acquired a sphere of influence over Kiangsi and, to a lesser extent, Hupeh. In July 1917, in the aftermath of the monarchist debacle, Feng succeeded Li Yüan-hung as the president of the republic, thereby further enhancing his political prestige.[11]

Only in Manchuria, Peking, and the Yangtze valley, however, were there such prominent figures ready to assume leadership of any large-scale political groupings. In the rest of the country, no one of comparable stature could be found. In the south, despite the presence of the KMT military government, there was no single center of gravity. One militarist was powerful in Kwangsi and parts of Kwangtung, another in Yunnan, still another in Kweichow. Similar situations existed in Hunan and Szechwan, except that there was more than one center of power within each province.

Therefore, in the formation of the Fengtien, Anhwei, and Chihli factions, there is a discernible correlation between the configuration of the militarists and the existence of a particular militarist whose capabilities were markedly superior to his neighbors'. In each case, he commanded enormous personal prestige, had wide political connections, and controlled a large army.

On the other hand, where no such sharp disparity existed among the militarists in a given area—such as the south, Hunan, and Szechwan—considerations of self-interest might dissuade militarists from joining any specific group. For instance, in the territory nominally held by the KMT, Lu Jung-t'ing was the most powerful militarist in Kwangsi and western Kwangtung. However, he could not serve as a rallying point, because there were local militarists in Yunnan and Kweichow whose personal stature and military or economic capabilities were not markedly inferior to Lu's. The southern militarists therefore had little motivation to integrate. These factors help to explain why the KMT was dormant as a political actor prior to 1924. The KMT existed largely by grace of the cooperation of the various local militarists for a very limited purpose, i.e. to preserve the legal façade of a constitutional movement to protect them against northern military encroachment. The KMT finally succeeded in integrating Kwangtung and Kwangsi only after the KMT's elite army had scored several impressive victories over these militarists and after financial and administrative reforms had greatly augmented its power. In other words, the southern militarists became reluctant supporters of the integration policy only after they had seen clearly that there was a great future for the KMT and that it would be better to jump on the bandwagon now than to be coerced onto it later.

In Hunan and Szechwan, a single center of power never developed. In both provinces, there were several semi-independent units, each ruling a small territory with equally meager resources. None of the militarists ever succeeded in enhancing his own capabilities enough to upset the existing distribution of power and to thrust himself forward as a leader. As a result, throughout the entire period, both provinces remained fragmented. The rare occasions when they displayed some potential for solidarity were prompted by imminent danger of invasion; as soon as the danger subsided, old divisions and rivalries returned to the fore. It was not until the very end of the period, when the possibility of KMT hegemony loomed large, that they reversed their independent lines of policy and joined the roll-up process.

Ideological Ties

The third factor that might affect a militarist's choice of faction is ideology. Almost immediately, we are confronted with the need for a functional definition of ideology. David E. Apter's definition, as "the explicit and derivative articulation of political norms," seems to imply that the articulation must also be coherent, systematic, and organized, because the formation of ideology itself represents a process of intellectual and moral maturation.[12] If such a rigorous definition is used, then very few Chinese militarists could be said to have had an ideology. If ideology is broadly defined as any system of beliefs or values, explicit or implicit, then many of them could be said to have had some ideology. We will use the broader definition in this discussion.

The Chinese militarists fall into two groups according to the degree of articulation of their ideological orientation. The overwhelming majority of them could be characterized as having implicit and unarticulated ideologies. That is, to some extent they

The Composition of the Military Factions 55

marshaled certain moral and political principles to justify their existence, and they had conceptions of right and wrong. But in general these militarists made little attempt to raise their political principles or moral standards to the articulate and conscious level. No major ideological differences distinguished one militarist from another. Consequently, no militarists in this group were in a position to utilize ideology to win over a large number of followers to their faction.

The second group includes a much smaller number of militarists who had explicit and articulate ideologies of some kind. Militarists like Chang Hsün, Wu P'ei-fu, Ch'en Chiung-ming, Li Tsung-jen, Feng Yü-hsiang, and Yen Hsi-shan all came to be identified with some ideas or programs. Their ideologies varied, from Chang Hsün's loyalty to the deposed Manchu monarchy and veneration of the imperial ways to Feng Yü-hsiang's and Yen Hsi-shan's mixture of many creeds, some moral, some political, and others religious in nature.

Among those who consciously cultivated an ideological image, there were two different approaches to the forms of indoctrination. One approach, of which Chang Hsün is an example, involved no organized attempt at systematic orientation of the rank and file. The ideological orientation of the army was determined by the top commander, who at most used informal indoctrination sporadically, such as through the occasional use of symbols and slogans, or through rewards for approved behavior. The other approach, typified by Feng and Yen, involved the conscious pursuit of systematic indoctrination. Formal indoctrination constituted an important part of the soldiers' daily routine. In Feng's army, for example, catechisms, songs, slogans, moralistic stories, lectures by officers, sermons by chaplains, and propaganda by cadres from the political department were orchestrated to drill the ideology into the soldiers' minds.[13]

Formal, systematic indoctrination seems to have been more conducive to enhancing internal solidarity than informal and intermittent indoctrination. The more the rank and file were exposed to an intense and deliberate indoctrination program and the more they acquired a sense of active participation, the more strongly they would identify with the unit. It was not at all accidental that

Feng and Yen commanded some of the most cohesive forces in the Chinese system.

Of more immediate concern to us in the present context, however, is the effect of ideology on recruitment or formation of factions. On this point the available evidence is very sketchy. Although Feng Yü-hsiang's army was quite well known for its ideological coloration, for example, most of the men joined it for nonideological reasons. Indeed, one of Feng's most impressive achievements was to convert men with a mercenary mentality into ideological soldiers.

Whether Yen Hsin-shan's ideological program in the Shansi army helped him to attract more followers is even more difficult to ascertain. Yen's regime was the only power structure in Shansi that could dispense political, economic, and social rewards. Ambitious individuals seeking advancement within the province had no alternative but to join him. It is therefore hard to establish the degree to which career and other interest calculations or personal or ideological ties brought them to support Yen Hsi-shan. The most that can be said is that Shansi represents a case where ideology might have attracted some individuals who otherwise would not have joined political forces with it.

Thus, up until 1923, when most military factions had already been formed, ideology as such played a minor role. And even after 1923, the only clear case of an ideological actor was the KMT. In the span of two years, between 1924 and 1926, the KMT became the champion of anti-warlordism, anti-imperialism, nationalism, responsible government, and the people's livelihood. Under Sun Yat-sen's leadership, the aim of the KMT reorganization was not only to improve internal solidarity by borrowing the Bolshevik model but also to develop into a broad-based multiclass national political movement. By the time it launched its Northern Expedition, the KMT's internal structure was already radically different from an ordinary military faction that drew its main support from the army. The KMT, in addition to having an army, had attracted significant elements from the workers, the peasants, and the new intelligentsia. Thus ideology and organization combined to attract many people into the KMT camp. The KMT was the only case in the Chinese system in which ideology was a major factor in the growth of a formidable political force.

The Effects of These Ties on Factional Cohesion

Having described the three groups of factors conducive to the formation of factions, we shall now turn to the question of how much they contributed or hindered the cohesion of these politico-military organizations. We shall begin with the factor that contributed the least to cohesion, self-interest.

The relationship between interest calculations and group cohesion is difficult to generalize. Under some circumstances, calculations of self-interest would be conducive to group cohesion. If a militarist joined a faction in order to achieve some nonaffective goals (such as power, wealth, career), then he would stay with the faction as long as these goals were achieved. Furthermore, even when a militarist's original motives were utilitarian, he might later develop affective attitudes to the leader or to the faction and then stay in the faction because of them.

Nonetheless, it is fair to say that interest calculations generally provided a rather weak incentive to uphold group cohesion, because the military factions were not ordinarily interest groups and the Chinese political system was different from ordinary national political systems. Most interest groups—farmers' associations, labor unions, chambers of commerce—have relatively stable and easily identifiable interests. They fight for limited stakes, for more or less share in the distribution of available resources, not for total interest or life or death. When people want to promote different interests, the logical thing to do is to join different interest groups. When each interest group is identified with one or a few specified interests, when the interest structure of its membership can be expected to stay constant over a long period of time, when the demands placed by the members upon the group are few and specified, and when the group's political activities are restricted to promoting these few well-defined interests, interest calculations can prove to be an exceedingly strong force for group cohesion.

The Chinese military factions were a different kind of political creature. Each militarist had a large number of interests (political, military, financial, territorial, social, private, etc.), but there were only a few military factions. None of the factions was identified with a specific interest, such as financial or territorial. Instead, every faction was a total-interest group. Since the interests were many and the interest groups were few, members inevitably tended to place heavy demands upon and entertain high expectations for the military faction, which naturally placed more stress on its cohesion. In other words, when the members expected a single faction (or interest group) to take care of many of their diverse interests, they had a greater chance of discovering that some of them were not served by the faction. Thus, when interest calculation *alone* was the reason for a militarist's joining a faction, his linkage with the faction was weak. As soon as his interests were significantly threatened, he would seek another faction.

Moreover, under the Chinese political system, participation in the political process involved more than the issue of how great a share of the resources a militarist was to get: it often involved his very existence. The Chinese militarists could not be expected to remain loyal to a faction in the face of serious threats to their personal interests. If they allowed themselves to suffer serious harm, they would not be around to fight the next round regardless of how the faction as a whole had fared. These militarists joined a faction not to promote one or two specific interests, but to fight for their political existence or total interest. Therefore, if a militarist joined a faction solely for self-interest, there was a high probability that he would feel dissatisfied with that faction. The division of labor, the distribution of rewards (in weapons, manpower, territory, offices, funds, etc.), personality conflicts, the threat of war and defeat, or any of a host of other reasons could persuade a militarist that his interest was being jeopardized and that he would do better by joining another faction. The abundant evidence of flux in military factions, of frequent defections, mutinies, desertions, and surrenders bears testimony to the fact that self-interest by itself was the least conducive to group cohesion.

Ideology presents an equally complicated problem. In its ideal form, ideology undoubtedly can be a very cohesive force. In the Chinese political reality, however, conventional social norms and relationships exerted a strong influence. Ideology was not locked in a fierec combat to dislodge and repudiate all traditional ties; rather, it operated in conjunction with them. Although ideology provided a basis for a radically different definition of its political goals, even the KMT, the foremost ideological power, did not hesitate to exploit personal, nonideological approaches whenever they served a useful purpose. Ideology had indeed introduced a number of structural mechanisms and innovations into the KMT's internal organization that contributed greatly to the party's cohesion, but its cohesion was also supported by extensive personal ties.

Since personal relationships were so pervasive and important in shaping Chinese politico-military factions, the remainder of this chapter will be devoted to a further exploration of their effects on the internal organization of the factions.

When we consider the effects of personal associations, we should remember that these associations existed as part of the larger social order. A faction that was formed principally on the basis of these associational ties was likely to achieve great internal cohesion, because its internal organization was consistent with the prevailing social order and ethical values and because its claim of legitimacy was sanctioned by them. This was most true when the faction grew from an original small nucleus of militarists who were closely related by such ties. These militarists owed personal loyalty to their leader. As the group expanded, they also grew in power and rose in rank; a centralized recruitment policy could further safeguard the homogeneity of the faction and prevent divergent centers of power from developing.*

These ties, however, did not always produce group solidarity. If the faction did not grow out of a parent unit but resulted from a merger of separate units, personal bonds might fail to bring any great stability to the faction's structure. Two factors contributed to this failure. First, there was difficulty in identifying the object of loyalty. The personal ties, being affective ties, worked best as guides to political choices when they were sharply defined, bilat-

* A case in point is Feng Yü-hsiang's army. The nucleus of his force consisted of men who served in Feng's unit either just before or immediately after 1911. The various ties among members of this nucleus were conscientiously preserved even after Feng's force had expanded into a huge army. Because of his stringent centralized control over recruitment, none of his lieutenants even tried to create a separate power base. As a regular practice, Feng often rotated his chief commanders among different units, possibly to prevent them from cultivating close institutional ties with the members of any unit over a period of time. When recruits joined Feng's army, they were instructed to be loyal to Feng, but their loyalty to their immediate superiors was never cultivated. Sheridan, p. 89.

eral, few in number as well as in kind, and noncontradictory. As these ties became more extensive, diffused, and multilateral, their utility as guides for political behavior diminished correspondingly. Consequently, when a militarist had to deal with a number of other militarists who were connected with him in different ways, it was very difficult for him to choose purely on the basis of personal or institutional relationships.

Worse still, as these ties multiplied, their relative importance became less susceptible to sharp definition. To be sure, a blood relationship was always paramount. Beyond that, it could be quite difficult for some militarists to rank other relationships on a scale and to state with certainty which relationships were more important. The difficulty was compounded when two militarists were related to each other in more than one capacity. The relations between Wu P'ei-fu and Ch'ü T'ung-feng illustrate this point. Both came from Shantung; there existed a teacher-student relationship between them, since Wu was a cadet at Paoting while Ch'ü was its commandant; Ch'ü was Tuan's protégé and Wu was Tuan's subordinate when Tuan was the commander of the 3d Imperial Division.[14] These relationships seem close enough and seem to reinforce each other. But, on the other hand, Wu also had institutional and patron-protégé relationships with Ts'ao K'un when he succeeded Tuan as the commander of the 3d Imperial Division. In the factional line-up after 1918, Ch'ü stayed in Tuan's camp while Wu followed his new master, Ts'ao. Wu and Ch'ü ended up fighting against each other in 1920. Thus, on the basis of the affective ties between these two men, their decisions to join different factions were anything but simple choices. In both cases the patron-protégé ties seemed to have overshadowed the other conflicting ties.

Therefore, as soon as the network of relationships became too complicated, its utility as a guide to alignment policies decreased correspondingly. Faced with many different claims, a militarist often felt at a loss to identify the proper recipient of his loyalty. Of course, looked at from a different angle, it may be argued that the complicated social web actually increased many militarists' flexibility in their alignment policies. When the connections were few and bilateral, it could be psychologically difficult for a militarist to depart from them. When the connections were many and multilateral, there was more room for exercising personal discretion and preference. A militarist could then bring his alignment policies into greater agreement with his self-interest, while still claiming to abide by the prevailing social norms.

Second, even after the object of loyalty had been identified, complications might arise in communication. For it was relatively easy for junior members of a military unit to direct their loyalty to their immediate superiors when identification was easy and face-to-face communication existed. When the unit became part of a larger group, the distance between the leader and the rank and file was lengthened, and new communication barriers were introduced. These barriers could affect group solidarity in two directions, horizontally and vertically. Since the larger group was usually composed of several militarists who had different kinds of relationships with the group leader, it was often hard for junior members of each military unit to extend the same kind of loyalty horizontally to the other militarists' units simply because they now belonged to the same larger group. There resulted a lack of horizontal coordination, and even of horizontal communication, among militarists on the same organizational rung. This peculiar situation, in turn, was related to the character of vertical communication within the larger military organization. Distance alone constituted a significant barrier in the flow of vertical communication; as the distance between the group leader and the members of the participating units lengthened, the identification of the object of loyalty was obscured, because the ties which bound the militarist to a particular group and to the group leader were usually not the same as those that bound him with his own followers. Although the militarist was supposed to serve as an intermediary between his unit and the larger group, in actuality he might not want to do so.

Here it is necessary to point out that in essence these armies were personal armies. The militarists realized that they owed their positions in a particular group to the troops they possessed. In this case, it would be foolish of them to tolerate a direct affective relationship between their troops and the group leader, for once their followers began to view the group as their own, then the group leader could exert direct pressure upon them and the intermediary role of the militarists would lose utility.

True to the style of personal armies, each militarist wanted to

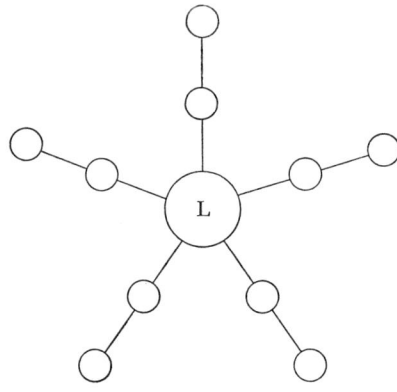

Fig. 1. The Krech-Crutchfield-Ballachey sociometric model

act as the sole spokesman for his troops. His troops were his clients and political capital, he their negotiator. He tried to satisfy their needs to retain their service; he in turn negotiated with the other militarists to serve his own interests. In order to insulate the troops from any pressure from the larger organization, the militarists must see to it that the vertical flow of communication was severely curtailed. As it went, the group leader could issue orders only to his immediate subordinates, who then relayed them to their immediate subordinates, and so on.

The desire for organizational insulation also caused most militarists to eye with suspicion any suggestion of increased horizontal communications, for they also had to guard against any attempt by their colleagues to swallow up their units. One easy way to augment one's influence within a group was to win over a colleague's troops, by persuasion, promise of promotion, the mobilization of affective ties, or bribery. There were many cases in which militarists suffered sudden political death because their colleagues swallowed up their troops. Hence, most militarists tried to discourage the development of friendly social contacts or of any other modes of communication between their own subordinates and other militarists.

The organization that emerges from our analysis of Chinese military factions bears a close resemblance to the star-shaped sociometric picture described by Krech, Crutchfield, and Ballachey (Figure 1).[15] The main characteristic of this type of organizational relationship is that the "intercommunication among the members is held to a minimum and wherever possible the avenues of intercommunication are through the leader or are under his immediate supervision."[16] And in the case of Chinese military factions, even the vertical communication flow was drastically reduced in many instances.

The Chinese military factions, like other Chinese organizations, were both hierarchical and authoritarian. A man should never try to communicate with a higher authority over the head of his own immediate superior, and even his contact with his immediate superior should be limited to periodic reaffirmation of his loyalty and silent obedience to his orders. To the average Chinese political actor, political issues came and went, but the basic personal relationships must remain intact at all times. In Richard Solomon's term, this "holding in" of feelings became the best way to preserve the interpersonal relationships between the leader and the led.[17] In this sense, a man's loyalty to the leader was measured not by how much he could contribute to the resolution of issues, but by how well he could restrain his expression of disagreement and swallow his pride. Literally, the leader was to lead and do all the worrying, while the others just waited to be led.*

The personal nature of many of the militarists' political relationships and their peculiar notions of how loyalty and subordination should be demonstrated posed great threats to the integration of the faction as an effective politico-military organization. Political conditions being as volatile as they were, there was great need for the leader and the followers of a faction to exchange views and to pool their collective talents in arriving at rational strategies. When his subordinates refrained from candid expression of their inner thoughts or merely told him what he wanted to hear, there was real danger that the leader would be cut off from political realities and make major decisions on the basis of false assumptions or erroneous information. As the leader became less and less aware of the sentiments and thoughts of his subordinates, the sub-

* For instance, according to the reminiscences of Ch'in Te-shun, a noted Nationalist general who had served in Feng Yü-hsiang's army, Feng saw that all his officers followed his orders, that they never ventured an opinion on important matters, and that all major military and political decisions were dictated by the commander in chief personally. *Ch'in Te-shun hui i lu*, p. 149.

ordinates became more and more estranged from him. Thus, for instance, while Tuan was a leader respected by his fellow militarists (including his rivals), his confidant Hsü Shu-cheng was widely hated. Tuan's loss of prestige within the Peiyang hierarchy was due in no small measure to his unlimited trust in Hsü. Similarly, Ts'ao K'un was misled by his brothers and close personal advisers into thinking that there was nothing wrong with buying the presidency, even though none of his important official subordinates was ever actively involved in the movement.

Therefore, when factions had been formed on the basis of particularistic affective ties, their integration was subject to two different forces that often worked in opposite directions. One was the traditional ethical standards which stipulated that a subordinate should never betray his superior, nor a student his teacher, and so forth. The other was the cultural inhibition on vertical communication between the leader and the led. This inhibition was strengthened by the personal nature of Chinese armies which gave militarists an additional motive for blocking direct vertical communication between their faction leader and their own followers. Consequently, although the military factions were often able to present an impressive show of strength in peacetime, they could seldom stand the test of trying times. When no vital issues were involved, all the militarists were eager to hide their differences and make everything look all right. The real strength of the faction, however, was much more limited. The estimates of military strength publicized by a faction before a major conflict were often much larger than the actual fighting force that it mobilized.*

The low degree of integration achieved by a faction as a result of its emphasis on personalized relationships and its inhibition on vertical and horizontal communications gave it a low tolerance for major stress. Nothing exposed this low tolerance more succinctly than a change of leadership. The removal of a faction's leader, caused by death, sickness, or defeat, etc., usually precipitated a major crisis over who should possess authority and upon

* For example, prior to the first Chihli-Fengtien war of 1922, the Chihli faction was supposed to comprise 370,000 troops, but it actually succeeded in mobilizing only 130,000. *Nu li chou pao*, no. 1, 1922, p. 2; *Tung fang tsa chih* (henceforth referred to as *TFTC*), 19, no. 9: 120ff.

The Composition of the Military Factions

what basis, especially if the faction had no legitimized and institutionalized system of leadership succession, which was frequently the case. For instance, when Feng Kuo-chang died, the difficulty of choosing a new leader was so apparent that many minor units in the Chihli faction at once contemplated desertion to Tuan's camp, believing that Chihli would fall apart.* To be sure, Ts'ao K'un had a respectable military machine, but he was not the only senior member in Chihli. On the same seniority scale with Ts'ao stood other Chihli militarists like Wang Chan-yüan, Li Shun, Ch'en Kuang-yüan, and T'ien Chung-yü.[18] And many considered Li Shun to be superior to Ts'ao in ability.[19] Alignment remained personality-oriented rather than institution-oriented; without institutionalization to give the leaders some impersonal basis of legitimacy, alignments had to change with each change in top personnel. The confusion was further compounded by the lack of horizontal communication. When members of a faction did not interact, they could not create an esprit de corps; without an esprit de corps, the members tended to split apart when their only common link, the leader, was removed.

In analyzing the organizational characteristics of China's military factions, many commentators have tended to liken them to families.[20] If we look at the political factions at close range, however, we find that the interpersonal relationships weaving their members into an organizational context were far from being parallels to relationships among family members. Furthermore, even when we are able to find seeming counterparts between family roles and political-military factions, we must not assume that they performed the same functions in both cases. Therefore, the crucial test of the validity of the family analogy does not lie with finding categories or analytical terms to apply to both cases, but with demonstrating that these categories and terms convey the same meaning and that our understanding of military factions will be enhanced by our knowledge about the family in Chinese society. It is against this test that the limitation of the family analogy is revealed.

* The most notable defector during the transition period was Liu Hsün, the commander of Feng Kuo-chang's personal guard division (the 16th Division) and one of his most trusted lieutenants. *NCH*, Jan. 31, 1920.

The term *ta-yüan-lao* (elders, senior members, usually referring to elders in a clan organization), for instance, has been used to describe certain militarists. In a military faction, one can indeed generally identify a group of people as seniors by virtue of their age as well as of their length of service in the Peiyang Army. Seniority derived from these sources undoubtedly bestowed prestige upon them, but power was not necessarily a concomitant component of their seniority. While socially they were accorded appropriate respect, politically their voice carried little or no authority if they commanded no troops. In the political game, it was clearly demonstrated that "power comes from the barrel of a gun," and not from seniority. This was a far cry from the role of ta-yüan-lao in the clan, which combined prestige and power.[21] In fact, a junior commander could reject or repudiate a senior's advice with impunity. While in the clan it would have been unthinkable for a junior member to unseat a senior and take over his position, this was done time and again in the military. Therefore, instead of constituting the decision-making power of the faction, the so-called *ta-yüan-lao* were usually retired militarists who were occasionally drafted to perform diplomatic chores.

Similar problems exist in the use of the term *ti-hsi*, or branch, another term often used to describe the military faction. In the clan, the *ti-hsi* are well defined by the distance of blood relationships; the ties are ascriptive and predetermined. In the military faction, however, most ties were purely incidental or deliberately contractual; they were also multiple in number, variegated or even conflictive in nature, and generally not well defined. As we demonstrated in the discussion of the evolution of the factions, for example, there was no a priori reason why Ts'ao and Wu must side with Feng Kuo-chang; yet common parlance often includes them in Feng's *ti-hsi*. The basis for doing so often remains ambiguous.[22] I suspect that the classification is based on a single dimension of interpersonal relationships, i.e. the institutional superior-subordinate relationship. When this relationship is taken out of context and treated as an isolated factor, it provides a very tenuous basis for deciding whether a militarist was a *ti-hsi* or should be a member of this or that faction. In actuality, as we have shown, the interpersonal relationships between militarists were diverse and often competitive.

It should also be pointed out that the inadequacy of the family analogy lies precisely in the fact that the emergence of the military factions was triggered by the breakdown of the "big family" concept that Yüan had fostered within the Peiyang Army. After Yüan's death, many militarists were genuinely concerned about preserving the cohesion of the Peiyang "family," and some of them, like Tuan, actually attempted to assume the father image. Yet it was Tuan's aggressive assertion that alarmed the Peiyang militarists and exacerbated internal division. Realizing that the once cohesive Peiyang "family" could not be reconstructed or restored, they joined different factions for different reasons. In the process of faction building, the leaders mobilized all resources at their disposal to attract adherents.

It seems, therefore, that the true organizational characteristics of the military factions can be better understood by analyzing the full range of complex interpersonal relationships among the key members of a given faction than by relying on a strained analogy with the Chinese family. From the average militarist's point of view, to decide to join a particular faction represented a reaction against and a disillusionment with the family image. Some residual familism might have influenced his choice, but other factors also entered his calculations. Those who had strong ties with other militarists that could not be evaded had to decide, either consciously or unconsciously, which tie was the most valuable one to uphold.

A ranking of these ties with mathematical precision is obviously beyond our ability, and was probably never even attempted by the militarists themselves. But given our understanding of how these ties had operated in traditional political systems, it is at least possible to achieve a crude and suggestive ranking that would apply under normal circumstances. With the exception of the father-son and brotherhood relationships, the relative strength of the ties is contingent upon many factors, some of which were mentioned in our discussion of the institutional superior-subordinate ties. It is thus difficult to assign a concrete value to each of these ties or even to assign each of them a definite place on a continuum. But some ranking is inevitable if we are to discuss them intelligently. As a compromise, I have first ranked twelve relationships on a continuum and then divided them into three broad ranges according to the strength of their integrative or cohesive value to the organization of the military factions. Ties grouped into the same range are more likely to possess cohesive values that are more difficult to differentiate from each other. In other words, the probability of error among ties within the same range is higher than across the ranges. Thus, for instance, to decide whether a teacher-student tie was more or less integrative than a patron-protégé tie would be subject to greater error than to say that either of them was more integrative than a colleague tie or schoolmate tie. Therefore, it is advisable to look at both the range and the rank order as complementary to each other rather than to rely on either of them alone.

The ties are divided into the following rank and range order, from strongest to weakest:

Range I   1. Father-son
          2. Brothers
Range II 3. Teacher-student (including cases where instruction was actually carried out and cases where one accepted another as a student without ever having given instruction)
          4. Patron-protégé
          5. Clansmen and kinsmen
          6. In-laws
          7. Sworn brothers (or membership in a secret society that implied sworn brotherhood)
Range III 8. Direct institutional superior-subordinate relationship
          9. Same county or district of origin
         10. Colleagues
         11. Same province of origin
         12. Schoolmate (classmate would rank slightly higher)

Because of the limitation of space and the lack of comprehensive information on all the militarists of the 1916–28 period, we can only offer analyses of the three most powerful factions—Anhwei, Chihli, and Fengtien—along the lines of reasoning suggested above. These analyses do not pretend to be definitive. They merely purport to suggest a fresh way of looking at the organizational characteristics of these politico-military groups. Our charts of the factions are constructed on the assumption that the basic communication pattern within a miliary faction resembles the star-shaped sociometric diagram described earlier, and that the network of interpersonal relationships can be systematically laid out to depict the organizational characteristics of the factions. See Figures 2–4.

A number of interesting points emerge from the sociometric

The Composition of the Military Factions

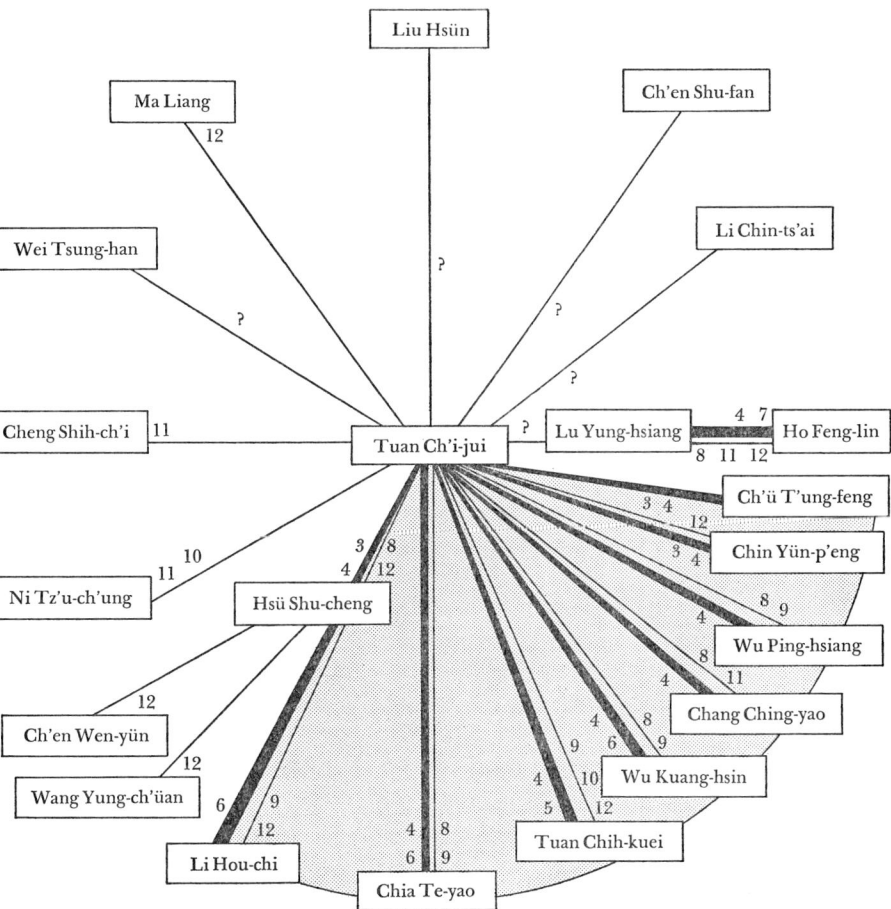

Fig. 2. Sociometric diagram of the Anhwei faction. Bold lines indicate ties #1–7 (Ranges I and II); thin lines indicate ties #8–12 (Range III).

charts. The militarists included were all important persons who had been identified with these factions. Almost all of them had held the positions of either division commanders, defense commissioners of strategic areas, or provincial military governors or their equivalents before 1922. A cursory look will immediately reveal that, in terms of sheer numbers, Chihli was the largest faction, followed by Anhwei and then Fengtien. On this basis alone, we might say that Chihli had the most complicated web of inter-

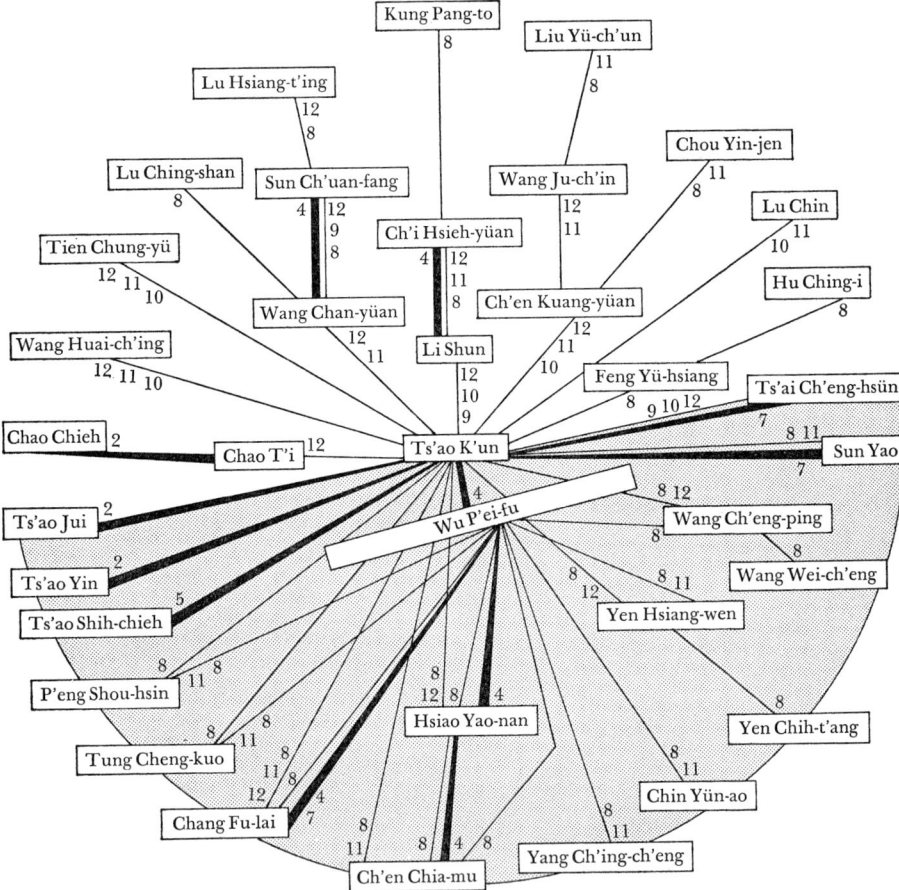

Fig. 3. Sociometric diagram of the Chihli faction. Bold lines indicate ties #1–7 (Ranges I and II); thin lines indicate ties #8–12 (Range III).

personal ties, and Fengtien the simplest. While this is certainly true, however, we cannot deduce that therefore Chihli was the least integrative faction. For multiplicity of number and heterogeneity of ties were not necessarily the same thing.

A closer look at the factions shows that although Chihli's Ts'ao K'un had more subordinates, there was usually more than one tie connecting Ts'ao with any subordinate. Even when these ties were

The Composition of the Military Factions

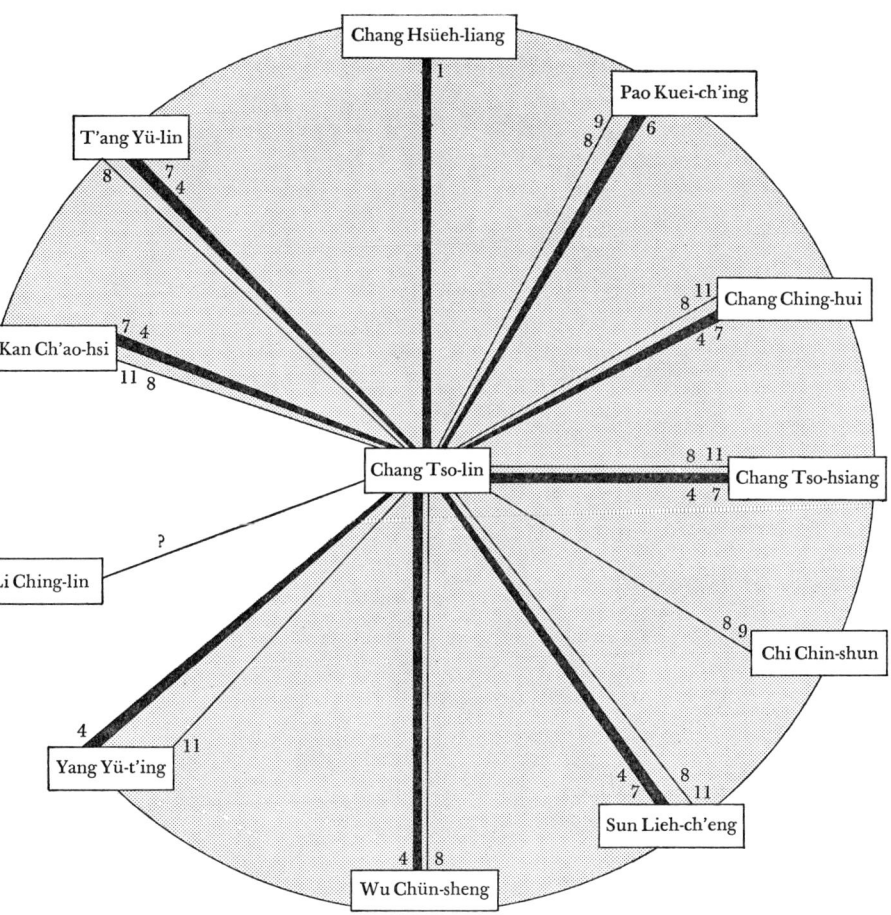

Fig. 4. Sociometric diagram of the Fengtien faction. Bold lines indicate ties #1–7 (Ranges I and II); thin lines indicate ties #8–12 (Range III).

low-range, their multiplicity tended to reinforce each other and made them collectively stronger than any single one of them. In contrast, Anhwei's Tuan Ch'i-jui had fewer direct subordinates, which seemingly gave him an advantage in control. Actually, we find that Tuan had no known tie (to the best of my knowledge) with five subordinates; with two others he had only one identifiable tie. If our information is correct, then Tuan had no, or very weak, ties with seven of his fourteen direct subordinates. Ts'ao K'un had at least one tie with all of his fourteen (this number is coincidental, not pegged) direct subordinates, and there were usually three ties. On this basis we can suggest that Chihli was more organizationally viable than Anhwei.

If we go a step further and look at the value of these ties and how they were distributed, the result is equally interesting. We find that overlapping ties constituted a significant pattern in Chihli, but not in Anhwei. The cause of this difference can be traced to the careers of Tuan and Ts'ao. The premiership and the ministry of army had given Tuan strategically favorable positions for gaining political allies, but they simultaneously had made it difficult for him to penetrate the organizational shell of his allies to reach lower-echelon commanders. On the other hand, Ts'ao was the commander of the 3d Division from 1906 until 1917–18, when he relinquished the division to the command of Wu P'ei-fu, who had led the division's 3d Artillery Brigade since 1911. Thus Ts'ao was in command for about twelve years, during which many of the militarists included in our chart had already become commanders of regiments or brigades—that is, they possessed positions high enough to have close face-to-face relationships with Ts'ao, which were further deepened as years went by. Thus, although it was Wu who made the 3d Division famous and strong, the members of the 3d Division were most likely to embrace Ts'ao as their leader, even without Wu's mediation. In fact, Wu was more loyal to Ts'ao than anybody else. Hence, the fact that Ts'ao as the leader of Chihli was able to establish meaningful ties with the lower-echelon commanders of the 3d Division made this segment more integrated into the faction than others.

These cases provide us with a way of gauging the organizational strength of a faction. We can use a shaded area to indicate where a high concentration of clusters of ties or highly integrative ties existed between a leader and his followers. If the shaded area included a few persons, then the internal organization of the faction was weak; if the shaded area includes many persons, then the internal organization of the faction was strong. The shaded area was where the organizational strength of the faction lay.

If we pursue the analysis still further to see how these differences

The Composition of the Military Factions

accounted for the overall strength and weakness of factions, we must bring in a new variable. We must try to correlate the distribution of military power and organizational strength (or integrative ties) within the same faction.

First let us look at Anhwei. There we find that the strongest military powers were connected with the faction's leader by the weakest links. Of the five division commanders—Ch'ü T'ung-feng, Ch'en Wen-yün, Wei Tsung-han, Ma Liang, Liu Hsün—only Ch'ü was closely related to Tuan. Of the five military governors—Li Hou-chi, Ni Tz'u-ch'ung, Cheng Shih-ch'i, Chang Ching-yao, and Lu Yung-hsiang—only Li and Chang were closely tied to Tuan. Chang, however, lost his military following in 1919. Ni, who had been at times quite vocal in his support of Tuan, was relatively weak in his own control over Anhwei province. Consequently, we see a separation of military strength from organizational strength: those who were most loyal to Tuan in terms of close personal ties did not have military power, and those in command of military power did not have close personal ties with Tuan.*

The Chihli faction presents a different picture. Although Chihli was composed of a larger number of units, the 3d Division constituted the backbone of its fighting machine. The Chihli divisions in Kiangsu, Kiangsi, and Hupeh under Li Shun, Ch'en Kuang-yüan, and Wang Chan-yüan had to spend most of their time and energy dealing with local military elements. Each of these three provinces had one or at most two Chihli divisions; they were widely dispersed and grew rather slowly. The 3d Division, on the other hand, expanded rapidly. Many of its brigade and regiment commanders were promoted to division commanders, and some of them, like

---

* Some may argue that there was nothing unusual about this anomaly, because Anhwei was basically a civilian faction with military allies. The Anhwei faction's link with the Anfu Club lends some support to this view. But we must not forget that Anhwei was never averse to using force whenever it believed force would achieve its political objectives. The Anhwei faction not only tried to acquire military allies; it also tried to create its own military force. In a way, it was Tuan's desertion of civilian political means and adoption of the policy of force (as in the Hunan campaign) that hastened the full development of militarism in Chinese politics. Therefore, to the extent that Anhwei regarded force as the final arbiter in the political process, it was no different from other military factions of its time. The only difference was that it was weaker than most other factions.

Chang Fu-lai and Hsiao Yao-nan, even reached a military governorship. There we see a high correlation between the organizational and military strength of the faction.

Our discussion of the military and organizational strength of the factions provides a good context for examining the accuracy of the geographical connotation of the factional labels. The charts suggest that the factional labels did not reflect the geographical origins of their membership or their military power with equal accuracy. There were twenty important members in Anhwei, of whom only eight came from the province of Anhwei. Of the 36 members of Chihli, 21 came from Chihli province. Fengtien had twelve members, of whom nine came from Fengtien and two others went to Fengtien province.

Again, if we use military power as a criterion, we find that the Anhwei faction's military power was largely in the hands of militarists who did not come from Anhwei province. Even in the Chihli faction, we are somewhat surprised to discover that of the twelve militarists associated with the most powerful 3d Division who later went on to higher posts, only five came from Chihli; five came from Shantung and one each from Hupeh and Fengtien. Only in the Fengtien faction was there a high correlation between military power and geographical origin.

These facts compel us to review the common conception of the labels these factions bore. If they were used in the sense that people from a particular province constituted the numerical majority of the membership of the faction bearing that province's name, they were misleading. They were also misleading if used to suggest that people from that province held dominant positions. In the case of Chihli, it would be more accurate to call it a "Chihli-Shantung" faction. However, if the labels were used merely to suggest that the leaders of these factions came from these provinces, then they were quite correct. This may not be as trivial a distinction as it appears. Once we realize these facts, we are made more aware of the personal character of Chinese factional politics. The identity of the rank and file was subsumed under the identity of the leader. It was the leader, rather than political ideals or institutions, who provided the rallying point for political loyalty. The use of "Anhwei" or "Chihli" as the name of the faction, even though it

The Composition of the Military Factions

clearly did not reflect the faction's membership or power, serves to focus our attention on the importance of the leader. This largely coincides with our sociometric analyses, for the leader was very much the same as the faction in terms of identification although not in terms of control. Without the leader, the faction would look quite different.

We must also reappraise the extent to which regional sentiments functioned in Chinese politics in the early Republican period. It is interesting to note that northerners in general were more able to work together within the same faction regardless of their provincial origins. Southerners were more often disinclined to work with each other when provincial differences existed. In this respect alone, both Chihli and Anhwei, as composite factions instead of factions with a single provincial base, were more able to mobilize resources and play a prominent role in the military politics of the early Republican period. So long as both northerners and southerners relied on the same traditional organizational techniques and personal ties, northerners held an edge over the southerners. If a military power was to launch an attack against the north from the south, it must offer new organizing principles and devise new organizational ties to transcend narrow geographical attachments. This was partly what took place during the KMT's northern expedition in 1927–28.

Of the three factions, there is very little doubt that Fengtien had the strongest organization. Chang Tso-lin had strong ties with almost all of his subordinates. Most men came from Fengtien and had known and worked under Chang personally for a long time; some were his sworn brothers, others protégés. The available evidence indicates that Chang was probably the shrewdest manipulator of human relationships among the three factional leaders. He demonstrated that he could be ruthless and magnanimous at the same time. Chang was generally able to exert a very strong psychological influence upon the men working directly under him, and he had a way of keeping them loyal to him. In sharp contrast to the rather lopsided and unbalanced picture that Anhwei and Chihli presented, Fengtien's internal organization very much resembled a wheel. Chang was the hub, connected to each of his lieutenants by a strong spoke of personal ties. The only weak spoke was between Chang and Li Ching-lin. Looking at this chart analytically, we would predict that the most plausible source of strain in this system would come from Li Ching-lin. History shows the truth of this prediction. Judged in terms of recruitment patterns and recruitment methods alone, we may say that Fengtien was the srongest faction *with* a geographical base.

CHAPTER 4

Military Capabilities: Recruitment

Since the military was the dominant political force of the 1916–28 period, an understanding of the composition and structure of the military establishment, the methods of recruitment, the manner of training, the types of weapons, and the prevailing tactical and strategic concepts should constitute a major part of our study. Unfortunately, very little reliable or systematic information on any of these subjects is available. Thus, in this and the following two chapters, it is necessary to treat these subjects in a highly tentative and generalized manner. I make no claim that this treatment is comprehensive; rather, I have tried to illuminate some of the central problems by piecing together whatever data are available.

All the Chinese militarists possessed standing armies and thus were faced with the necessity of recruiting soldiers. The total number of recruits needed at any given time, however, is difficult to estimate. Although there was a standard table of organization for all military units (which would stipulate the number of men in a division, for example),* it was seldom followed. Nor can we deduce a rough estimate of an army's total strength from the number of its weapons, because many armies were notoriously underarmed. While these problems should not discourage us from trying to reconstruct the total size of the military establishment, they do compel us to accept the possibility of a large margin of error, no matter how credible the sources of information might be.

* As the *China Year Book* once observed (1926–27, p. 1044), "In theory the division should number 12,512 officers and men. In practice, it is customary to credit a division with 10,000 all told, and this often proves to be an overestimation. On the other hand, there are divisions in which the number of men enrolled greatly exceeds the theoretical figures."

In the last years of the Ch'ing dynasty, the total size of the newly created army units, the provincial armies, and the Green Standards was less than half a million men. The revolution brought a great expansion in the ranks of existing units and of the new revolutionary units; although probably a million more men were recruited into the various forces.[1]

Under the Republic, a process of demobilization was introduced in January 1913 and was accelerated after the suppression of the Second Revolution. By 1915, the total number of soldiers was reduced to about half of the 1913 figure.

The real momentum of growth began only after Yüan's death in 1916 and continued unabated until 1928. A study of the various numerical estimates available shows that it was next to impossible to determine with accuracy the size of the army in any given year and that there is little basis for choosing one set of figures over another. However, these figures do show a general trend over the years. Consequently, at the risk of gross simplification, we have estimated the growth of the armies in this period as follows: 1916, slightly over 500,000 men; 1918, over 1,000,000; 1924, over 1,500,000; and 1928, over 2,000,000.

Therefore, with each passing year, the military's need for manpower increased. The increase was especially sharp during major wars. Thus, while these wars contributed greatly to rural poverty, at the same time the resulting expansion of the army provided increased employment opportunities for the uprooted and impoverished people. The two phenomena were closely related.

The overwhelming majority of soldiers were recruited by two methods: coercion or profit incentives. A militarist might simply seize a number of able-bodied men and put them in uniform or he might give the local bureaucrats a quota to fulfill. However, coercion was probably used on a very small proportion of the total recruits, because the supply of soldiers was usually more than adequate to meet the militarists' demands.

The primary method of recruitment, then, was to offer opportunities for a stable profession and pecuniary rewards. The uprooted peasants and unemployed urbanites were often only too glad to join the army, since it required no special skills. The worsening population-land ratio, the lack of technological innovations in farming techniques, poor marketing and credit systems, and primitive means of transportation all created serious poverty in the Chinese rural areas, where 70 to 80 percent of the population resided, and there was extensive unemployment and underemployment throughout the country. The poverty and social stagnation of rural China combined to make the military profession attractive to the peasants in comparison with the other opportunities provided in their environment. After they entered the army, poverty was also the most powerful force keeping them there.

It is of course true that in the traditional society, there had always been powerful cultural and ideological forces at work to discourage people from joining the military profession. Such sayings as "Good iron should not be used to make nails," "Good men should not become soldiers" were undoubtedly deeply entrenched in the popular mind. On the other hand, it is also true that throughout history various dynasties maintained large armies. When economic conditions were favorable, these traditional inhibitions might be effective in dissuading people from a military career, but when times were hard, the military often provided the only outlet for survival and mobility. As one scholar has observed, "A major function of military roles in Chinese culture is the provision of alternative possibilities to individuals of ambition who desire to improve their social, political, and economic fortunes but who realize that humble tilling of the soil, thrift, and virtue do not often bring success."[2] Given the economic and social realities of the 1920's, Chinese farmers had little grounds for scorning the army; in fact, joining the army increased their social status.

Unfortunately, there is very little information about the social, economic, and cultural characteristics of the Chinese soldiers. We can only get glimpses of these characteristics from widely scattered and often impressionistic records. The most important sociological study of Chinese soldiers that I have been able to uncover was conducted by Professor T'ao Meng-ho in 1929.[3] He studied a sample of 946 men from a garrison brigade of 5,000 located "somewhere in north China." The first thing that attracts our attention is that it was a young force: almost all were under 30, and the largest group (43.3 percent) were aged 20–24. The second feature was the high turnover rate of its personnel: about two-thirds had joined within the previous two years, and almost no one had been in the unit longer than four years. Between 1926 and 1928, new recruits were taken in every month, thus indicating that recruitment was a continuous concern of the unit.

The high turnover rate is intriguing and is open to several plausible explanations. First, battle casualties could have depleted its ranks, creating the need for new recruits. Second, many of the soldiers might simply have decided to quit for personal reasons after a brief period of service. Here the social background and economic conditions of the soldiers could give us some clues.

The interesting thing is that men with peasant background or no profession constituted 87.3 percent of the total membership of the brigade. About the same percentage were illiterate. Although the net income of a soldier was meager (about five dollars a month), 68 percent of the respondents reported that they sent money home to help their families. On a self-evaluative (subjective) basis, 73 percent of the soldiers regarded their families as poor.

Of course, we cannot ascribe universal validity to T'ao's data, but they provide us with some preliminary impressions. In the first place, they indicate that the overwhelming majority of soldiers were in their most productive age and came from peasant families. Their presence in the army can be taken as a partial reflection of the unfavorable conditions in their villages. They were barred from the educational channels of mobility, since most of them were illiterate. More fundamentally, they were very, very poor. The most telling connection between rural poverty and entry into the army was suggested by T'ao, who noted that traditional Chinese culture placed such an extremely high value on the single son in order to protect the lineage and to honor the ancestors that under a conscription system, a poor family with a single son would be willing to offer a large sum to buy a replacement for him. Yet, in his sample, 21.3 percent of the soldiers were the only sons in their families, which suggests that the families must have been in abject poverty to allow this to happen.

The linkage between army recruitment and general poverty produced several interesting consequences. On the one hand, in the 1920's desertion was very common. Chiang Fang-cheng, probably the best authority on military affairs of the early Republican period, estimated that the annual nationwide desertion rate for all units was somewhere between 15 and 25 percent.[4] Desertion was most likely to occur in combat or when life in the army became unbearable (physical brutality by superiors, suspension or reduction of pay). But desertion became a realistic alternative only when there was some means of living outside the army. Thus a man usually would desert only after he had stayed in the army for a few years and had gathered a small personal fortune through saving or looting. (This might partially explain the high turnover rate in the brigade that Professor T'ao studied.)

On the other hand, there were also numerous reports that soldiers resisted dismissal or disbandment. Although individual units were undoubtedly plagued by large-scale desertions, it was the soldiers' refusal to be discharged from military service that presented the most serious national problem.

The crux of the matter was that the poverty-stricken soldiers simply did not want to leave the army when there were no prospects of a better livelihood elsewhere, and many deserters drifted back into the army when their fortune was gone, thus giving rise to the expressions *yin-hun-tzu* or *ping-yu-tzu*, meaning a man who drifted from one barrack to another in search of a living. Consequently, the reaction of the soldiers to disbanding was usually unfavorable and often violent. For instance, after the war between the Chihli and Anhwei factions in 1920, when one of Anhwei's Northwestern Frontier Defense Army brigades was ordered to disband, the soldiers mutinied, caused considerable damage to the T'ung-chow area in Chihli, and were finally incorporated into the Fengtien army.[5]

It became increasingly difficult to distinguish between soldiers and bandits in many cases. So long as a soldier remained below the poverty line, he would try to stay with his unit or drift among units to sell his services. If he could not attach himself to a unit, then he might temporarily become a bandit. And there were many cases of defeated army units or individual soldiers setting themselves up as bandits or bandits becoming part of regular armies.*

Hence, contrary to both traditional cultural heritage and the

* For instance, when Chao T'i was defeated by Feng Yü-hsiang during the first Chihli-Fengtien war of 1922, his disbanded troops turned to banditry. Despite the presence of the huge armies of Wu P'ei-fu and Feng Yü-hsiang, these bandits became a very serious problem in Honan after 1922, numbering some 10,000 strong. *NCH*, Dec. 30, 1922; Feb. 3, 1923. Likewise, the famous Lin-ch'eng robbery was perpetrated by former Anhwei soldiers disbanded after defeat. It is of considerable interest to note that apart from the ransoms they asked of their victims' families, they also demanded that the government give them full pardon and incorporate them into the regular army. Reluctantly, the government agreed. *NCH*, May 12–19, 1923.

prevailing contemporary belief that military life repulsed the Chinese, we find that the abject economic conditions caused the Chinese peasants in this period to view a military career not as a curse but as a welcome opportunity to escape from starvation and to lift themselves from an otherwise hopeless situation.

But although it is easy to establish a close connection between rural poverty and the peasants' embrace of a martial life when we look at China as a whole, it is more difficult to establish a direct causal relationship between the recruitment pattern of any region and the economic conditions of that region. In theory, if it is true that peasants flocked to the army because of their poverty, it must also be true that the poorer a region, the more likely its peasants were to seek military employment.

In reality, however, we cannot make such an inference. The size of an army was affected not only by the supply of peasants who wanted to be soldiers but also by the militarists' demand for their services. The militarists' needs, in turn, were influenced by the level of political stability in their region and the kinds of goals they wished to pursue. To analyze these needs, we need reliable information on population figures, crucial economic indicators, measurements of political stability, and the political objectives of most militarists in a given region. Unfortunately, we do not have such information on a region-by-region basis.

However, there are some grounds for suggesting that the north probably produced more soldiers than the south. Here we can only rely on indirect evidence, but a number of factors seem to have produced this interesting phenomenon.

The first factor that led the north to produce more soldiers than the south was that political events in the late nineteenth and early twentieth centuries favored military expansion in the north. During these years, a northern army, Peiyang, was the most modern and best trained and generally the most powerful army. This predominance of northern power over the rest of the country constituted one of the most crucial political facts of the early Republican years. For many writers, the 1916–28 period was simply referred to as the "period of Peiyang warlords." With the exception of Kwangtung, Kwangsi, Yunnan, and Kweichow, all the provinces had northerners as military governors at one time or another, mostly throughout the whole twelve years. Thus, northern troops were present in some eighteen provinces during this period.[6]

There were other factors that produced more soldiers in the north. Not only was the north poorer than the south, with lower agricultural productivity and lower living standards; it also was the area where the heaviest damage was inflicted by wars.[7] Between 1916 and 1928, the northern provinces constituted the major battleground for nearly all the important wars. Natural calamities also exacted heavier tolls from the north than from other parts of China. The famine of 1920–21 left millions of people destitute in five northern provinces.[8] Other cases of drought and flood caused many more deaths and forced millions more to desert their homes.[9]

These facts tend to bear out Chiang Fang-cheng's claim that of all the provinces in China, Shantung produced the largest number of soldiers, followed by Chihli and Honan.*

No matter what their provincial origins, however, most of the soldiers had no conscious collective cause. They rendered their services to a militarist not out of any personal or ideological attachment to him, but out of a desire to acquire material benefits or to avoid physical pain. These armies were most at home when they dealt with an impotent population, but were reluctant to face enemies in the field unless their own preservation was at stake. In ordinary situations, they would try to outmaneuver their enemies but avoid hard fighting. Very often, soldiers would defect or desert rather than do battle.

Much of this mercenary mentality can be attributed to the arbitrary methods of recruitment. Szechwan provides some of the most extreme examples of arbitrary recruitment.

Local recruiters might trick gullible peasants into joining their "armies" and then sell their services to the commanders of real military units. When a deal was made, the recruits were formed into a new unit under the militarist. The recruiter became the commander of the unit, and pledged his allegiance to the militarist in return for money, weapons, and supplies. Since Szechwan had a number of contending militarists, each of them was anxious to prevent these units from falling into his rivals' hands. Such a process of army formation necessarily occurred at the expense of

---

* Chiang Fang-cheng, *Ts'ai-ping*, 1: 10–11, 13. Sonoda, a Japanese journalist with wide knowledge of Chinese political and military affairs, came to the same conclusion: "Shantung has become the most famous soldier-producing province. Whenever there was war, warlords from other provinces would come to Shantung to recruit soldiers. Consequently, innumerable young men from Shantung became soldiers or bandits and moved into other provinces." Sonoda, p. 141.

internal organization and discipline. Consequently, the Szechwan armies were famous for three things: there were more officers than soldiers, more soldiers than weapons, and more weapons than ammunition.[10]

Some militarists were acutely aware of the shortcomings of a recruitment process that indiscriminately accepted people regardless of their motives and qualifications. A few of them even tried to take corrective measures.

Shansi seems to have been the only province to preserve a regular conscription system after 1916. Shansi was too poor to maintain a large standing army strong enough to ward off neighboring militarists' intrusions. Through conscription, however, it was able to keep an inexpensive military establishment in peacetime for the purpose of training new recruits who would then return to civilian life. The program was stepped up after 1923, when the province faced increasing danger of aggression from neighboring provinces. Shansi was thus able to have a force of about 100,000 men trained in the skills of war without disrupting normal peacetime productive processes. When a state of emergency existed, the "reserves" could be mobilized swiftly.[11]

Although conscription worked well in Shansi, it was not feasible in other areas, for several reasons. In the first place, a successful conscription program required a stable territorial base with a stable social system, so that some form of census could be conducted. Furthermore, without such stability, the ruling militarist had no incentive to plan a strategic allocation of human resources on a raional basis, which was the main attraction of a conscription system.

In the second place, a conscription system also required a relatively efficient bureaucracy to handle the statistics and the planning, and mechanisms of rural control to implement the program. Shansi was the only province that had had a stable regime since the founding of the Republic and that had an efficient bureaucracy by contemporary Chinese standards.

In the third place, most militarists considered rotational conscription to be too costly. After a militarist had made the initial investment in a soldier's training, he could draw dividends on the investment as long as the man stayed in the army. In this way, he would have a veteran army. A conscription program, on the other

Military Capabilities: Recruitment

hand, required continuous investments in training at certain intervals. Furthermore, the existing force would always be small, while most militarists wanted a large standing army because of the constant wars.

The counterproductive effects of indiscriminate or coercive recruitment, on the one hand, and the impracticability of a conscription program, on the other, led some militarists to devise other ways to improve the quality of their recruits. Feng Yü-hsiang, for example, was one of the few militarists who emphasized physical fitness and imposed a number of minimum standards for his recruits.[12] Moreover, Feng was careful to preserve the social and geographical homogeneity of his force. Because his soldiers came mostly from the provinces of Honan, Shantung, Chihli, and Anhwei, he preferred to recruit from these provinces, sending his officers and men to their home towns to encourage relatives and friends to join the army. The merit of this method was that all the recruits were screened to eliminate those who had served in other military units and acquired a "mercenary" mentality. Instead, a network of close social relationships was woven among these recruits and the existing members of Feng's army to promote good working relationships and enhance the army's solidarity.[13]

Many other militarists also used particularistic ties to guide their recruitment policy. In the previous chapter, we discussed the ways in which these ties affected the recruitment and integration of militarists into the factions. In the recruitment of rank-and-file soldiers, there were necessarily some differences. Since most recruits came directly from the rural areas, they had no existing institutional superior-subordinate ties. Since most of them were illiterate or poorly educated, the teacher-student and classmate ties were seldom relevant. The family, clan, friendship, and sworn brotherhood ties undoubtedly were more important, but the most important and pervasive ties were probably the locality ties, because of the sheer number of people involved. When so many men were needed, it was quite difficult to recruit only men who were closely and personally related to the existing members of an army. It was not so difficult to recruit men from the same geographical area.

The relative importance of geographical ties in the recruitment of the rank and file probably had its drawbacks. Since the geographical tie was the least particularistic of the personal ties, the militarist could not expect it to play a highly integrative role. It could not be mobilized as effectively as the other ties to impose a socially and culturally defined set of rights and obligations upon the soldiers. Geographical ties would be at their strongest when members of an army found themselves surrounded by a hostile alien population. Thus, the armies of most militarists in the Chihli faction were composed of soldiers from the northern provinces even when their territories extended to both banks of the Yangtze River; in the south, for a long time Kwangtung was ruled by a Kwangsi militarist who commanded a predominantly Kwangsi force.[14] But even then the feelings of solidarity existed only in the short run, when dangers were present. By itself the geographical tie was not as integrative as the other particularistic ties in the long run. In this sense, the generally low level of solidarity and lack of discipline displayed by most Chinese armies can at least partially be attributed to the recruitment process itself.

As one might expect, the KMT, as a political party with a distinct ideological outlook, stressed ideological enthusiasm as well as physical fitness in its recruitment policies. In bulding its military power, the KMT originally tried to recruit in Kwangtung, but its recruiters were driven away, jailed, or murdered by the local militarists.[15] Barred from this nearby source, the KMT government set up clandestine recruiting stations in the big cities in central China, inside the territories of hostile militarists. The Whampoa Military Academy set up recruiting centers for junior officers in both north and south China.[16]

Since the KMT army was still in its infancy, it offered little prospect for individual profit-making. Nor did the KMT use coercion in its recruitment. Consequently, we may assume that the many young men who approached the recruiting stations were attracted primarily by the ideological appeal of the party's programs. Therefore, the KMT had a very strict system of selection and its recruits may have been superior to those of other militarists.

The KMT, however, was an exception. There is little doubt that the recruitment patterns adopted by most militarists offered significant incentives to the large mass of the poverty-stricken rural population to take advantage of the opportunities offered by a military career. By doing away with most physical and intellectual criteria, the armies made it possible for people from the lowest economic classes, who otherwise would have had an extremely difficult time competing for the limited opportunities offered by farming, to make a living. Many soldiers were even able to improve their social position, through increases in their education or wealth or by rising in the military hierarchy.

While the educational opportunities offered by the military way of life were not very great, nevertheless the army provided in many cases a peasant's only chance to escape from his village confines. For a farm boy from the mountainous regions of eastern Shantung to accompany an army into Kiangsu, Hupeh, or Szechwan inevitably broadened his range of experience. He might even have a chance to improve himself through some formal education. If he was lucky enough to have joined the army of one of the more enlightened militarists, he might learn a few hundred characters, some songs, a more efficient way of managing his activities, and possibly even a trade.

The financial opportunities offered by the military were more important. If a man stayed in his village as a farmer, his chance of economic improvement was nil. But if he joined the army, even when the pay was very modest he might still save a fraction of it to assist his family. If he joined a well-managed and well-financed army or an army in control of a rich area, he would do even better. In either case, a soldier's financial status was much better than that of the average peasant.

Even in poorly managed armies, the opportunity to gain sudden wealth was always possible. In fact, for many soldiers this was the major reason for staying in the military. Many armies had no qualms about plundering the populace, or they might engage in some illicit trade like gambling, prostitution, or opium. The leaders and the rank and file would all profit from such activities. A good example was the extensive opium trade carried out by the Yunnan troops in Kwangtung in the 1920's, which made the Yunnanese the wealthiest of all troops in Kwangtung.[17] Bravery in action could bring a large share in the booty, and even in defeat the soldiers could go on individual forays to loot the civilians. Although we do not know precisely how much wealth could be accumulated in this manner, we can at least state that the average soldier was conscious of the possibility that an illegal "killing" could give him a greater fortune than he could acquire by saving through a lifetime of hard work on the farm.

Last, there was the most formal and most visible kind of upward mobility: rising in the army hierarchy. We must remember that in twentieth-century China the military organizational ladder did not represent merely professional status; it had much wider ramifications. Generally speaking, the higher military status one reached, the more respect and deference one commanded, the greater wealth one acquired, the more political power one wielded, and the greater number of people's lives one could affect. These facts made upward mobility in the military more valuable than in other professions.

In China in the 1920's, there were no insurmountable barriers between officers and soldiers. A considerable number of soldiers could expect to become officers, and some moved all the way up. Thus to a certain extent the officers and soldiers could be considered as different parts of the same and continuous mobility ladder. To be precise about this subject, we need to have reliable information about the total number of soldiers, where they were distributed on different hierarchical levels at a given time, and how fast they could move from one level to the next and with what probability of success. Unfortunately, we do not have such information.

However, it is easy to find numerous cases of men rising from rags to riches. The very existence and high visibility of these cases must have had considerable impact upon the common soldiers' conception of their opportunities within the military profession. For they could see that a humble social origin was certainly no major hindrance to their own careers.

If we look at all the topmost militarists of the period (inspectors general of several provinces or commanders in chief of a force occupying several provinces), we find that obscurity of social origin was a shared feature. Chang Tso-lin (Manchuria) and Lu Jung-t'ing (Kwangtung-Kwangsi) came from the outlaw's world. Wang Chan-yüan (Hunan-Hupeh) and Chang Hsün (Yangtze valley) joined the army as foot soldiers. Ts'ao K'un (Chihli-Shantung-Honan) had been a cotton cloth peddler, and Chang Tsung-ch'ang (Chihli-Shantung) had earned his early living as a cymbalist and a helper in a gambling den. Wu P'ei-fu (Hunan-Hupeh, Chihli-Shantung-Honan) and Feng Yü-hsiang (northwest) both came from impoverished families. All these men joined the army (either directly or via banditry) to escape hardship in civilian life. Five of these eight militarists joined the army as soldiers, three as reformed outlaws.

If a soldier cared to look around, he would have no trouble finding one or more of his immediate superiors who came from as lowly a social background as his own. For instance, Feng Yü-hsiang's most important subordinates came from very humble backgrounds. Surveying Feng's top 25 commanders in 1925, Sheridan found that only two had graduated from military academies, while 23 had risen from the ranks. The lack of formal education was shared by commanders on all levels of Feng's army.[18]

There is reason to believe that the rate of upward mobility at all levels accelerated during the latter part of the period. As the armies expanded, new units came into existence and more wars were fought. These conditions were favorable for a large number of lower-level officers and men to move upward at a faster rate.* As the discussion of military training in Chapter 5 will show, the number of cadets graduated from China's military schools could not possibly meet the increasing needs for officers. As supply lagged behind demand, the soldiers' opportunity to be promoted increased correspondingly.

Certainly, this discussion of upward mobility is not intended to imply that soldiers and officers enjoyed equal opportunity for advancement. But the lack of rigid organizational stratification, the inadequate supply of officers, and the low level of the military art all tended to blur the distinction between officers and soldiers as two separate groups of personnel. This blurring allowed a signif-

* In 1916, there were only 32 division commanders in the country; in 1924, there were 84. After the wars of 1924, a period of reorganization and realignment led to the creation of so many new divisions that it became quite impossible to determine their exact number; possibly 200 divisions were in existence between 1925 and 1928. *CYB*, 1926–27, pp. 1068–86; 1928, pp. 1291–97. Furthermore, the majority of top officers stayed in their positions for only a few years and then moved out because of death, defeat, dismissal, or promotion, leaving vacancies for lower-level aspirants. As a result, the high-ranking officers were fairly young. My preliminary study of those division commanders whose ages were known for 1916 (15 out of 32) and 1924 (37 out of 84) shows that the median and mean ages of both groups were 43 years.

icant number of soldiers to move up the mobility ladder, and some even managed to reach the very top.

In sum, this chapter purports to show that, contrary to popular impression, the peasants who constituted the bulk of the armies were not impressed but joined voluntarily. While the growth of the armies was not caused by the peasants' demands for employment but by the militarists' needs for more power, the growth was facilitated by the existence of peasant masses in dire economic conditions. Compared with farming, the military offered not only some measure of occupational security but also some realistic hope of social and economic advancement. However, the fact that the majority of soldiers were drawn to military life by remunerative motives also created many problems in morale, discipline, and training. We shall turn to these problems in Chapter 5.

CHAPTER 5

Military Capabilities: Training

From a modern point of view, we would expect that a period of training would follow the induction of recruits into an army. A comprehensive training program would include discipline, that is, a body of basic rules and regulations, and technical training, to teach the recruits how to use their weapons. In this chapter we shall examine the amount and quality of training provided to officers and soldiers in the armies of the militarists.

Disciplinary Training

In most of the armies, disciplinary training was very poor. By and large, there was a high correlation between the militarists' indifference to recruitment standards and their neglect of training. Those who recruited by any available means also tended to regard training as a long, tedious, and expensive job. In many cases, the recruits were assigned to regular combat units immediately upon arrival and were expected to acquire the necessary skills and discipline during active service.

This laxity in discipline was attributable to the commanding officers, whose indifference implicitly encouraged the soldiers to act as they pleased. More significantly, the militarists' personal life-styles were usually unprofessional and set bad examples for their men. Many of them were notorious with women, and gambling was the most popular way of socializing among the militarists.[1] Greed and corruption were pervasive; and most important militarists were able to amass a huge personal fortune after a few years in office, invariably through irregularities.[2] When corrupt and incompetent militarists led the armies, they could neither inspire confidence nor expect respect and discipline from their ranks. No greater harm was done to the armies than that caused by the widespread addiction to opium among officers, which also affected their soldiers. Frequently, a whole army became a collection of addicts. This greatly impaired both its fighting strength and its morale. The opium habit in some cases may have been deliberately encouraged by the commanding militarist, for once the soldiers had acquired this habit they had to stay in the army and fight harder for the militarist in order to pay for their opium. In some cases, opium addiction helped a militarist to tie down a large number of followers who had to rely on their commander for supply. The most notorious case of addiction was reported among Yunnan troops. Huang Shao-hung, the noted Kwangsi general who had experience working with Yunnan troops, reported that when Yunnan troops went on expeditions into other provinces, they were usually issued opium in lieu of food and wages. The addiction to opium became so demoralizing that even when the commanders realized the harm done they could not rectify it.*

Another factor that induced sagging morale and discipline was the officers' embezzlement of funds, especially the soldiers' pay. Since the primary motivation of most soldiers in joining the army was money, they naturally resented any reduction in their already meager pay. After Yüan Shih-k'ai's death, the last threads of centralized control were broken, and the soldiers' income came to depend more on the honesty of their commander than on the soundness of the system. In some units the pay scale was reduced, or the pay might not even be issued for months.†

One of the most immediate consequences of the prevalence of corruption among officers was that it became increasingly difficult for the higher command to keep track of its soldiers. Almost all commanders inflated the size of their forces, sometimes to intimi-

---

* When Fan Shih-sheng of the Yunnan army decided to ban opium smoking, he aroused such fierce resentment that one of his top lieutenants was assassinated. After several battles, his army simply withered away. Huang Shao-hung, 1: 98–99.

† An officer's irregularities might take many forms: he might render false accounts of expenditures and pocket the funds appropriated for his unit; he might reduce the percentage of salary paid in cash; he might pocket all surpluses; or he might simply expropriate all the money and leave his soldiers payless for months. *NCH*, Oct. 18, 1919; Ts'ai T'ing-k'ai, 1: 133–39.

Military Capabilities: Training 93

date enemies, but quite often simply to cheat their own superiors by drawing pay for nonexistent subordinates. Thus it was not unusual for a division or brigade to be credited by shrewd political observers of the time with only 70 percent or even 50 percent of its professed strength. When the top commander did not know exactly how many soldiers he actually possessed, he could exercise little supervision over their payment, and his command of their loyalty was impaired correspondingly. In fact, disputes over pay were one of the primary causes of the recurrent tension within the armies, which sometimes erupted into open riots or mutinies.*

Although such open acts of defiance as riot or mutiny provide us with a glimpse of the seriousness of the decline of discipline in some armies, they do not give us the whole picture. For each mutineer or rioter there were even more soldiers who became so disaffected that they simply deserted, as the high desertion rate cited earlier demonstrates. But the most telling indicators of the deterioration of discipline were the soldiers' conduct in war and their treatment of the civilians.

The lack of disciplinary training tended to reinforce the mercenary mentality that had prompted so many soldiers to join the army in the first place. Soldiers went into battle in the hope of being rewarded by their commanders or allowed to loot. To that extent, the soldiers had a stake in their military unit, whose continuity was instrumental to their personal well-being. But the army lost its instrumental value when it was placed in an unfavorable military situation. For in the final analysis, few mercenaries would accept high risks, since the first condition for making a profit was to stay alive. The implicit contractual relationship between the commander (employer) and the soldiers (employees) dictated maximizing material gains and minimizing battle losses. Such a strategy was scrupulously observed by a large number of Chinese soldiers. Consequently, some "marginal units" frequently

* According to a survey published in *Ku chün*, a journal devoted exclusively to military problems, between 1912 and 1922 there were recorded 179 mutinies, of which 38 cases involved a direct dispute over pay increases or pay in arrears. A large number of the other mutinies attributed to disbandment, insubordination, or unspecified reasons also involved an indirect dispute over pay. (Looting, for example, would often be caused by failure of prompt payment.) Ai Shih, "Min-kuo i lai ping pien piao," *Ku chün*, 1, 4–5 (Jan. 1923); Shou K'ang, "K'o p'a ti ping pien," *ibid.*

changed sides during battles, through defection or surrender. The presence of these units posed enormous difficulties for the military factions in coordinating their war plans: they undermined the factions' internal control, made the outcome of each war highly unpredictable, and jeopardized the stability of the power relations among the factions.

Since these armies surrendered or defected only in order to avert disaster on the battlefield or in exchange for better treatment, they would resist any faction's attempt to impose tight control over them. If too much discipline was demanded, they might defect again. Consequently, there was little mutual trust between the faction and these units, or between the unit commander and his soldiers. The units remained unreliable no matter which faction they joined.

While the soldiers acted cowardly on the battlefield, they acted arrogantly toward the civilians. In the absence of a lofty cause to inspire the soldiers to risk their lives, the only substitute was the vision of personal enrichment. Under such conditions, the people were victimized. Looting, burning, raping, and killing were regular features of the conduct of most Chinese soldiers. When a town was taken, the commander of the victorious army would sometimes deliberately stay out until the soldiers had had a chance to loot systematically. Or he might simply declare a three-day period when the soldiers were allowed to act freely. If the townsfolk wanted to be spared random violence, then they had to pay a protection fee.

Although provincial troops sometimes committed acts of violence against their own people, the most flagrant cases usually occurred when an army operated in another province. During the northern troops' expedition into Hunan in 1918–19, the soldiers of the 7th Division, under the command of Chang Ching-yao, rampaged through the Hunan countryside, seizing or destroying everything in sight.[3] In Kwangtung during 1919–20, Kwangsi troops also behaved very badly.[4] And in Fukien in 1918, the northern troops adopted many of the ordinary practices of bandits, carrying off young women, holding young men for ransom, and looting. The people were forced to hide in the hills until they passed.[5] Even the Yunnan forces, which once had been known for their high professional standards, deteriorated into a band of unruly thugs during their stay in Szechwan. Between 1917 and 1920, the Szechwan and Yunnan forces were constantly at loggerheads. In 1920, when a fierce battle took place between them over the control of Chengtu, the Yunnan forces wantonly destroyed and burned several thousand houses, systematically looted the residential and commercial areas, and killed innocent civilians in large numbers.[6]

Needless to say, such lack of discipline was bound to be highly counterproductive for any army. It posed enormous problems of control. To exploit the soldiers' eagerness for profit might give the commander a temporary advantage in luring them into battle, but it was eventually self-defeating, because when duty and profit clashed, they would not hesitate to choose profit. More seriously, the atrocities perpetrated by the soldiers with their commanders' implicit encouragement eventually turned even the most docile civilians to fierce hatred and resistance. If these atrocities were committed by an outside army, as they most often were, they helped the local militarists to mobilize latent regional sentiments and to weld an otherwise apathetic population into a strong force. In the cases cited above—Szechwan, Hunan, Kwangtung, and Fukien—the lack of discipline proved the undoing of the armies. In each case, a smaller local force, with inferior weapons and fewer resources but enjoying mass support, finally drove the undisciplined troops out of their territories.

Although the lack of discipline we have described was true of most armies, there were some militarists who were alive to the need for training. In general, these were the militarists who also paid more attention to the recruitment process. For instance, Wu P'ei-fu was known to be a strict disciplinarian. Of all the northern troops operating in Hunan, only his 3d Division behaved properly and won the respect of his enemies.[7] Yen Hsi-shan and Feng Yü-hsiang also exhibited great enthusiasm for intensive disciplinary training and ideological indoctrination.

In Shansi, Yen Hsi-shan's soldiers were organized into various kinds of special groups such as "heart-washing societies" (*hsi-hsin-she*), "introspection halls" (*tzu-sheng t'ang*), "lecture meetings" (*chiang-yen-hui*), and other instructional or research classes, small study groups, and discussion groups to inculcate a "spirit of enthusiasm, loyalty, obedience, and self-sacrifice."[8] Officers were expected to know their soldiers. Instructors were installed in all battalions and companies to improve the soldiers' physical condition and to prevent idleness and other bad habits from taking root. Furthermore, soldiers were subject to a rather intense program of political indoctrination which in the early years was based predominantly on orthodox Confucianism. Lectures, posters, songs, discussions, and other methods were used to transform the mentality of the half-literate soldiers and to establish a harmonious relationship between the military and the civilian population. After 1927, Sun Yat-sen's Three People's Principles were added to the teaching material to provide an explicit political orientation for the Shansi army.

Feng Yü-hsiang also believed in a vigorous program of disciplinary training. He laid down several simple rules for his men: they could not smoke tobacco or opium, they could not drink or gamble, and they could not use obscene language or visit brothels. Even high-ranking officers had to live and dress like the common soldiers and to participate in the same daily drills and exercises and other forms of manual labor. Consequently, there was little status consciousness or resentment in the ranks. Strict discipline was enforced, and even senior officers were publicly punished for wrongdoing. Although Feng's army was strewn with primary and secondary associations on the lower levels, nepotism was scrupulously avoided; only achievement counted. But Feng was also a compassionate and understanding leader and he expected his officers to be the same. The rapport he was thereby able to achieve with his officers and men constituted a firm ground for the development of discipline and loyalty within his army.*

The content of Feng's political indoctrination program was more varied than Yen's; in addition to orthodox Confucianism and later Sun Yat-sen's political theories, Feng also used some parts of fundamental Christianity and Lenin's theory of revolution. Like Yen, Feng made profuse use of booklets, songs, slogans, sermons,

---

* Feng took pains to familiarize himself with as many soldiers as possible. When he was a regiment commander in 1913, he knew the names of about 1,400 of the 1600 men under his command. Officers were required to know most of their men by name and to be familiar with their family background as well as personal characteristics. They were expected to look after the welfare of the soldiers and treat them as members of the same family. Unlike other militarists, Feng tried to avoid using corporal punishment as much as possible, and even went so far as to list the circumstances under which corporal punishment was not to be used. Sheridan, pp. 83-87.

Military Capabilities: Training 97

catechisms, posters, and wall papers to convey his messages to the poorly educated soldiers. Hence, in their waking hours, the soldiers either attended religious sermons, recited catechisms on the need to serve the people, or watched plays depicting exemplary lives. Ultimately, the goal was to establish a rationalization and a sublimated sense of mission for his soldiers and to teach them how to relate their existence and their behavior to the prevailing political problems. After Feng's return from the Soviet Union in 1927, he organized a political department with branch offices in each army, division, and brigade; political officers were sent all the way down to the platoons, who in turn organized their own political cells. The addition of this new political arm apparently further consolidated the development of discipline in his army.[9] They certainly recognized that a lasting affective bond among their men could be cemented not by severe corporal punishment or lust for money, but by comradely ties and understanding, and that discipline could best be maintained if they inspired their men with lofty ideals instead of purely acquisitive and exploitative instincts.

Yen and Feng's hard work was certainly not in vain. The longevity and stability of Yen's regime in Shansi bore eloquent testimony to the discipline of his army. During the 1916–28 period, there was not a single case of internal unrest or open revolt against Yen's authority. Even when he later suffered several setbacks in fighting external enemies, his soldiers never forsook him.

Feng's army maintained its reputation for good discipline throughout the whole period. When Feng's 16th Mixed Brigade was stationed in Wuhsüeh (Hupeh) in 1918, his soldiers were well received by the local peasants; even their Hunanese enemies unreservedly voiced their respect and said that they would not attack Feng's forces. They were honest in their dealings with the people, did not commit thievery, and settled all debts before they left. In fact, communities either were sorry to see them leave, or invited them to take over their administration.[10] The supreme test of the army's discipline and loyalty came in 1926, after it was defeated at Nankow. Despite repeated harassment during its retreat, the overwhelming majority of the army traveled hundreds of miles to the Northwestern Territory and regrouped under Feng's leadership. By September 1926, when Feng declared his determination to launch another series of campaigns against his enemies, he had effectively established a new force out of the badly beaten remnants of the Kuominchün. Not only was there no reported case of a power struggle, but some of his subordinates, like Han Fu-ch'ü and Shih Yu-san, who had been obliged to find refuge under Yen Hsi-shan, were persuaded to return to Feng's fold. Thus within a few months, the army was again ready to go to war with undiminished vigor.[11]

Probably no militarist organization succeeded more thoroughly in its training program than the KMT. From the very beginning, the Whampoa project was given the utmost priority in the KMT's rebuilding program. A major characteristic of the disciplinary training in Whampoa was its intensive ideological indoctrination and heavy emphasis on strict discipline, implemented through the political educational program established in October 1923.* Whampoa offered the best political educational curriculum of its time. It included courses on political economics, the theory of imperialism, the history of China, and the history of the revolutionary movement in the West.[12] But it is obvious that the ideological indoctrination revolved primarily around the theses espoused in Sun Yat-sen's Three People's Principles. These principles tried to blend certain salient aspects of the traditional Confucian political creed, the four bonds and eight virtues (*ssu-wei, pa-te*), with elements of Western democratic theory; they embodied a sweeping attack on foreign imperialism, a bellicose assertion of national independence, and finally an earnest advocacy of a constructive program for the salvation and rejuvenation of China. Sun's theory provided the KMT military personnel with a set of conceptual tools to explain the contemporary social and political evils that were everywhere readily visible.

In addition to heavy dosages of political instruction, the cadets were also subject to constant political supervision. The KMT, borrowing the organizational techniques of the Red Army, instilled

---

* This training was placed in the hands of some of the best political minds at the party's disposal. Liao Chung-k'ai was the resident representative of the party, Tai Ch'uan-hsien was the head of the Political Department, Teng Yen-ta the acting head of the Training Department. Other party luminaries who frequently lectured the cadets included Wang Ching-wei, Hu Han-min, and Shao Yüan-ch'ung. Ch'en Hsün-cheng (Ch'en Pu-lei), *Kuo-min ko-ming chün chan shih ch'u kao*, 1: 90.

Military Capabilities: Training

the political commissar system in November 1924, when the training regiments (*chiao-tao-t'uan*) were created.[13] The system was later introduced into all units under the KMT's effective control.

The "Regulations of Political Departments in the National Revolutionary Army" drafted in December 1925 created a political hierarchy of commissars parallel to the military hierarchy, in order to "promote political education, instill a national revolutionary spirit, raise fighting capacity, solidify discipline, and realize Sun Yat-senism in the Army."[14] The commissar was equal in status to the military commander of the unit to which he was assigned. Theoretically, they had separate fields of responsibility;[15] actually, the political commissar was there to check the commander. The political commissar was given power not only to act for the military commander in his absence but to control promotions, recommendations, and punishment of all military personnel. Under extraordinary circumstances, commissars were empowered to veto a commander's orders or forbid subordinates to obey them if they thought the orders were unwise or illegal.[16] They not only helped train the recruits; they also served in combat units. Commissars existed in platoons, companies, battalions, regiments, divisions, army groups, army headquarters, commanders' offices, the various organs of the National Revolutionary Army, Naval Headquarters, the General Staff, and the arsenal. The commissars, in turn, were assisted by political workers in their units, organized into party cells.*

The existence of such an extensive network of political control and supervision enabled the KMT to accept the nominal allegiance of militarists of questionable loyalty. Often the only condition the KMT imposed was that they allow the KMT-appointed party representative with his own team of commissars to be assigned to their units. These commissars would then lay the groundwork for organizing the soldiers into party cells, educating them politically, teaching them to read and write, and acting as their guardians and spokesmen. Once the commissars had won the sympathy and confidence of the common soldiers, they would then

---

* In an army corps, for example, each commissar had about one hundred such political workers to help him, so that there was approximately one political soldier to every one hundred fighting men in the combat units. F. F. Liu, *A Military History of Modern China*, p. 18.

mobilize the soldiers to put pressures upon their commanders.*

As F. F. Liu, the military historian of the Nationalist Army, notes, the political commissar system enabled the KMT to fill its ranks with heterogeneous groups of men, and it also contributed to rectifying such defects in the armies as irregularities in spending, favoritism, and nepotism. Their work not only helped improve the army's public relations during peacetime, but also contributed directly to the party's military success by using organization and propaganda to arouse popular support behind enemy lines.[17]

In addition to ideological indoctrination, the KMT military leaders also stressed conventional martial virtues. The Whampoa cadets were exhorted to achieve four martial qualities—bravery (*yung*), daring (*meng*), authority (*wei*), and austerity (*yen*). In his lectures to the cadets, Chiang constantly reiterated several other themes: he admonished them to learn to persevere regardless of hardship, to be uncompromising on matters of principle ("rather be a crushed gem than a whole piece of tile"), and to be ready to sacrifice and die for the revolutionary cause.[18]

To further enforce discipline, the KMT put into effect in January 1925 the so-called *lien-tso-fa* (military law of collective responsibility), which was to apply to the commanders and soldiers of all military units. Under this law, if a regiment retreated without orders, then the commander in chief would execute the regiment commander. Or if a regiment's commander was killed in action, then any of his battalion commanders who had retreated without orders would be executed to pay for his life. Therefore, the commanders would not dare to retreat. This type of collective responsibility was carried down to the individual members of the smallest military unit. Thus, if a squad leader did not retreat but his entire squad retreated without orders, thus causing the death of the squad leader, then all the privates of the squad would be executed.[19]

---

* A good case in point was the KMT's absorption of Lai Shih-huang's force, which was composed mainly of natives of Kiangsi province. When Lai's force became the 14th Division of the National Revolutionary Army, the KMT appointed Hsiung Shih-hui, a native of Kiangsi, its political representative in the division, in which capacity he organized political work in the division and worked his way into the command structure. When Lai was later executed by the party, Hsiung was appointed commander of the 14th Division. The transition was smooth.

Military Capabilities: Training 101

Shortly after the *lien-tso-fa* went into effect, the Whampoa cadets were incorporated into the KMT forces for the army's first major expedition, the so-called Eastern Expedition. This campaign merits our attention because it set a pattern that was to be followed in the KMT's future campaigns. In the first place, collective responsibility was strictly enforced. During this very first campaign, a company commander was executed for having violated the *lien-tso-fa*. A regimental political commissar and a deputy company commander received severe punishment for the same offense.[20]

Second, the leadership showed great concern for the welfare of the soldiers, in sharp contrast to the callous attitudes of many militarists toward their men. The dead were buried and their families notified; Chiang Kai-shek personally led a memorial service in their honor. The wounded were given extra cash. Third, a thorough investigation of battlefield performance was conducted, and reports were made with recommendations for promotions, demotions, honors, rewards, and punishments.[21] This may be routine for a modern army, but in the context of the 1920's and in comparison with other military units, the KMT's policies were very unusual and made the soldiers feel that their efforts were appreciated. Fourth, the Whampoa cadets and their followers showed extraordinary enthusiasm for fighting and performed heroic deeds beyond the call of duty. It was in this campaign that they first employed the dare-to-die groups (*kan-ssu-tui*) to scale city walls, with very simple instruments and practically no cover. Finally, strict control was exercised over the soldiers' behavior toward the civilian population. The soldiers were forbidden to enter or board in civilian houses or take their property without appropriate compensation. Violators were severely punished.[22]

The KMT force won a resounding victory. In subsequent years the Whampoa-trained officers and soldiers went on to face larger and better equipped enemies, and they continued to score one victory after another. Their bravery won them a reputation for being invincible, and their good conduct also won them the enthusiastic support of the people wherever they went.

Thus, the meticulous inculcation of martial virtues accompanied by the enforcement of iron discipline in the ranks of the Whampoa cadets and the revolutionary forces under their leadership made the KMT army into a formidable force. The political indoctrination gave them some definite principles to fight for, and the *lien-tso-fa* ensured the observance of strict responsibility between superiors and subordinates and necessitated close coordination among commanders, both vertically and horizontally.

Technical Training

The military educational system that existed in the early Republican years was inherited from the Ch'ing dynasty. The imperial edict promulgated by Emperor Kuang-hsü in 1905 established a three-level system for military schools. On the lowest level, each province was to have a three-year primary school at its capital for the training of officers. On the next level, there were to be four military middle schools for the entire country, located at Peking, Sian, Wuch'ang, and Nanking. Students must be graduates of the provincial primary schools and would spend two years in the middle schools. On the highest level, there was a Military Officers' Academy at Paotingfu. Graduates of the military middle schools must first complete one year's service in the army before enrolling in Paotingfu's two-year course.[23] According to the edict, an entrance examination was to be held once a year to select candidates for the primary school, with the proviso that each *hsien* would be guaranteed one student in the school. Although this process of selection seemed fair and objective, the qualifications were actually set by provincial authorities, which led to considerable differences.

By the time of the 1911 revolution, only four classes had graduated from the primary schools, and one from the middle schools. Therefore, the total number of graduates from the new military schools was quite small. In the confusion caused by the revolution, some of the provincial primary schools were either closed or were so poorly supported that they existed in name only. In addition, the qualifications, requirements, and timetables had undergone some minor changes.

By and large, however, the Republicans kept the Ch'ing military educational system essentially intact. Their only structural change was the creation of a Military College as the highest institution for military education. Theoretically, only Paoting graduates who had served in the army for more than two years were eligible to take the entrance examination. Once admitted, they would under-

TABLE 1
Educational Background of Division Commanders,
1916 and 1924

School	1916	1924
Peiyang Military Academy	9	7
Shikan Gakko	10	4
Paoting	1	6
Other schools	4	8
No information	8	10
Total number of commanders	32	35

SOURCE: "Chih yüan piao," *Tung fang tsa chih*, 14, 1 (Jan. 1917); *China Year Book*, 1924, pp. 927–49.

go three years of advanced training to become high-echelon line officers or staff officers.[24] According to regulations, seven years of academic training were required to produce an officer, or ten years for top commanders and staff positions.

Concerning the quality of military leadership in the early Republican period, there seem to be two different views. Powell, on the basis of his examination of the late Ch'ing army program, suggests that many military leaders were fairly well educated.[25] Others argue that most leading military figures were ignorant. Jerome Ch'en, for example, studied the biographical sketches of 1,300 men who held the rank of brigadier or higher between 1912 and 1928 and concluded that "the number of 'educated' war lords is unlikely to have exceeded 30 percent of the total and the rest were mostly illiterate or semi-literate people from extremely modest origins."[26]

My own studies indicate that many of the militarists on the higher levels had had some form of education. Table 1 shows that more than 70 percent of the division commanders in 1916 and 1924 (the years for which we have a complete national listing) had attended some military school. Moreover, the other 30 percent includes men whose educational background could not be ascertained; the actual number of men without any formal education might be even smaller. Thus, although the illiteracy of such militarists as Chang Tsung-ch'ang and Han Fu-ch'u was well publicized, often in comical terms, such men were rare among the top leaders. It is true that no first-rate scholars were to be found among the militarists, but many of them were quite educated. Feng Kuo-

TABLE 2
Educational Background of Highest Provincial
Military Authorities, 1916–1928

School	Number of militarists
Peiyang Military Academy	18
Shikan Gakko	19
Paoting	12
Other schools	22
No information	36
TOTAL	107

NOTE: Sinkiang has been omitted, since it was remote and never figured importantly in the military politics of the period.

chang and Wu P'ei-fu were *hsiu-ts'ai* (successful candidates of civil service exams), Tuan Ch'i-jui was quite immersed in the exposition of Buddhist theology, and Hsü Shu-cheng had a very solid training in classics and was the author of *Chien kuo ch'uan cheng*, a treatise on a new political system.

Of course, it may be argued that the division commanders, a relatively small group, were not necessarily representative of the other high-ranking militarists. To try to meet this objection, I have analyzed the educational backgrounds of those militarists who occupied the highest military positions in the provinces during the 1916–28 period; see Table 2. In this group, too, the educated militarists outnumbered the uneducated ones, by 71 to 36 (or 66 to 34 percent), even if we treat all those for whom we have no information as uneducated.

Unfortunately, existing information does not allow us to carry this type of aggregate national statistical analysis all the way down to the lower ranks. However, we are able to conduct such an analysis on a regional basis. For the three provinces in Manchuria, we possess fairly reliable and complete information on the educational background of all the important militarists of the Fengtien faction in 1924. As Table 3 shows, two-thirds of the division and brigade commanders, three-fourths of the regiment commanders, and almost all (93 percent) of the other officers above lieutenant colonel had had some education.

The consistency of all these findings compels us to reject the view that the leading militarists of the 1916–28 period were generally uneducated men. We must not confuse humble origins with lack

TABLE 3
Educational Background of Fengtien Militarists, 1924

School	Division commanders	Brigade commanders	Regiment commanders	Others above lt. colonel
Shikan Gakko and Japan War College		1	3	12
Paoting and National Military College	1	3	11	
Manchurian Military Academy	1	7	20	7
Other		5	12	9
No information	1	8	16	2
TOTAL	3	24	62	30

SOURCE: *Tosan-sho Kanshin roku*, ed. by Tanabe Shujiro, pp. 1–77. The Manchurian Military Academy included the Tung-san-sheng chiang wu t'ang and Feng-t'ien chiang wu t'ang.

of formal education. Many military schools, because they were publicly funded, did not discriminate against the poor. In addition, frequently talented soldiers would be sent to military school for a period of formal training. Quite a few officers in Manchuria went to school only after they had risen through the ranks to become company or battalion commanders.

Thus, literacy is too simple a measure of the quality of military leadership. We must look at the kind of education that prepared men to be military leaders.

By and large, the education reform initiated in the late Ch'ing and carried on in the 1916–28 period did not produce the desired improvement in the quality of military education. Ting Wen-chiang, a distinguished geologist who was also intensely interested in the military affairs of his time, categorically declared that military education was the most backward branch of Chinese education, lagging behind civilian higher education by at least twenty years. He further claimed that the officers being produced by the schools not only lacked modern knowledge and training; they could not even read military maps.[27]

Although the system looked good on paper, the government lacked the administrative machinery and technical expertise to carry it out fully. In the first place, the quality of students enrolled at the military schools was difficult to control; there were no uniform standards. Even an advanced military school like Paoting suffered from an unevenness in the quality of its students, since it had to accept any serving officer.[28] Second, political instability during the 1916–28 period often forced many schools either to suspend operations or to shorten the duration of training.

More serious shortcomings were the backwardness of the instructional material and the inefficiency with which the schools were administered. In the military primary schools, the amount of military knowledge and skills imparted to the students was usually small and superficial.[29] The courses taught at the military middle schools were apparently more advanced, but the quality of instruction was probably not very good.[30] During the Republican period, a graduate of a middle school served in an army unit for six months before going to Paoting, but the educational value of this in-service training was nil.[31] The Paoting Military Academy, which was supposed to be the highest training ground for line commanders, presented a similarly dismal picture. Because the cadets came from diverse geographical backgrounds, and some of them had even participated in the 1911 revolution, the academy was given a low priority by Tuan Ch'i-jui and the other Peiyang militarists who were in control of the central government.* In addition, there was a general refusal to take the educational process seriously. Instructors and cadets alike believed that the characteristics of a good military leader were contempt for death and the judicious application of simple strategy and tactics. Science and technology were neglected; there was no attempt to integrate and synthesize military science with other related disciplines. This invariably led to a very narrow perspective. For instance, students showed little interest in studying weaponry, because it was considered a field only for specialists.[32] There was also a pervasive cynicism about the purpose of the whole educational process. Both instructors and students regarded the schooling period as a formality, not a time to really learn something. Thus, so long as a student fulfilled his minimum academic requirements, he would be graduated.

The worst problem facing higher military education, however,

* When Chiang Fang-cheng was commandant of Paoting, he became so frustrated by the central government's unwillingness to improve the school that he attempted to commit suicide in protest. The situation remained poor after Chiang's departure. Ts'ao Chü-jen, pp. 7–8; T'ao Chü-yin, *Chiang Pai-li hsien sheng chuan*, pp. 36–42, 48.

was the inadequacy of the instructors. Most of the Chinese instructors had themselves been inadequately educated at the same poor schools in which they were teaching; a few had been educated in Japan. And when foreign instructors (mostly Japanese) were employed, new psychological strains and instructional problems were created.* In addition, most ambitious and educated officers shunned desk jobs, and an academic position was the worst of the desk jobs. The military school was a place for premature retirement, and only the hopeless ones would accept such an assignment. Even the militarists who appreciated the importance of military education were reluctant to send their able lieutenants to teach in military schools. A militarist, regardless of his intellectual and leadership potential, wanted a combat assignment, since this was the surest way to rapid promotion and greater power. The best indication of the contempt for teaching is the appallingly small number of instructors employed by the military schools. In June 1916, there were only about 350 instructors known to be employed by all the military schools above the provincial primary school level in the entire country.[33]

The basic cause of the neglect of military education during the Republican years was not financial, for the country certainly could afford to finance a few good schools. Nor was it the lack of talent, although talent was not in abundant supply. The basic cause was to be found in the concept of what constituted a good military leader and in the constraints imposed by the nature of the political game. It seems that the image of a military man was still shaped in traditional terms. The militarists tended to define themselves in terms of the traditional Chinese hero (such as Han Kao-tsu or Ming Hung-wu), who elevated himself from humble background to fame and power by sheer personal valor and political acumen. This was particularly true in a time of chaos, when there was no orderly system of promotion but much chance to fight. The opportunities were abundant if only one could command some troops.

So far we have been analyzing the quality of military education, but we can also approach our problem from a different angle. The

* The students regarded foreign instructors as spies and treated them with hostility. Moreover, interpreters had to be used, which made the instructional process very cumbersome and unproductive. Ch'in Te-shun, pp. 128–29; Hu Shih, *Ting Wen-chiang ti chuan chi*, pp. 61–62.

distribution of the educated militarists among the different echelons also had an important bearing on the functioning of the military system. Instead of quality, here we are primarily concerned with quantity—the number of graduates from the various military schools, where they went, and how their number might have affected the character of military operations.

Throughout the 1916–28 period, the theoretical ratio between officers and men stipulated in the organizational charts remained relatively stable, never exceeding 1:20.[34] If we apply this ratio to the rough estimates of the total size of the army given in Chapter 4 (p. 78), then we arrive at the following estimates of the number of officers needed to lead China's armies in various years: 1916, over 25,000 officers; 1918, over 50,000; 1924, over 75,000; and 1928, over 100,000. These figures represent only the officers needed to serve in combat and various combat-support activities. They do not include such military personnel as the military police or the staffs of the Ministry of War, the Chief of the General Staff, the defense commissioners of military districts in all parts of the country, and the arsenals and other supply depots. Thus our estimates represent the bare minimum number of officers required according to the prevailing theory of military organization.

Our next task, then, is to find out whether the military educational system was capable of meeting this rising demand for officers. A comprehensive survey of China's military educational institutions shows that, for the four-year period 1912–16, the total of all military school graduates above the primary-school level came to a figure of less than 10,000, or less than 2,500 annually.[35] Since the number of combat officers required in 1916 was over 25,000, even if all of the 10,000 graduates produced in the previous four years were given combat assignments, they could only fill the top positions within each combat unit, leaving the middle and lower levels to men with no formal military training.

The situation deteriorated after the beginning of the 1920's. Several northern provinces either closed their primary schools or supported them so poorly that they served no useful purpose.*

---

* In some provinces, a new form of military education arose, known as the "lecture halls," or *chiang-wu-t'ang*. Generally, these took the place of the provincial primary schools or even the middle schools, when regular facilities for training officers were unavailable. *CYB*, 1921–22, p. 513. But, as a whole, this

One middle school, at Ch'ingho, was closed, and even the Paoting Military Academy was closed after producing nine graduating classes. Both the quality and quantity of military school graduates remained stagnant or declined during most of the 1920's.

At the same time, the number of troops was increasing rapidly, and the demand for qualified officers became more pressing. During the 1920's, the frequency of wars increased, and more troops were fighting than ever before. Consequently, the depletion of officers caused by battlefield casualties must have increased significantly as well. Under these conditions, the number of officers with some form of formal military training must have constituted an even smaller percentage of the entire officer corps.

There is little doubt that this lack of competent officers eventually made the task of training the soldiers extremely difficult, if not impossible. The greatest obstacle presented by the Chinese soldiers was their widespread illiteracy.* The more illiterate soldiers there were in any unit, the greater was the need for face-to-face communication, detailed oral instruction, personal demonstration, and supervision. This, in turn, required a greater officer-to-soldier ratio.

Furthermore, as the sophistication of the weapons increased, the need for trained officers to instruct the soldiers increased correspondingly. In this respect, the supply of competent officers was even more inadequate. Almost half of the military schools were general-purpose schools of various levels. There were two military police schools, one logistics school, one medical school, one veterinary school, one aviation school. Although there were nine or ten army survey schools, there was no artillery school, no signal, engineering, quartermaster, or ordnance school. Thus almost no officers received specialized training in the more important branches of military science. The Chinese armies fought with constantly improving weapons, but the military organization was tailored

---

new institution failed to improve the quality of military education or to increase the output of graduates.

* James Yen's investigation of Fengtien troops during the 1920's showed that only 25 out of every 150 soldiers (16.6 percent) were literate; T'ao Meng-ho's investigation of a northern brigade showed that only 13 percent of the soldiers were literate. Worse conditions probably existed in other troops. For instance, Feng Yü-hsiang declared that during 1919–20, over 95 percent of the officers and men in his army were illiterate or semiliterate. F. F. Liu, p. 142; Feng Yü-hsiang, *Wo ti sheng ho*, 2: 107.

to a more primitive mode of warfare and was very slow to change. The deficiency in the number of qualified specialized officers made the technical training of the soldiers almost impossible.

Under these conditions, it is not at all surprising that some militarists simply omitted technical training altogether, especially when they considered training to be of little value anyway. To these militarists, the best way to use a recruit was to give him a rifle and to throw him into action as soon as possible. If he got killed, there were always more men than rifles.

The backwardness of the Chinese armies, I submit, was due less to any lack of education among the top militarists and more to the high rate of illiteracy and the insufficient technical training of the lower-echelon officers and the overwhelming majority of the soldiers. For the inadequacy of top leaders could sometimes be ameliorated by outside assistance, such as personal secretaries or foreign military advisers; the services of soldiers of fortune or foreign career officers acting with the implicit encouragement of their governments could be enlisted with relative ease.* Thus, high-level planning posed no serious problem if the militarists were willing to employ outside talents. At the middle and lower echelons, however, foreign advisers were unavailable and the lack of well-trained indigenous staff members had its full impact. Each battle had to be improvised. The commanders themselves, because of their misconception of the requirements of a military leader, were not in a position to assume the role of staff officers. Sometimes, they were simply incapable of commanding a large force.†

The strategic and tactical mistakes committed by the officers showed that they were woefully deficient in the basic requirements imposed by the contemporary technology. Under such leadership, it was unrealistic to expect the soldiers to behave any more effi-

* For instance, Feng Yü-hsiang "had at least one German, one Italian, and one Japanese officer in his army besides his Russian advisers." Japanese military experts served in the armies of Tuan Ch'i-jui, Chang Tso-lin, and Wu P'ei-fu. Sheridan, p. 29.

† Commenting on the reasons for the dismal failure of the Second Kuominchün under the leadership of Hu Chin-i, Feng Yü-hsiang said, "Many of Hu's subordinates were ... hardworking men and displayed extraordinary bravery at the front. But many of them also had no understanding of military strategies and tactics. Therefore, whenever the force exceeded one thousand men, they simply did not know how to command it." Feng Yü-hsiang, *Wo ti sheng ho*, 2: 25–26.

Military Capabilities: Training

ciently. Whenever technical training was not given appropriate emphasis, the majority of the soldiers were unfit to fight. They did not know how to handle their weapons properly, or how to use the terrain, or how to coordinate with their fellow soldiers. They often fought individually, rather than as parts of a formation. They used their weapons for the wrong purpose or in the wrong way, causing rapid depletion of ammunition and destruction of weapons. What otherwise would have been a mere reverse in fortune on the battlefield could become a major defeat, and a major defeat an annihilation.

It must not be assumed, of course, that all armies were alike. There were militarists who were alive to the need for technical training at a very early time; by and large these were the same men who were exceptions in recruitment and discipline. Wu P'ei-fu was known as a thorough trainer. Right after the 1920 victory over Anhwei, he established a serious training program at Loyang that by 1923 included an officers' school, schools for the men, and a cadet school for several hundred small boys. He also had specialized training in such areas as armored cars, bombs, and aviation.[36]

Yen Hsi-shan was equally enthusiastic about technical training. His junior officers were required to complete two years of middle school education. Before being given senior assignments, officers had either to attend the Paoting Military Academy or to enlist in Yen's own Military Instruction Corps. One significant feature of the training in Shansi was the use of live ammunition for target practice, which was extremely rare among northern armies and which earned for Shansi soldiers the reputation for the best marksmanship.[37]

Feng Yü-hsiang also had a vigorous technical training program. Nearly all his low-ranking officers had risen from the ranks, and the majority of the middle- and high-ranking officers were not graduates of military schools.[38] He first organized intensive training classes for commanders in 1913; soldiers were instructed through booklets, songs, daily pep talks, and periodic examinations. Later Feng established a Military Training Corps, which offered courses for both officers and noncommissioned officers on military tactics, troop leadership, topography, weaponry, military history, fortifications, and regulations. In 1925 Feng added a "Qualifications Examining Group" to check the knowledge and performance of his officers, and its reports usually had great influence over the promotion and demotion of officers.[39] In the same year, Feng's training program received a boost from Soviet military advisers, who inspected and evaluated Feng's army in terms of military knowledge and efficiency and made suggestions for improvement. They also organized and served as instructors in the artillery, advanced infantry, engineering, cavalry, and intelligence schools.[40]

Of all the armies, however, the KMT gave the most serious attention to military technical training. As early as August 1923 the party dispatched a delegation headed by Chiang Kai-shek to visit the Soviet Union, and one of its important missions was to study the Soviet military system as a possible model for the establishment of the KMT party army. Soon after his return, Chiang was appointed by Sun to supervise the preparations for the creation of an officers' training school, the Whampoa Academy.

From the beginning the quality of the Whampoa cadets was high. Of the 3,000 men who applied for admission to the first class, fewer than 500 were accepted. Only a small fraction of the students were selected from among the officers of the KMT armies (Hunan, Honan, Yunnan, Kwangsi, and Kwangtung) in Kwangtung; the majority were recruited on the basis of their performance in entrance examinations held clandestinely in other provinces.[41] This fact marked the Whampoa force as the first significant case of breaking way from the narrow geographical pattern of recruitment set by other provincial forces in the south, and the policy undoubtedly had a beneficial effect on the quality of recruits. For Whampoa's applicants were superior to those of all the military schools in the nation, and in some cases they were even superior to the graduates of other military schools.*

The Whampoa faculty also showed marked superiority to most

---

* In a telegram to Chiang Kai-shek dated March 13, 1924, Liao Chung-k'ai reported that one-third of the 1,200 applicants in Kwangtung had already graduated from either a regular high school or a specialized school. Even after the examination officials had added trigonometry, geometry, and algebra to the examination in order to be more selective, many were still able to answer all questions, and Liao complained about the difficulty of choosing from among so many qualified applicants. If in Kwangtung alone there were some 400 applicants with high school education, it would not be wide of the mark to speculate that almost all of the 500 cadets selected from the 3,000 applicants had had a high school education or better.

other military schools. The instructor-student ratio was higher at Whampoa than at other schools. And, unlike other militarists, the KMT put its best military talents into educational training.[42]

The quality of Whampoa's technical training was enhanced by the presence of heavy foreign influences. Many top-level faculty members came from the Japanese school, Shikan Gakko, and many of the instructional materials were obtained from the Japanese.[43] Most important, however, was the role played by the Soviet Union, which sent some of its best military commanders to establish a foothold in the KMT military structure.[44] The Soviet advisers were actively concerned with all major aspects of the training program. Although they could not personally conduct any classes, the senior advisers in fact developed all the academic courses, while the junior advisers worked with drills, weapons firing, and tactical preparations. In sum, the Soviet advisers exerted a very strong influence in shaping the training program at Whampoa.[45]

There is little doubt that the extensive support given by the KMT to Whampoa, the high quality of its Chinese faculty, the high standards of its cadets, and the able advisers and advanced teaching material provided by the Soviet Union together made Whampoa into the best military school of the 1920's. It was also the largest.

By January 1926, the first four classes of Whampoa had graduated some 5,540 cadets.[46] The expansion of the school had been phenomenal, from a first class of fewer than 500 cadets to a fourth class with over 3,500 cadets.[47] Even the Paoting Military Academy never had more than 1,500 cadets in a single class.[48] By June 1926, Chiang claimed than some 6,400 cadets had been trained by Whampoa.[49] Thus, in less than two years, the KMT had trained approximately the same number of officers produced by all the military schools (above the primary school level) in the nation in any three of the years between 1912 and 1916, and had trained them better as well.

During this period, the activities of the school went much beyond the classroom and the training field. In October 1924 the cadets were used to suppress the rebellion of the Canton Chamber of Commerce. With the seized weapons, the Whampoa Academy proceeded to organize training regiments in November and December 1924, using the cadets as officers, and recruiting soldiers in

Shanghai as well as in Kwangtung. By the spring of 1925, two training regiments, totaling about 4,000 men, had become fully established. These training regiments, with Whampoa graduates serving as junior officers, became the nucleus of the new KMT army which was organized in August 1925.[50]

Conclusion

Our inquiry into the disciplinary and technical training of the Chinese armies shows that wide discrepancies existed among them. The majority of them, the mercenary armies, were poorly trained. The armies that were better trained were guided by some form of idological commitment, ranging from a strict personal code of proper conduct to a comprehensive body of political doctrines. The fact that *some*, but not all, armies had a mercenary character had a dysfunctional effect on the stability of the Chinese political system.

Since only some armies had a strongly mercenary character, they could not effectively impose on the entire system a set of rules for conducting warfare that would be most conducive to their own major interest, which was self-preservation. When there were ideological armies that aimed at the destruction of enemies, wars could not be fought in accordance with a "conservationist" policy. Unable to change the terms of warfare and unwilling to fight hard, the Chinese mercenaries resorted to plots, counterplots, defections, and surrenders to preserve themselves in the system.

Precisely because of the commercial orientation of many of these units, they were used but seldom trusted. Their resistance to strict military control often created internal stresses and strains in the military organizations to which they belonged. The presence of "unreliable" mercenary armies made military calculations extremely difficult. Highly integrated and better trained units seldom changed sides; mercenary units did. When the latter happened, the militarist to which these units belonged faced the threat of annihilation. Hence we find that the demise of the Anhwei faction was brought about in 1920 not because its troops were defeated in the battlefield, but because many units lost the will to fight soon after hostilities began and went over to Chihli and Fengtien factions. Even as late as 1926–27, the KMT's task of fighting Sun Ch'uan-fang was made easier when many southern militarists in

Fukien, Kiangsi, and Chekiang were bought off and defected at opportune moments. In this sense, the existence of mercenary elements made the Chinese system inherently unstable.

Toward the last three or four years, armies like that of the Shansi faction, the KMT, and the Kuominchün came to acquire a rather pronounced ideological character. As a result, the hard core of these armies displayed a high degree of group solidarity. Faced with this solidarity, even the northern militarists were driven to become somewhat ideological, in the broad sense of the term. They developed a distinct tendency to view their war against the KMT as a regional struggle between north and south. Northern leaders like Chang Tso-lin and Wu P'ei-fu began to refer to the KMT as "reds" and warned their followers that the forthright and honest northern soldiers could never expect to receive a fair deal from those cunning and treacherous southerners.

It is interesting to note that the northern troops, which had never been known for good discipline or high morale, put up fierce resistance against the KMT offensive throughout the duration of the Northern Expedition. The overwhelming majority of militarists who surrendered to the KMT were provincials of Kiangsu, Chekiang, Kiangsi, Hunan, Hupei, and Fukien. Few high-ranking northern militarists defected or surrendered to the KMT without a serious fight. Compromise was considered impossible because there existed a wide gap in political style, ideological outlook, and educational background, as well as in personal relationships, between these two groups, the Peiyang militarists and the KMT.

CHAPTER 6

Military Capabilities: Weaponry and Tactics

MILITARY modernization constituted an important part of the late Ch'ing reform programs in response to Western challenges. The Ch'ing court spent considerable sums of money on foreign equipment and aspired eventually to produce its own. The court relied equally heavily upon foreign, especially German, assistance to train Chinese officers and soldiers. It is clear, however, from the quick defeats the Chinese forces suffered during the first Sino-Japanese War and the Boxer Rebellion that the Ch'ing government failed to achieve its objectives.

In the waning years of Ch'ing, some improvement occurred. On the whole, however, military technology and tactics advanced very little, and even this modest gain was probably more than vitiated by the political chaos of the ensuing years. This situation had a profound impact on the military in the 1916–28 period. In a sense, military technology and tactics imposed a set of constraints upon all Chinese militarists. Additional constraints were imposed by China's communications system and geography. Eventually, these constraints affected the distribution and transformation of political power. This chapter, then, attempts to describe these constraints and to assess their significance for the Chinese political system.

Weapons

Although spears, swords, and shotguns were widely used in some units, the infantrymen's most important modern weapon was the rifle. But the rifles were not of uniform quality or standard specifications, for three reasons.[1] First, most Chinese arsenals had been established and managed under regional auspices. Second, the for-

Military Capabilities: Weaponry and Tactics 117

eign supply of arms came from many different countries. Third, procurement was the personal problem of each militarist; he had to take whatever weapons he could get and afford. The consequence was near-chaos; it was quite common for an army to be equipped with different types of rifles whose parts and ammunition were not interchangeable. In addition, the rifles were often obsolescent and poorly maintained. Most important, the number of rifles of any kind was usually inadequate.[2]

The most powerful weapons employed in the field were the artillery pieces. Here, too, the weapons were of diverse descriptions.[3] Again, the diversity did not reflect technological sophistication, but rather decentralized procurement policies. According to one investigation, in early 1918 there were only 1,480 small pieces and 46 heavy pieces of artillery in the entire country; the possession of artillery was the privilege of a limited number of militarists and a matter of great envy.[4] After the mid-1920's, fairly large quantities of mortars were produced by domestic arsenals.

Machine guns were not used in Chinese armies on a large scale until after they had demonstrated their value in the First World War, although the exact time of their introduction has not been determined. From the beginning, there was a wide variety of models and calibers.[5] In 1920 there were reported to be 1,394 machine guns in use throughout all of China; many of them were Chinese products patterned after Western models that had long been discarded as impracticable or even dangerous. After 1920, machine guns became increasingly popular in Chinese armies and their number increased substantially.[6] The exceedingly high price of machine guns, however, was a powerful deterrent to most militarists. (In 1923, a machine gun sold for $450, while a rifle cost only $17.)[7] Consequently, the number of machine guns used by Chinese militarists probably never exceeded a few thousand pieces, most of them owned by the leading militarists, during the entire 1920's.[8]

Together, these three types of weapons constituted the essential equipment for the Chinese armies, although some new weapons were introduced from time to time. Airplanes were first used in military engagements during the anti-restoration campaign of 1917.[9] At this time, there were very few airplanes in the whole country. On the eve of the Chihli-Fengtien war of 1924, the number of planes had increased to about 170, with more than 100 of them in the hands of the Chihli militarists.[10] The total number probably reached 240 by 1928.[11] Other new weapons included tanks, armored railway cars, poisonous gas, and grenades.

A review of the state of military technology of the 1916–28 period shows that although differences existed among militarists at a given time, they were greater between different time periods. In keeping with the expansion of the size of the army during these years, there was a continuous expansion and improvement in weapons. This continuous, and in some cases phenomenal, progress in the armaments of the rapidly expanding Chinese armies raises an important question: How were these armies able to meet the increasing demands of expansion and modernization? To answer this question, we must examine the domestic and foreign sources of supply of military hardware.

The domestic armament industry rested on a very feeble foundation. The Ch'ing government made very little headway in its program to expand the armament industry to meet the needs of the proposed New Army program, except for the creation of the Kiangnan and Hanyang arsenals. In all of China in 1916, there were only eight arsenals with any capacity for producing armaments.[12] There were 21 other so-called "arsenals" under national and provincial management, but they were mainly concerned with storage and simple repair and should more appropriately be called "armories."

The operating budgets of the arsenals reveal that even the larger arsenals had a very small output. Only Hanyang Arsenal had an annual operating budget of over one million dollars; three others had budgets between $500,000 and $600,000. The rest operated with very small funds.

All the arsenals with productive capabilities were located in six provinces (Hupeh, Shantung, Szechwan, Kwangtung, Kiangsu, and Honan), leaving the vast majority of provinces without their own arsenals. When the central government collapsed in 1916, the arsenals became the private property of the militarists in control of these areas; a large number of armies were left with no assured sources of supply. Many militarists responded either by expanding the facilities of existing arsenals or by creating new ones. By

TABLE 4
Monthly Output of Armaments, China
and Manchuria, 1923 and 1928

Type	1923	1928
China proper:		
Rifles	7,000	8,500
Cartridges	5,500,000	9,500,000
Pistols	750	1,250
Machine guns	33	72
Artillery	6	300
Shells	1,200	96,000
Manchuria:		
Rifles	—	7,500
Cartridges	—	9,000,000
Pistols	—	—
Machine guns	—	70–80
Artillery	—	Large quantity
Shells	—	120,000

SOURCES: *China Year Book*, 1923, pp. 592–94; *China Year Book*, 1929–30, pp. 751–53; "Feng-Chih ping li chih pi chiao," *Tung fang tsa chih*, 21, 19 (October 10, 1924): 160–61; Donald G. Gillin, *Warlord: Yen Hsi-shan in Shansi Province, 1911–1949* (Princeton, N.J., 1967), pp. 26–29.

the early 1920's almost every provincial capital had an arsenal equipped to manufacture small quantities of pistols, rifles, machine guns, and some artillery pieces. Furthermore, lesser militarists also resorted to every possible means of self-help, such as using local blacksmiths to make weapons.[13]

Since the vast majority of these arsenals were makeshift operations and did not affect national total output to any significant degree, we can regard the figures cited in Table 4 as approximating the total arms output by domestic sources in China in 1923 and 1928. These figures allow us to make several further observations about China's armaments industry in the 1920's. Insofar as China proper is concerned, the increase of output in all areas except artillery pieces and shells was less than threefold. The modest nature of this increase becomes obvious when we compare the production figures of China proper with those of Manchuria. Although their combined total represented a definite increase over the early years, the fact that the Manchurian output almost equals the output of China proper conclusively shows that the development was an extremely uneven one.

Of all the arsenals in China, three—Mukden (Manchuria), Tai-yüan (Shansi), and Hanyang (Hupeh)—could produce adequate quantities of small arms to meet the needs of the local militarists. Hanyang could even supply other Chihli faction armies as well as sell small quantities to neighboring provinces.[14] The other arsenals, however, present a different picture. Many of them originally had old machinery imported from abroad; as time went on, their obsolescence increased. Many arsenals also deteriorated as a consequence of wars between militarists, even when they were not directly exposed to war damages.[15] Production became irregular and output declined.

As the total number of Chinese soldiers quadrupled from half a million in 1916 to over two million in 1928, the production of about 200,000 rifles per year (the peak figure for 1928) hardly sufficed to meet the needs of more than a tiny fraction of the armies. In fact, production was probably not sufficient to replace battle losses as wars became both more frequent and more devastating toward the latter part of the period.[16] Under these circumstances, the militarists found that the only alternative was to seek foreign supplies.

Foreign arms had played a prominent role in China since the beginning of the programs for military modernization. Their importance steadily mounted, reaching a peak during the heyday of militarism. However, an accurate assessment of the importance of foreign arms is difficult.* The best we can do is to describe some of the practices and tentatively suggest the proportions and political consequences of foreign arms deals.

Japan seems to have been the only country whose government had a clear record of deep involvement with the Chinese military prior to the 1920's. While the West was preoccupied with the First World War, Japan established a close relationship with the Peking

* There are several reasons for this. First, foreign governments wanted to prevent full exposure of arms transactions between them (or their agents) and the Chinese militarist-buyers. Second, when transactions were purely commercial and private, they usually involved a large number of agents and operators without coordination or centralized control, thus making it difficult to track them down. Third, the parties involved shared a common interest in shielding their deals from the public view; the Chinese did so to protect military secrets and their reputation, and the foreigners to avoid prosecution under the laws of their own countries. Not infrequently, transactions were conducted on a cash basis, with no written records. Even when banks and credit were utilized, the banks protected the anonymity of their clients.

government, then under the domination of Tuan Ch'i-jui and his Anfu Club. Through the Sino-Japanese Mutual Defense Pact (May 1918) and its extension (February 1919), Japan became the sole foreign government to supply and train Chinese troops.[17] With the defeat of the Anhwei faction, Japan's official involvement in arms supplies began to decline. After 1920, there was little evidence of further massive governmental arms support to any Chinese militarist.

In fact, Japan was one of the signers of the Arms Embargo Agreement reached on May 5, 1919, in which the signatory powers formally pledged to halt all arms supplies to Chinese militarists so as to discourage further civil strife.[18] Implementation of the document encountered obstacles almost from the very beginning, however. In the first place, the embargo's enforcement was undercut by reservations and interpretations individually attached to the agreement by some countries. Japan, for example, claimed that the embargo should not forbid the importation of arms into the Japanese territory at Port Arthur; the French claimed the right to import arms for the police force and volunteers in the French concessions at Shanghai and elsewhere.[19] These governments thus were able to ship large quantities of arms to China on the pretext that the arms were meant for their own forces.

In the second place, the nationals of the signatory powers were allowed to engage in arms transactions without legally violating the terms of the agreement. Airplanes and arsenal machinery, for instance, were sold openly by the nationals of the powers most eager to enforce the spirit and letter of the agreement.[20]

In the third place, some of the world's leading arms producers—Germany, the Soviet Union, Austria, Norway, Denmark, and Czechoslovakia—had not signed the agreement. Consequently, the nationals and governments of these countries could engage in arms transactions openly with their Chinese clients without fear of reprisal or punishment.

These shortcomings prevented the embargo from fulfilling its original intentions, although the agreement might have had some limiting effects on the amount of foreign arms shipped to Chinese militarists during the first few years. After 1924, however, violations became so frequent and flagrant that the embargo ceased to exist for all practical purposes.[21] Since all parties involved in arms smuggling or transactions jealously guarded their business secrets, we may never be able to gauge the full scope of such activities in China. However, several general observations can be made on the basis of the available information.

First, the supply of foreign arms figures prominently in any explanation of China's civil strife. Most certainly, foreign countries were a more important source of supply than domestic production. It is no exaggeration to say that most Chinese armies were confronted with two alternatives: they could remain poorly equipped or they could rely heavily on foreign arms. The heavy depletion and attrition in the later years of the period often compelled even militarists with their own arsenals, such as the Fengtien faction, to import foreign arms. The deciding factor in the arms race among Chinese militarists was their ability to procure foreign arms. The sudden shift in power relationships brought about by one side's acquisition of large quantities of arms was often viewed with great alarm and often triggered a chain of reactions that eventually led to war.[22]

Although the exact proportions of the foreign supply of arms are not readily assessable on a year-to-year basis, the general trend is unmistakably one of steady increase over the years. As conflict among the militarists became more intense, their need for arms also soared. Their scramble for foreign arms reached a frantic pace, especially after the spring of 1927 as the KMT forces were about to carry the war into North China. By 1927, according to a report published in *The North China Star*, a total of over a hundred million dollars worth of foreign arms had been imported into China.[23]

The question of which country was the most to blame for the arms trafficking has never failed to arouse interest. While there has never been a lack of controversy, there have been very few hard facts. In the absence of reliable statistics, no one can determine with any degree of confidence which country was the chief culprit. Both the Nationalists and Communists maintained that the leading imperialistic nations like Japan and Great Britain were the major exporters of arms to support their favorite militarists in their respective spheres of influence. Their argument assumed that foreign governments and private individuals worked in collusion and should be lumped together for practical purposes.

Available evidence, however, does not support the thesis that the

Military Capabilities: Weaponry and Tactics

foreign arms dealers operated as a front for their governments; nor was there a client-sponsor relationship between Chinese militarists and a particular foreign power insofar as arms supplies were concerned. It is generally assumed, for example, that Chang Tso-lin depended on Japan for arms because Manchuria was in the Japanese sphere of influence. There is no doubt that Fengtien bought Japanese arms, since the source of supply was close by and the transaction was facilitated by the numerous Japanese commercial firms and banks in Manchuria. But Fengtien also purchased extensively from other countries, and the Mukden arsenal was equipped with European machinery and supervised by European experts.*

The transactions show no pattern of preference or dependence between the Chinese buyers and the foreign suppliers. It is fair to suggest that under normal circumstances the profit motive was the most important factor in the transactions. All the Chinese militarists wanted to buy foreign arms when they could afford them. Foreigners of many nationalities were equally eager to sell arms to the Chinese. The record seems to suggest that arms dealers were as diverse in national origin as the merchandise they peddled.

Although foreign governments certainly were concerned about their rights and interests in China, they did not openly intervene on behalf of a particular militarist. Before Japan changed its policy in 1927–28, it did not intervene to prevent the defeat of Tuan Ch'i-jui in 1920 or Chang Tso-lin in 1922, although both were supposed to be "pro-Japanese" militarists. It is also hard to cite any evidence of the British helping Sun Ch'uan-fang and Wu P'ei-fu, or the French helping T'ang Chi-yao. It is very possible that many more weapons were made available to these Chinese militarists through private transactions than through any secret official channels.[24] Together, the arms dealers and the militarists sustained China's civil wars.

It is against this background that we must evaluate the role of

---

* Chang Tso-lin bought a large shipment of German arms manufactured at the Krupp plants in 1923–24. Then in the midst of the 1924 war, he bought 18 airplanes from France. In May 1925, he also bought from Italy arms and ammunition valued at 6 million Mexican dollars. He even tried to buy arms from the United States, but without success. See Jowe, "Who Sells the Guns to China's War Leaders?"; *CWR*, Oct. 11, 1924; *TFTC*, 21 (Oct. 2, 1924): 147; Report of the American Consul in Mukden dated May 1925, in 893.24/26 of *Records of the Department of State*.

the Soviet Union, whose behavior constituted an important departure from the general pattern delineated above. The Soviets provided the KMT with a considerable quantity of arms, although the exact contribution of these arms to the KMT's success is not easy to assess.

In its early years, the KMT commanded no arsenal of its own; when Sun Yat-sen waged a punitive war against Ch'en Chiungming, he had to rely heavily on foreign gunrunners.[25] By the end of 1925, the KMT had more than 85,000 men organized into six army corps, but their combat preparedness was still very low. At that time, the chief Soviet adviser, Kisanko, complained that the entire National Revolutionary Army had only 13 cannons of various models and calibers, some of them obsolete; rifles and machine guns were also insufficient, and there was a general shortage of ammunition of all kinds, particularly for artillery weapons.[26]

Thus, in this initial stage of army-building, the injection of Soviet military assistance assumed added importance, because it helped the KMT to put the new forces on their feet.[27] Among the documents seized during the raid on the Soviet Embassy in Peking on April 6, 1927, there were indications that the value of Soviet supplies handed over to Canton in the first eleven months of 1925 amounted to 2.5 million rubles, and that another 2 million rubles' worth of hardware was concentrated at Vladivostok for shipment to Canton during the spring of 1926.[28] It is possible, as F. F. Liu contends, that after the March 1926 purge of communist elements within the KMT, Soviet assistance in arms became meager in quantity, low in quality, and high in price.[29] But the exact amount of reduction is not clear. In July 1926, the Soviet military attaché in Peking transmitted to General Galen the Soviet government's policy on arms delivery to the KMT: the KMT must pay immediately for the transportation from Vladivostok to Canton, make payments for the supplies already delivered or to be delivered on a fixed time schedule, and must henceforth pay in cash as far as possible.[30] These were undoubtedly unfavorable terms. Nonetheless, they still left open the possibility of arms deliveries so long as the KMT could pay cash. And some Soviet ships loaded with military supplies continued to call on the port of Canton.[31]

In sum, the facts clearly indicate that Soviet arms played a critical role in hastening the birth of the KMT army and continued to play an important, albeit somewhat reduced, role in

Military Capabilities: Weaponry and Tactics 125

helping the army to launch its drive northward. We cannot say, however, that Soviet arms alone enabled the KMT to defeat its northern enemies. In fact, the distribution of Soviet arms benefited only a small portion of the armies engaged in the Northern Expedition.[32] With the seizure of larger territories and better arsenals, the KMT was able to become more self-sufficient.

Soviet arms were also instrumental in reviving another army, the Kuominchün, which made significant contributions to the Northern Expedition. This assistance was particularly important because Feng Yü-hsiang never controlled a large arsenal of his own and his territories had no access to the sea for importing arms. The Soviet shipments to Feng, from Siberia across Mongolia, began in early 1925, and by June 1926 Feng probably had received almost 6.5 million rubles' worth of Soviet arms.[33] After its Nankow defeat, the Kuominchün lost most of its equipment and retreated to the northwest, with no local source of arms supply. But Feng managed to obtain additional Soviet supplies.[34] With these replacement supplies, Feng was able to regroup his soldiers quickly, in time to attack the northern militarists from their western flank. The re-entry of the Kuominchün into the battlefield, which would have been difficult without substantial Soviet assistance, took considerable pressure from the KMT front and brought the campaign in the northern plains to a speedy conclusion.

The uneven geographical distribution of domestic arsenals and the heavy reliance on foreign arms put some militarists in some areas in an unfavorable competitive position. The few provinces with large arsenals of their own, and the coastal provinces with easy access to foreign shipping, usually had little trouble getting at least some supplies of arms and ammunition. The interior provinces, on the other hand, had great difficulties. Provinces like Hunan, Szechwan, Yunnan, Kweichow, Shensi, western Honan, and Kwangsi, western Kwangtung, and the other northwestern areas were at a particular disadvantage. Their great distance from the coast hampered dealings with foreign arms smugglers. If they turned to the few arsenals in China that had the capacity to produce surplus arms for sale, they not only had to cultivate friendly relationships with the militarists who owned the arsenals; they also had to pay exorbitant prices for small quantities and inferior quality.

When militarists in these areas attempted self-sufficiency, they encountered equally insurmountable obstacles. Foreign machinery and raw materials had to face the same transportation problems as finished products.[35]

The primitive nature of arms procurement and arms production during the 1920's had considerable influence on the structure of political power. Our information provides support for three general observations. First, the crucial importance of foreign arms gave the coastal provinces a decided military advantage; second, the few provinces with their own arsenals were also well armed; third, the interior provinces that were denied access to either of these two sources were the worst armed. Geographical differences in the distribution of armaments were important variables in explaining the tactics used by the militarists, the pattern of conflict among them, and thus the transformation of political power within the system.

Tactics and Strategy

The increased number of weapons and the introduction of new and better weapons into China substantially altered the mode of warfare. Before examining these changes, let us briefly establish the relative importance of the main types of weapons used during this period.

The total number of airplanes was too small to bring about any change in the strategic concepts of the time. Even on the tactical side, their impact was quite modest, for a number of reasons. The planes imported by Chinese militarists often were of inferior quality, and mechanical troubles were common. Spare parts were difficult to obtain, and maintenance facilities and mechanics were inadequate.[36] The bombs were too small, and many of them failed to explode at all. Pilots were poorly trained (there was no qualified flying school), and they tended to fly too high for accurate target observation or bombing.[37] When planes were first used, they at least had terrorized the soldiers; after a few years, even this effect wore off.[38] Consequently, the combat value of airplanes was very low. Their primary value was limited to reconnaissance.

The machine gun likewise had no substantial impact on the character of Chinese warfare. This contrasts quite sharply with the weapon's impact in Europe in the First World War. There, its introduction destroyed fighting in a close disciplined order and necessitated heavy reliance on trenches, transforming the war into battles of attrition and long periods of stalemate. In China, despite the use of machine guns and trenches, no such stalemate ever took place, primarily for economic reasons. To be strategically significant, machine guns had to be used in large numbers, and few militarists could afford to buy very many. Nor could they afford to provision and maintain the large armies required for trench warfare. Moreover, even some of the best trained troops were unfamiliar with the revolutionary nature of the machine guns.* In the majority of cases, machine guns were just another weapon for the infantrymen, certainly increasing their firepower, but not achieving a revolutionary change in warfare.

Compared with machine guns, artillery figured more importantly in Chinese warfare. During the anti-restoration campaign in 1917, only a few rounds of artillery shells were fired, causing negligible damage. At the height of the first Chihli-Fengtien war in 1922, however, Fengtien forces were reported to have lobbed thousands of rounds over one Chihli target in a single day.[39] The widespread use of artillery made untenable the traditional strategy of city defense. Mud and brick walls were no longer sufficient to withstand the pounding of heavy artillery shells. Constant bombardment and severe shortages of food and ammunition quickly demoralized the civilian and military populations. In 1917, Chang Hsün held the city of Peking for merely five days before capitulating, although the artillery fire at that time was only intimidating, not really damaging. Toward the end of the period, there were no more than two or three instances when important cities were held for a prolonged period of time, and in these cases special circumstances prolonged the siege. By and large, city defense had by the 1920's been rendered valueless as a strategy wherever artillery was employed in quantity.

---

* For instance, in an inspection of Feng Yü-hsiang's troops, Soviet advisers found that machine guns were moved with the men instead of being used to produce a screen of fire to cover their advance, and that machine gunners were inefficient in assembling and dismantling their weapons. Sheridan, p. 166. Lawrence Impey, who witnessed much of the fighting of the 1924 war between Chihli and Fengtien, observed that "the higher command appeared to have no idea of the value of the Maxim from a strategic angle," and did not know how to utilize them to enfilade the enemy troops or to harass their lines of communication. "Chinese Progress in the Art of War," *CWR*, Dec. 27, 1924.

The inability of machine guns to achieve results comparable to those of the First World War and the combined use of rifles and artillery caused the wars to become gradually more mobile in character. The railway and highway system, though underdeveloped by Western standards, greatly facilitated the mobilization and transportation of troops and heavy equipment. As the importance of communication networks increased, the militarists became more interested in controlling these networks. The defense of main communication arteries became a paramount concern as the militarists recognized that without them their territories would be vulnerable. Furthermore, the widespread use of artillery and the concentration of large numbers of troops during later campaigns made it almost impossible to fight battles except on relatively flat land along railway lines and main highways.

Thus, there evolved a pattern of warfare in which communication networks—especially the railways—not only became the most hotly contested military objectives, but also determined the location and size of the battlefields. Names of cities of historic fame gave way to those of obscure towns (such as Ch'ang-hsin-tien, Lang-fang, Ting-ssu-ch'iao, and Lung-t'an) on or near vital communication lines as the sites of the bloodiest battles. In fact, in some cases much of the fighting was actually done within a few miles of the railway tracks. The restricted area of fighting helped make armored trains, equipped with heavy machine guns and artillery, an extremely potent implement of war. Mobility and concentrated firepower were the two greatest assets. Armored trains were "decisive weapons" in some cases precisely because both antagonists had to rely heavily on the railways and thus had to risk concentrating their troops in the immediate vicinity of these lines.[40]

Good communication facilities also greatly expanded the area that could be affected by military power. Conflicts of a strictly local nature tended to diminish in proportion to their proximity to major communication routes. Communications increased the militarists' ability to reach trouble spots more swiftly and forcefully. Other things being equal, the better the communication facilities a militarist commanded, the larger the territory he could govern.

In order to understand the effect of China's communications network on military strategy and tactics, let us first briefly describe the development pattern of the transportation system.

TABLE 5
Highway Mileage in China, 1928

Province	Mileage	Province	Mileage
Anhwei	1,010	Kiangsu	1,036
Chahar	1,562	Kwangsi	1,336
Chekiang	559	Kwangtung	2,440
Fukien	336	Kweichow	—
Honan	687	Manchuria	—
Chihli	1,742	Shansi	1,307
Hunan	291	Shantung	1,535
Hupeh	808	Shensi	107
Jehol	733	Szechwan	735
Kansu	1,787	Yunnan	267
Kiangsi	312	TOTAL	20,973

SOURCE: Estimate made by the Good Roads Association of China, quoted in *China Year Book*, 1931, p. 217.

The construction of modern highways did not begin until after 1916.[41] Conditions improved after the launching of the Good Roads Movement in May 1921; by 1923, at least 1,800 miles of roads had been built. Most of these roads were built in the provinces of North China—Chihli, Shantung, Shansi, and Honan. Some roads existed in Kiangsu and Szechwan, and none at all in Yunnan, Fukien, Kweichow, or Kwangsi.[42] As Table 5 shows, this pattern of development was followed until 1928, with few exceptions.

In addition to the shortage of modern highways, there was an equally serious lack of motor vehicles. According to Silas Strawn, the American representative on the Chinese Tariff Conference and on the Commission of Extraterritoriality, there were only about 8,000 motor vehicles in all China in 1926, compared with 20 million in the United States at the same time.[43] Most of the motor vehicles were concentrated in or near the major port cities in the eastern section. Motorized traffic in the interior was extremely inconvenient.

The railroads in the early twentieth century were also inadequate, both in terms of length and distribution. The preoccupation with defense and the heavy reliance on foreign capital resulted in a highly uneven distribution pattern which largely ignored China's domestic economic needs.[44] By the end of the 1920's, only approximately 5,000 miles of railway were owned by the Chinese

TABLE 6
Mileage of Government-owned Railways, 1930

Province	Length (main line, miles)	Province	Length (main line, miles)
Chihli	790	Hupeh	210
Honan	790	Hunan	160
Kiangsu	487	Kiangsi	80
Shantung	510	Chahar	235
Shansi	200	Suiyuan	125
Anhwei	175	Manchuria	1,100
Chekiang	125	TOTAL	5,237
Kwangtung	250		

SOURCE: Bureau of Railway Statistics, Ministry of Railways, report released in June 1930, in *China Year Book*, 1931, p. 178.

government. A comparison of Tables 5 and 6 reveals the interesting fact that all the provinces with low mileage in highways also had little or no railway mileage. In fact, railways were even more concentrated in the plains of northern China than were highways.

The military significance of the communication systems can best be illustrated by comparing selected areas in these two regions, the interior and the northern coastal provinces. For instance, Chihli province had a total of 790 miles of railway and 1,742 miles of highway in 1928. Altogether this frequently contested area could be approached from four major railway lines: Peking-Hankow, Peking-Mukden, Tientsin-Pukow, and Peking-Suiyuan. In 1924, these four lines radiating from Peking contained more than 70 percent of the total rolling stocks in all of China proper (excluding the southern Manchurian railways).[45] The distances between the terminals and Peking could all be covered in from two days to less than a week's time. And the amount of personnel and war matériel that could be mobilized along these lines would be adequate to meet any logistic demands for fighting a major war in the Peking-Tientsin area.[46] In addition, the terrain was flat enough to allow travel on foot with relative ease; even heavy artillery pieces could be hauled by draft animals where no road existed. These conditions made it possible to concentrate fairly large numbers of troops and heavy equipment to fight a war.

If we examine logistic conditions in the interior, we find a totally different picture. In Kwangsi, for example, land communications were virtually impossible, since there was no railway at all and only about sixty miles of highway prior to 1925.[47] Rivers consti-

Military Capabilities: Weaponry and Tactics 131

tuted the only important means of communication. Because most rivers run from the northwest to the southeast, travel between the northeastern and southwestern parts of the province was extremely difficult. Even traffic along the rivers between northwestern and southeastern portions was unreliable, because the water level fluctuated radically between seasons.[48] Furthermore, while it was easy to travel in a southeasterly direction with the current, sharp increases in altitude made it difficult to travel in a northwesterly direction against the current. Even on the main tributaries, the average speed was painfully slow; more than three weeks were required to cover 700 *li* when traveling against the current.[49] Consequently, although Kwangsi's navigable rivers totaled about 11,700 *li*, and reached 80 of its 99 *hsiens*, the traffic volume was very small.*

The situation in Kwangsi's neighboring provinces was even worse. Almost all of Yunnan was cut up by mountain ridges running in parallels in a north-south direction, with deep valleys in between. Traffic was extremely difficult, and many parts of the province were simply inaccessible. More than half of Kweichow was hilly country 2,000 meters above sea level. Here, even water traffic was nearly nonexistent, not to mention railways or highways. Whatever traffic there was occurred mainly on narrow foot trails. The relatively wealthier province of Szechwan was hardly in a better position. Prior to 1928, there was not a single mile of railway. There was no highway linking the two most important cities of the province, Ch'engtu and Chungking, which were separated by a distance of about 250 miles. Most traffic was conducted along the Yangtze River and its navigable tributaries within the small basin, while the borderland on all sides and the vast western part of the province were inaccessible because of high mountains.

The sharp differences in communication facilities that existed between the eastern and interior parts of China gave rise to different modes of warfare in the two areas. We shall begin our comparison with a description of the type of warfare that prevailed in the interior.

* We do not have any figures for the 1920's, but as late as 1938 a survey shows that there were 6,084 boats of all descriptions in the whole province, with a total loading capacity of only 62,985 tons. The river section between Wuchou and Kuei-lin, the most important city in the north, was the most heavily traveled section in the province, but there were only 553 boats in operation, with a total loading capacity of 5,580 tons. Ch'en Hui pp. 36–37.

In provinces like Shensi, Szechwan, Yunnan, Kweichow, Kwangsi, western Kwangtung, and Fukien, where modern communications were grossly inadequate, we find small armies fighting each other in a highly concentrated area. Lack of railways, highways, and motor vehicles made it necessary for soldiers to approach a battlefield by water in some areas, or on foot in others. Usually, therefore, most battles involved only a few hundred men, or at most a few thousand. The reliance on boats and draft animals made it exceedingly difficult to maneuver heavy field equipment. Even the transportation of a few million rounds of rifle ammunition presented a major logistical problem that many a militarist could not solve. Reconnaissance perimeters were restricted, and coordination between friendly units was difficult.

Geographical factors alone excluded large areas from the scene of combat. Generally, battles tended to take place in the few level areas of relatively low altitudes. Since armies of even modest sizes could move only along navigable tributaries and a few footpaths and cart trails, the points of military contact were also few. In this region, city defense was more common, because cities were usually also centers of communications. Ch'engtu, Chungking, Wuchow, Kueilin, all figured importantly in military strategy during this period.

Another concomitant of the interior location and harsh terrain of this region was the general backwardness of its military technology. Both domestic and foreign arms were difficult to obtain. The same weapons were used for years without substantial replacement or renovation. These obsolete weapons were unable to inflict irreparable damage on the enemy. Seesaw battles were commonplace throughout this whole region.

The logistical obstacles tended to discourage militarists from conducting long-distance campaigns. When we review the history of this period, we find that the militarists in these provinces seldom pursued military ventures beyond the neighboring provinces. For brief periods, Yunnan forces were in Szechwan, Kwangtung troops were in Fukien, and Kwangsi troops were in Kwangtung. Such troops were often placed in a predicament; logistics made it difficult to supply a large expeditionary force far from home. Living entirely off the conquered land, however, inevitably aroused the hatred of the local populace.

Military Capabilities: Weaponry and Tactics

As long as militarists were separated by an adequate distance, and as long as the weapons remained below a certain technological level, defense held an advantage over offense. Points of contact existed only at the narrow open spaces between the warring parties, along a river valley, or at a mountain pass. Under such adverse circumstances, battles were fought inconclusively, and the victor was usually unable to follow his initial success by mopping-up activities. The defeated militarist seldom had to fear total annihilation, because he was able to retreat to a secluded area to nurse his wounds and rebuild his forces.* Such geographical features and inadequate communication systems tended to enhance the status quo among the militarists in these areas and thus were conducive to political fragmentation.

In this connection, we must note that the low level of military technology also provided a favorable climate for the existence of many small forces. Since a militarist with modest means could raise and maintain a force on that unsophisticated level, a large number of militarists sprang up in that area. Furthermore, since all the soldiers used practically the same kinds of crude instruments of war and since the skills required were either directly transferable from civilian life or very easily acquired, there was little need for a host of intervening ranks between the commander and his men. The relationship between commander and men could be reduced to a simple and direct relationship without impairment of the strength of the military unit. Under the commander, almost all men performed the same task with the same instruments. This situation was hardly conducive to military centralization or the formation of large units. By the same token, it was difficult for ambitious militarists to integrate and incorporate lesser armies by force because such simple weapons made it difficult to achieve decisive victories.

Thus many of these provinces had two, three, or sometimes six

---

* In Szechwan, for example, the local militarists had trouble for years in trying to dislodge the Yunnan army. In late September 1920, when the Yunnan army of about 10,000 men was finally forced to evacuate Chengtu, it simply went into the hills east of the city. Although the coalition of Szechwan generals gathered no fewer than 45,000 men, they could not dislodge the Yunnan troops from their securely fortified heights. After a week of unsuccessful assaults, the Szechwan troops were exhausted and went back to Chengtu, whereupon the Yunnanese immediately followed them and laid countersiege. *NCH*, Oct. 1920.

or seven militarists contending with each other for hegemony. The frequency of wars was high in these areas precisely because the cost of waging wars was relatively low. The ease with which a modest army could be raised, maintained, and equipped and the meager consumption of war matériel made it possible for militarists to indulge in frequent tests of strength without bleeding themselves to death either militarily or financially. Therefore, on the superficial level, the impression one gets is that these areas experienced more years of war than of peace. Indeed, in the newspapers of this period, it is hard to find a month passing without some report of war activities in Szechwan.* To a lesser extent, the same was true in Shensi, Fukien, and Kwangsi.

The high frequency of wars and the general difficulty in military and political control in this region merit some explanation. Although we have no statistical data, available evidence indicates that the warring parties probably spent more time in maneuvering for position than in joining battle. From reading contemporary accounts, one gets the impression that the militarists more often made threats and counterthreats, mutual denunciations, and other dramatic gestures than actually fighting. Furthermore, even when militarists actually did fight, the wars were usually of low intensity. Most of the time wars affected only the immediate vicinity of the battlefield and the direct participants, and there were few casualties. Thus, "skirmishes" described the situation more accurately than "wars." Under these circumstances, it is not surprising that a large number of relatively weak militarists managed to survive and continue to engage in hostilities.

But this situation required that the status quo with respect to the level and quality of armaments and military training and leadership be maintained at all times. No local militarists could suddenly acquire large increases in these capabilities. The civil wars in Szechwan provide an illustration of what could happen when the local balance of power was upset. For years, the province was divided among six or seven military groups, all equally handi-

---

* One source suggests that between 1912 and 1933, there were more than 700 wars in China, of which 500 took place in Szechwan. Teng Yün-t'e, p. 102. Another source estimates that over 400 large and small civil wars were fought in the province after 1911. Ho Ping-ti, *Studies on the Population of China*, pp. 248–49.

Military Capabilities: Weaponry and Tactics 135

capped by poor technology and insufficient attention to logistics. But in 1923 Yang Sheng secured the support of Wu P'ei-fu and entered Szechwan with a large army much better equipped and supplied than those operating under local generals. Yang followed the Yangtze, rapidly dislodging his enemies from the cities along the river and appearing capable of unifying the province. But when one of his two steamers shipping supplies from Hupeh was captured and the other was sunk, his fortunes ran out. Denied access to the main communication line and outside assistance, his forces were bogged down in the overland fighting, and eventually they were forced to abandon their previous gains.[50] With that, the internal division of Szechwan was preserved.

In sum, a low level of military technology, relatively mild fighting among many militarists with small armies, and general political stability prevailed in this region with poor communication and logistics. In sharp contrast, the region with superior communications and logistics witnessed rapid progress in the art of warfare, fewer but more devastating wars, and an extremely volatile political situation. Here, the wars involved increasingly larger armies, wider areas of conflict, and greater casualties.

At the beginning of the period, no militarist could exercise assured control over a large number of troops. The first modest improvement came during Tuan Ch'i-jui's Hunan campaign. Altogether, Tuan probably mobilized between 60,000 and 80,000 soldiers during the entire span of the campaign. The Hunanese had about 20,000 soldiers, plus some contingents from Kwangsi.[51] It would not be too wide of the mark to suggest that some 100,000 troops were involved during this campaign. But this increased mobilization was brought about by intense political bargaining and compromise, rather than by the existence of a sound and powerful command system. Although the militarists now found greater need for cooperation, the manner in which the campaign was executed left little doubt that the level of mobilization was still very low, since the numerical superiority of the northern forces was not exploited to its full potential.

With the crystallization of the factional line-up and the advent of a progressively intensifying arms race, military mobilization became more effective. The first demonstration of this was the

Chihli-Anhwei war of 1920. A conservative estimate of the total Anhwei strength, according to Wen Kung-chih's account, would put it at 60,000 or 70,000 men. On the Chihli side, the total strength was probably somewhere between 40,000 and 50,000 men. In addition, Fengtien dispatched two divisions to help the Chihli forces in their common struggle. This added at least another 20,000 men. In sum, the Chihli-Anhwei war directly involved at least 120,000, perhaps 140,000, men in major battlefields in the north alone.[52]

In addition, provinces like Chekiang, Kiangsu, Hupeh, and Honan were intensely interested in the war and adopted some measures of preparedness. The Chihli-Anhwei war can be regarded as the first truly large-scale civil war among the military factions because it had nationwide ramifications. Unlike the previous campaigns, many more militarists participated in the conflict because they now believed that their interests were seriously affected by its outcome.

This trend continued down to 1928 and beyond. It is clear from the data that civil wars in China were radically escalated, in the sense that more and more combatants participated in them. In fact, our figures in Table 7 suggest that their magnitude increased nearly twenty-fold within this time period. This phenomenal expansion in combat manpower was made possible only because the logistical system could support such a mobilization system. It is no accident that progress in military mobilization occurred only in the eastern region, where the best communication facilities existed.

The existence of these facilities also made it possible to expand the area of conflict and allowed militarists to exert their influence over remote areas. Unlike the militarists in Szechwan or Yunnan, who fought skirmishes in areas not exceeding several counties, the militarists in the east extended their operations into several provinces simultaneously. If we review the major wars, we can see a clear progression from conflicts involving one province to those involving many provinces. The expanding size of the war zones over the years is summarized in Table 8.

So far we have demonstrated that during the 1916–28 period there was a clear trend for wars to involve a greater number of participants and to cover ever-larger areas. It remains to be de-

TABLE 7
Number of Troops Mobilized for Major Wars, 1916–1928

Year	Number of troops	Index
1917	55,000	100
1918	100,000	181
1920	120,000	218
1922	225,000	409
1924	450,000	818
1926	600,000	1,090
1928	1,100,000	2,000

SOURCE: Wu-liao-tzu, *Ti erh tz'u Chih Feng ta chan chi* (Shanghai, 1924), chap. 2, p. 5. Wen Kung-chih, 2: 53; 3: 119, 167–68, 185–88; 1: 226. Chang Chün-ku, *Wu P'ei-fu*, pp. 358–59. *China Weekly Review*, Sept. 1924. *Feng Chih chan shih*, pp. 20–23. T'ao Chü-yin, *Wu P'ei-fu*, pp. 100–101. *Tung fang tsa chih*, 21 (Oct. 10, 1924), pp. 152–57. *China Year Book*, 1925, pp. 836–40. *Pei fa chan shih*, 2: 321. James E. Sheridan, *Chinese Warlord: The Career of Feng Yü-hsiang* (Stanford, Calif., 1966), p. 191.

TABLE 8
Size of Major War Zones, 1916–1928

Year	Name of war	Provinces in war zone	Other provinces affected	Total provinces involved
1917	Anti-Restoration	1	—	1
1918	Hunan Campaign	1	4	5
1920	Chihli-Anhwei	3	3	6
1922	Chihli-Fengtien	4	6	10
1924	Chihli-Fengtien	5	9	14
1926	Fengtien-Kuominchün	8	5	13
1926–28	Northern Expedition	12	8	20

SOURCE: Wen Kung-chih, 2: 19, 53; 3: 168–78. Chang Chün-ku, *Wu P'ei-fu*, pp. 358–59.

termined what kind of fighting was actually done. Some journalists and scholars have characterized Chinese civil wars as "comic operas."[53] In fact, many of them were neither "civil" nor "comic."[54] As the years went on, the fighting became increasingly fierce, as is demonstrated by the escalating numbers of casualties suffered by the warring parties (see Table 9).

The Anti-Restoration campaign against Chang Hsün does indeed appear to have been a comic opera. As soon as contact was made, Chang Hsün's soldiers quickly abandoned their positions and withdrew to the safety of Peking. Although the war lasted officially for six days, actual fighting occurred on only two days. When the city gates finally fell, Chang Hsün's soldiers readily cut

TABLE 9
Casualties in Major Wars, 1916–1928

Year	Participants	Total strength	Casualties
1917	Chang Hsün Tuan Ch'i-jui	55,000	100
1918	Anhwei faction Hunan	100,000	1–2,000
1920	Anhwei faction Chihli faction	120,000	3,600 (high) ? (low)
1922	Chihli faction Fengtien faction	225,000	30,000 (high) 10,000 (low)
1924	Chihli faction Fengtien faction	320,000	20,000 (high) 15,000 (low)
	Kiangsu Chekiang	147,000	6,000
1926–28	Sun Ch'uan-fang (Lung-t'an)	70,000	20,000 (high) 10,000 (low)
	KMT Wuhan govt. (East Honan)	70,000	14,000
	KMT 3d Army Group (Fang-shun-ch'iao)	70–80,000	19,840

SOURCE: *North-China Herald*, July 21, 1917; Dec. 15, 1917; March 18, 1918; Aug. 7, 1920; June 18, 1927. Lai-chiang-chu-wu, *Chin tai shih tzu liao*, no. 2 (1926), pp. 99–101. Wen Kung-chih, 3: 132, 192–93, 274–81, 333–40, *China Year Book*, 1923, pp. 573–76. *China Weekly Review*, Nov. 29, 1924. *Wu P'ei-fu hsien sheng nien p'u*, pp. 30–32. *Feng Chih chan shih*, p. 94. James E. Sheridan, *Chinese Warlord*, pp. 184, 224, 346n45. *Ko ming wen hsien*, 11: 212; 16: 843; 20: 1493–1509. Mao Ssu-ch'eng, p. 988. Huang Hsü-ch'u, "Kuo min ko ming chün ti ch'i chün shih shih," *Ch'un ch'iu*, no. 247 (October 16, 1967), p. 20. Kao Yin-tsu, *Chung-hua min-kuo ta shih chi* (Taipei, 1957), p. 267. Ch'en Hsün-cheng, 3: 214–15, 722. T'ang Leang-li, *The Inner History of the Chinese Revolution* (London, 1930), p. 278. Feng Yü-hsiang, *Wo ti sheng ho* (Shanghai, 1947), 3: 202–3.

their queues, dropped their rifles and opium pipes, and fled. Total casualties amounted to one hundred killed and wounded, mostly civilians.[55]

The Hunan campaign lasted officially from August 1917 to August 1918, but fighting was only intermittent. With the exception of Wu P'ei-fu's 3d Division, most northern troops showed little disposition to engage the enemy, and many units simply disintegrated after skirmishing with the less numerous and poorly equipped Hunanese armies.*

During the Chihli-Anhwei war of 1920, the Chinese soldiers be-

---

* The lack of interest in fighting among northern troops is evidenced by the fact that in less than four months before the end of 1917, the north lost 10,000 rifles and 8,000 soldiers taken prisoner. *NCH*, Dec. 15, 1917.

Military Capabilities: Weaponry and Tactics　　　　139

gan to show some capability for serious fighting. The warring parties now had more effective command of their own troops, and did not have to rely exclusively on the good faith of their allies. Although there were still instances where whole units ceased to fight because of low morale and inept leadership, the general tenor of fighting was serious, and some engagements were considered "the fiercest fighting since 1911."[56]

By all standards the first Chihli-Fengtien war dwarfed the Chihli-Anhwei war of two years earlier. Both the number of troops and the war matériel committed by both sides far exceeded the quantity of the 1920 war.* Fengtien relied heavily on artillery power, but its commanders had little understanding of strategy and thus its artillery had only minor effect.[57] The poor performance of Fengtien soldiers on the battlefield prompted a number of foreign military observers to suggest that the commanders were completely ignorant of the rudiments of modern military strategy. The war did indeed show that Chinese soldiers and commanders still had much to learn about modern warfare, but considerable human and material sacrifices occurred. Although exact battle losses cannot be ascertained, partly because commanders on both sides were inclined to underestimate their own losses and exaggerate the enemy's losses, probably a total of at least 10,000 casualties were sustained by both sides. In addition, on the Fengtien side, four high-ranking officers (regiment commander or above) were killed, and seven were wounded.[58] These casualties among officers at the higher levels indicate the ferocity of the fighting, since Chinese generals did not usually participate directly in front-line activities unless absolutely necessary.

The 1924 war proved to be a replay of 1922, involving the same antagonists but on a much grander scale. Fengtien's army was much better trained and equipped. Mine fields were extensively laid, and electric barbed-wire fences were set up to protect fortifications. Armored trains and tanks were employed, and artillery fire was extremely heavy. The fighting itself was occasionally fierce. Some key points changed hands several times a day, and both sides

---

* It was estimated that the Fengtien force of 120,000 men was equipped with 150 field guns and 200 machine guns, while the Chihli force of 100,000 men was equipped with 100 machine guns and 100 artillery pieces. Wen Kung-chih, 3: 132.

used machine-gun corps to kill their own troops who retreated without orders. Furthermore, victorious forces pursued defeated units and covered as many as forty or fifty *li* a day to mop up the remnants.[59]

After 1924, it became increasingly difficult to estimate casualties, because wars were fought continuously among a larger number of militarists. It was hard to determine when a war started or ended. Fengtien and Kuominchün were enemies from late 1925 until 1928. From 1926 on, the KMT also enlarged its active participation, which further complicated matters. Hence, it is more realistic to view these years as one period of prolonged war consisting of many different battles. The size of armies increased, weapons improved, and battles were often marked by personal animosities among the militarists and by ideological overtones.

The qualitative and quantitative changes in war after 1925 brought mounting casualties to all parties involved. Heavy losses occurred among officers as well as among the rank and file. Before 1920, it had been very unusual for commanding officers to be wounded or killed in action; after 1925, casualties among high-ranking officers showed a conspicuous rise. This trend accelerated after the advent of the Northern Expedition, when the KMT troops often forced enemy commanders to fight or face total annihilation. During the two years of the Northern Expedition (June 1926–June 1928), 55 of the KMT's commanding officers with the rank of colonel or above (which included commanders of regiments, brigades, divisions, and army corps) were killed in action.[60] During the Kiangsi campaign alone, nine regiment commanders and one division commander were killed in battles, mostly in the month of October, 1926, when the fighting was most intense.[61]

While there is no comprehensive figure for the KMT's enemies, there is no doubt that their higher ranks suffered dearly. At the battle of Ting-ssu-ch'iao, the brigade under Liu Yü-ch'un suffered very heavy losses: all three regiment commanders and 24 of his 39 company commanders were killed. In fact, the fighting became so fierce that in a desperate move to stem the imminent collapse of his defense, Wu P'ei-fu dispatched teams of soldiers to block all escape routes and executed nine battalion and regiment commanders who had retreated without permission.[62] Such enforcement of battlefield discipline had never been exercised in previous wars.

Thus, wars had vastly changed during the twelve years. In 1916, every province in the country (except Manchuria) was carved up by two, three, or more militarists, none of whom commanded a force larger than 20,000 soldiers. By early 1928, the KMT probably had as many as 700,000 men on the front line, while the northern militarists had no fewer than 400,000. Whereas war casualties in the early years never amounted to more than a few hundred, after 1928 it was common for a single battle to claim several thousand lives.[63] Fighting also became a continuous phenomenon, and fierce battles followed each other in quick succession. When so many casualties were inflicted so often, war necessarily became more decisive.*

Conclusion

Warfare in the eastern portion of China increased dramatically because logistic conditions made possible the concentration of ever larger numbers of troops and the employment of ever more sophisticated weapons. The rapid introduction of more destructive and more widely applicable weapons had certain effects on the political system. For one thing, the character of military organization changed. After 1920, most armies in areas with good communication systems employed rifles, machine guns, light and heavy artillery, armored vehicles, and even airplanes. As the weapons became more variegated and sophisticated, some minimal measure of coordination was necessary for their maintenance and use. Specialization of skills and differentiation of tasks became imperative. The simple and direct commander-to-men relationship gave way to a more complex hierarchy of military command.

The complexity of weapons also paved the way for greater integration of larger military units. Small units found it increasingly more difficult to lead an autonomous existence, because they lacked the variety of weapons needed to fight more versatile enemies. Unlike rifles and shotguns, artillery pieces and armored cars could be manufactured only in modern arsenals by highly skilled labor, or procured abroad only with large sums of money. Both resources were concentrated in the hands of the few most powerful milita-

---

* For example, the battle of Lung-t'an totally annihilated Sun Ch'uan-fang's army and foiled his attempt to regain his power base in the lower Yangtze delta. Likewise, the battle of Fang-shun-ch'iao dashed Fengtien's hopes of defending the Paoting area, thereby making Chang Tso-lin's position in Peking untenable. Ch'en Hsün-cheng, 3: 722, 734–35.

rists, and these individuals thus had greater power over their subordinates and over lesser militarists. In the final analysis, only militarists who controlled large arsenals or had access to foreign supplies could control a large standing army; the militarists who had to depend on other militarists for arms had to be subservient to them as well.

In addition, machine guns and artillery made it feasible for an army to rule over a larger territory than before. In contrast to the division of one province by several militarists of meager but equal strength, one finds in the advanced military areas the tendency for several provinces to coalesce around one militarist. At the zenith of their careers, Chang Tso-lin, Feng Yü-hsiang, Wu P'ei-fu, and Sun Ch'uan-fang each controlled five or six provinces and directed the affairs of these spheres of influence as they saw fit. This tendency toward concentrated political and military power kept the number of primary contenders down to a small number at all times.

To sum up, notwithstanding the fact that the potentiality of some weapons was vitiated by the militarists' inability to appreciate them and the soldiers' inability to handle them properly, the general trend toward increasing sophistication and larger quantities of weapons introduced enough revolutionary features into warfare to upset the prevailing equilibrium. Our comparison of the two distinct geographical regions with different levels of communication systems and military technology showed that the militarists in the more advanced areas, aware that the stakes were high, had to fight harder in each battle. The accelerated pace of conflict and its usually decisive resolution, coupled with its increasing destructiveness, gravely undermined the stability of the political system in which these militarists played the leading parts. The system was disturbed by the emergence of the KMT, a new power with a great deal of military vitality and an eagerness to engage other militarists in ever bloodier and more costly battles. It is little wonder that under these circumstances the mercenaries finally lost out.

A Note on the Importance of Geography

The patterns of communication, logistics, and weapons distribution we have described are all related implicitly to geographical factors. It is regrettable that few analysts of modern Chinese political history have chosen to dwell on the country's geography, which is one of the most significant and stable aspects of China's national life. This omission may stem from the belief that geographical factors are too static and too obvious to need elaboration. It may also reflect a desire to avoid "geopolitics." But the complex geography of China cannot be ignored. These features are not static; they assume different meanings under different conditions. They necessarily had a bearing on the development of political events. Here, we shall consider only those aspects of geography that are immediately related to the larger question of political stability.

As we have shown, geography certainly affected the initial composition of military factions by influencing the militarists' choices of allies. At the initial stage, one visible pattern was for militarists to combine with distant militarists to deal with a common threat. The upshot was the emergence of military factions with fragmented territories, of which the Anhwei faction was doubtless the prime case. Although Tuan Ch'i-jui's base of power was in Peking, he had the support of Lu Yung-hsiang and Ho Feng-lin, whose territories (Chekiang and Shanghai) were separated from the faction's core area. The Chihli faction also suffered from fragmentation. Before 1920, the territories in the Yangtze valley and Chihli provinces formed two distinct and incontiguous parts. Even at the zenith of its power, the Chihli faction never effectively controlled Shantung and Anhwei. This initial fragmentation left indelible marks on the factions, for even later conquests did not wholly succeed in rectifying the situation. Up to the eve of the Northern Expedition, only the Fengtien faction enjoyed a high degree of territorial cohesion.

Territorial fragmentation necessarily entailed certain disadvantages. For one thing, serious logistical problems occurred when a faction's separate parts came under military pressure simultaneously. In addition, a faction with fragmented territories usually lacked depth and therefore had to halt enemy attacks at the frontier or expose its core area to grave danger. In 1920, for example, as soon as Anhwei's front line was penetrated, the whole defense collapsed and all its northern territories fell into enemy hands. The defeat came so abruptly that militarists in Shanghai and Chekiang had neither the means nor the time to send reinforcements. Thus, the various militarists within a faction were often compelled to set up independent defenses when they controlled separate territories. This fact sometimes undermined the unity of the faction.

In contrast, a territorially integrated faction possessed ample flexibility in defense policy as well as advantages in administrative consolidation. It was more resilient in the face of enemy pressure. Its ability to absorb enemy penetration into its own territory allowed it to fight a prolonged rear-guard war and offered it a good chance of mounting a counterattack. Even after the front line was broken, it was still possible to wear the enemy out inside its own territory.

The difference between territorially fragmented and integrated factions carried wider implications with regard to the policies they might pursue in the system. Since the fragmented faction lacked a territorial resilience against enemy penetration, the most urgent and minimum defense prerequisite at all times was the security of the frontier. The frontier was, in effect, both the first and the last lines of defense; it had to be protected at all costs. But such a policy involved a great deal of uncertainty. A bolder and more rewarding policy was an attack, especially a surprise attack, that would carry the war into enemy territory and away from home. The faction had to be sensitive to changes in relations among other factions and to be decisive and aggressive in meeting challenges. Procrastination might lead to irreparable loss of time and thus to disaster.

The fragmented faction also had to plan its defense with little prospect of coordination. In most cases, the transfer of troops from one part to another was exceedingly difficult. Whenever the fragmented faction entered a war, it expected to fight on several fronts. Therefore, although the fragmented geographical configuration of the faction was originally a product of the political pressures felt by many of its components, these components were never able to become parts of a fully integrated defense system. By joining the faction, each component had expected to bolster its defense posture; in the final analysis, however, the chance of obtaining mutual support was more illusory than real. The fragmented faction was highly vulnerable to piecemeal aggression, especially when its outlying parts were the targets. It had to face the perennial dilemma of either allowing these parts to be chipped off one at a time while preserving sufficient force to defend the core area or coming to their rescue and thus exposing the core area to enemy pressure. Thus a fragmented faction was ill-equipped to deal with either large-scale or limited but selective aggression.

In contrast, the ability to sustain a prolonged war was an invaluable attribute of the external policy of a territorially integrated faction. The faction did not have to attack or to remain ever on the offensive as the only way of ensuring its security. It could afford to be calm when tension was mounting, because it had many alternatives for defense. This facilitated peaceful resolution, because delay would not mean disaster. An interesting comparison is provided by the two major wars among the factions. In the 1920 war between Anhwei (a fragmented faction) and Chihli (a more integrated one), Anhwei gave a very quick and decisive response after its position was challenged. In the 1922 war between Chihli and Fengtien, both integrated factions although not equally so, a long period of preparation preceded. During the first phase of preparation, when Fengtien seemed successful in gaining allies in the south, Chihli did not feel compelled to strike out immediately. In fact, Ts'ao K'un made every effort toward a peaceful settlement. This might seem a little overcautious for a faction that had just won a resounding victory over Anhwei barely two years before. But the most significant policy implication of Chihli's geographical character is that it could afford to show restraint and to keep open all policy options precisely because it did not have to fear a sudden breakdown of its defenses. It could fight a protracted war and minimize the effects of an enemy surprise attack. If the tripartite alliance among Fengtien, Anhwei, and the KMT had worked out, Chihli might still have had time to decide whether to compromise or to resist.

In time of war, the territorially integrated faction was usually more capable of coordinating all efforts. It had shorter lines of communication which were well protected within its territory, and consequently easier logistical problems. Whether an integrated faction could be attacked at more than one point depended on its relations with its neighbors. For instance, Chihli had to guard against the threat of invasion from the KMT, Anhwei, or Fengtien, while Fengtien had only to guard against its southern neighbor.

However, when compared with a fragmented faction, territorial integration provided a much more propitious environment for more integration in other aspects, political or economic.

A look at a map instantly reveals that all the powerful factions were congested in the eastern part of the mainland, each sharing a section of the coastline. All the lesser factions were landlocked. In order to understand how the location of the factions constrained their behavior, it is necessary first to describe their geographical characteristics.

Fengtien, the northernmost faction, with only one side bordering China proper, had the most defensible boundary.

In the south, the KMT was separated from Kiangsi and Fukien by mountains. The other two neighbors to the north, Hunan and Szechwan, were anxious to maintain their neutrality and took special care not to offend the north or the south. The KMT's borders with them were also well defined.

Thus, both Fengtien and the KMT enjoyed a measure of geographical seclusion, which allowed them to stay away from the larger political conflicts and to concentrate on their own internal affairs if they so chose. This advantage was crucial to Fengtien between 1922 and 1924. Had Fengtien been contiguous with Chihli on more than one side or sandwiched between two factions, it would have been extremely difficult to maintain its independence and undertake major reforms without Chihli's intervention. The KMT benefited from its geographical location to no less an extent. The repeated threats of invasion by northern militarists never materialized, perhaps partly because of the strategic difficulties involved in such a long-distance overland expedition. This fact proved to have far-reaching ramifications for the whole system. The KMT used these precious years to consolidate its grip on the southern provinces, and then to use them as a springboard for launching the Northern Expedition. If, instead of being located at the southernmost pole of the mainland, the KMT had been in central China, it is hard to imagine how it could have managed to pursue a provocative program and still survive.

Thus the geographical attributes of both Fengtien and the KMT offer clues to their behavior. These geographical attributes gave them a great deal of leeway in their policy maneuvers. At the least, they were able to exercise a greater control over the scope and

Military Capabilities: Weaponry and Tactics

extent of their interaction with other militarists in the Chinese system.

In sharp contrast, both Anhwei and Chihli were located in central China and shared entangled borders with each other as well as with at least one other faction. Such a border situation provided many points of potential conflict. It is hardly surprising, then, that they were the first to engage in a major clash. From the geographical point of view, it could hardly have been otherwise. They were both placed in a setting from which neither could recoil. In order to carry out either an integration program within its own domain or an expansionist program into the deep south, Anhwei's first task was to clear Chihli from its advancing path. From Chihli's point of view, the most efficient way to deal with the threat of Anhwei would be to launch a strike directly at the source of provocation—Peking—which it did.

This analysis is borne out not only by the relations between Anhwei and Chihli, but by all subsequent events. As the history of this period shows, almost all the major wars took place in the area between the southern border of the Fengtien faction and the northern border of the KMT. Thus the central part of China must be identified as the area where military activities took place and where political decisions were made. Within that area, the Peking-Tientsin area could be regarded as the geographical "pivot" of the Chinese system. This was where the factor of geographical location came into full play. Had Fengtien, Anhwei, Chihli, and the KMT been arranged in a unilinear order with simple border relations, and had there been no Peking-Tientsin area, the two middle factions would still have had more complicated external relations than the two polar ones. But at least they might have been much freer to develop their external policies. In reality, however, their external relations were compounded not only by the entangled nature of their common zigzag borders but also by the fact that they were close to and were drawn toward the Peking-Tientsin area. The pattern of wars among the factions suggests that the faction controlling the Peking-Tientsin area was always alone in facing an alliance of other factions. It was Anhwei vs. Fengtien and Chihli in 1920, Chihli vs. Fengtien and its abortive alliance with Anhwei and the KMT in 1922, Chihli vs. Fengtien and Anhwei in 1924, and the Kuominchün vs. Chihli and Fengtien in

1926. In these wars alliances were concluded among factions far apart against the one in between.

From this train of events, some further observations can be made. First, the faction that possessed the Peking-Tientsin area had the highest frequency of wars, and in most cases had to be prepared to fight alone. Second, in all wars, whether localized or involving many factions, it was most advantageous to isolate one's opponent, or better still, to find allies and fight the opponent collectively. Since there was potential conflict between factions that were territorially contiguous, and since conversely there was little likelihood for conflict with remote factions, an alliance among the latter seemed most logical. It had the added advantage of forcing the opponent to face a two-front war. (This was exemplified by the relationship between Fengtien and Chihli before 1920 and that between Fengtien and the KMT before 1927.) But if the relative geographical positions changed, the political relations tended to change correspondingly. Therefore, as soon as Chihli replaced Anhwei as Fengtien's southern neighbor, it also inherited Anhwei's role vis-à-vis Fengtien. Even the KMT, which had been Fengtien's ally on many occasions, came into direct conflict with Fengtien when its territory extended to Fengtien's border.

The geographical location of the Peking-Tientsin area and of the factions is important to the stability of the system in two more ways. In the first place, it was the geographically central position of Peking-Tientsin that enabled the factions to adopt the policy of aligning with a distant actor to fight the one in between. Otherwise, the pattern of conflicts might have been more dispersed and more evenly distributed. Or if the political center had not been at the geographical center, but had been at, say, Canton or Mukden, then the policy of two against one would not have worked. A more equal distribution of capabilities among the opponents would have been possible. And the system as a whole would have been more stable, or transformed into a bipolar situation.

In the second place, it is apparent that there was a great advantage in possessing a polar location, as both the KMT and Fengtien did. It was more isolated, more defensible, and it allowed them more flexibility. On the other hand, this location by no means hampered their prospects of making encroachments upon the territories in the middle. The full strategic implications of such a geographical position are shown by the fact that by the end of 1928, only the territories of the KMT and Fengtien remained unviolated. The final political unification of the country was achieved not by military conquest, but by political bargaining between the KMT and Fengtien. On the basis of these observations, I would like to offer the conjecture that had the KMT occupied a nonpolar position (say either in the Yangtze valley or on the northern plains), the Chinese system might well have ended in a quite different way.

CHAPTER 7

Economic Capabilities

MATERIAL resources affect the capabilities, performances, and goals of the actors in any political system, and the Chinese militarist groupings were no exception. First of all, the important figures in the factions, the commanders of divisions and brigades, had to be paid handsomely for their allegiance. The allocation of resources could be a delicate business, especially in cases where self-interest constituted the cornerstone of a group's solidarity. Second, militarists needed money to maintain vast standing armies, to pay, feed, and equip them. Third, they needed money to meet the mounting cost of fighting wars and replenishing battle losses. Fourth, they needed money as a diplomatic instrument, to buy the cooperation of their rivals or to induce their rivals' subordinates to defect. It was always cheaper to engineer a coup within the enemy camp than to fight it out on the battlefield. And finally, militarists needed money for personal enrichment. Frugality was a virtue rarely found in the military profession during these years. Professionally insecure, military leaders were also anxious to seize any opportunity to accumulate personal wealth as insurance against the loss of office and power. All these needs called for money, and the militarists had to find the means to tap the financial resources of Chinese society.

By and large, a centralized fiscal system operated during much of the nineteenth century. The provinces collected various taxes under the explicit authorization of the central government. After all authorized provincial and local expenditures were deducted, the rest was remitted to the central government or to designated

Economic Capabilities 151

neighboring provinces as subsidies from the central government. Thus the system made the central and local governments interdependent. After the middle of the century, however, the prolonged internal upheavals denied the central government revenues from the southern provinces; the rise of the Hsiang-chün brought about a further decline in the central government's authority by shifting the financial power to the provinces. As time went on, provincial officials were able not only to increase existing taxes and add new taxes, but also to mint copper coins, collect *likin* (internal transit taxes), circulate currency, and finally to keep the revenues that should have been remitted to the central government. By the beginning of the Hsüan-t'ung reign (1908), the court had practically lost control of the nation's finances and had to rely heavily on foreign loans.[1]

The financial authority of the central government suffered another serious setback when the Ch'ing government was overthrown in 1911. It was slightly improved after the suppression of the Second Revolution in 1913, when Yüan Shih-k'ai dispatched some of his loyal Peiyang troops into southern provinces.[2] But when the anti-Yüan revolt broke out in 1915, many provinces simply halted their remittances, and some even seized the proceeds of the special taxes that should have belonged exclusively to the central government.[3] Order was partially restored after Yüan's death, when some provinces renewed their remittances, but these were mostly token amounts. Even these remittances ceased altogether after 1918, when civil wars engulfed the country.

Therefore, the central government's financial power reached its nadir at the time when the militarists became most powerful. The traditional fiscal relationship between the center and the provinces was destroyed. In order to understand how the militarist regimes were able to survive and flourish, let us turn to a more detailed examination of the sources of their revenues. Their regular sources of income included the revenues yielded by land taxes, the customs service, and the salt gabelle. Special sources of income included bonds, loans, currency manipulation, opium profits, and various forms of emergency exactions. After we have described these revenue sources, we shall then evaluate the impact on political stability and integration of the financial weakness of the Peking government, the rising costs of war, and the financial policies of the militarists.

Regular Sources of Income

Traditionally, the land tax was the single most important source of government revenue. Therefore the withdrawal of this source could hit the central government financially harder than anything else and could facilitate the growth of local power bases. The heavy reliance of the central government on this single item had made it highly vulnerable to challenges emanating from the provinces.[4] In the twentieth century, almost all militarists realized that in order to strengthen their own position, they had to deny land tax revenues to the central government and exploit these resources to increase their own power.

Almost without exception, land tax rates were among the first to rise, and new taxes were attached to them from time to time. In North China, figures show substantial increases in land taxes during the first several decades of the century.* In some areas in the north, the tax was increased simply by raising the original tax schedules. In other areas, a surcharge was attached to the original land tax and collected at a different time. Over time these surcharges were steadily increased, and particularly large increases were made during the 1920's.†

A further means of extracting revenue from the land was to collect taxes for many years in advance. If the militarist who had already collected the current year's tax was driven away, his successor would find that he could support his troops only by taxing the land for future years. When several militarists succeeded each other in quick order, which was by no means uncommon during this period, the peasants might be forced to pay for many future years out of the current year's earnings and savings.

The actual manner of collection in most cases imposed additional burden on the taxpayers. The lack of up-to-date information on landholding, the possibility of collusion between the local gentry and tax officials to shift the tax burden, and the severe lack

---

* The Japanese survey conducted by Amano Motonosuke estimated that the average land tax per *mou* in Shantung rose from an index of 100 in 1902 to 268 in 1925 and, even more steeply, to 468 in 1927. Myers, *The Chinese Peasant Economy*, p. 264.

† Liu Shih-jen estimated that 673 different kinds of taxes were levied on land throughout the country during this period. See his *Chung-kuo t'ien fu wen t'i*, pp. 172–73.

of qualified and honest magistrates and other functionaries all made the situation worse.

Whenever possible, the militarists converted the existing local bureaucracy into a tool for collecting taxes. If the bureaucrats failed to meet the revenue goals, the militarists appointed tax farmers to do the job. Since profit was their only motive, tax farmers were often extremely arbitrary and corrupt. The actual amount of taxes collected almost always exceeded the terms of their contract, and they pocketed the excess. But the militarists were satisfied so long as they got their share.

Although we know that land taxes increased substantially during the 1910's and 1920's, when militarism was at its height, we do not have any reliable figures for the overall national increase. After 1916, we can only get a glimpse of the increase by looking at individual provinces. In Kiangsu, for example, the land tax rose from $5,922,000 in 1921 to $6,981,814 in 1923. In Szechwan in 1925, the tax was $6,861,394; in the following year, the provincial militarists drew up a plan calling for a total land tax of $14,000,000 by collecting one year's tax in advance.[5] Although such drastic increases were not common, substantial increases occurred in all other provinces.

Since 1854, the Maritime Customs had been under foreign management. Over the years, the customs receipts steadily increased until they reached very substantial proportions during the early twentieth century. However, the Chinese government was not able to use these funds freely; by the beginning of the century, the bulk of these revenues had been reserved as securities for the government's obligations to foreign governments and business. After 1912, when the Peking government surrendered to the foreign powers the right to interfere with the internal disposal of customs duties, only the surplus (called *kuan yü*) was turned over to the central government. Consequently, between 1912 and 1927, only HK.Tls 132,441,000 was turned over to the Peking government for its own disposition; this was about 18 percent of the total revenue net of first charges.[6]

Small as the amount of the *kuan yü* was, it was extremely important to the central government because it was the most reliable source of regular income with which the militarists in the provinces could not effectively interfere. (The only significant exception was Kwangtung, where the Constitution-Protection government under Sun Yat-sen claimed that it was entitled to the *kuan yü* for the territory under its nominal control; after 1924, it received some of this money.) The central government used this money as security for foreign loans, domestic bonds, or borrowing from domestic banks. By July 1922, the entire customs surplus was pledged for the future payment of the interest and principal of such loans.[7]

In sharp contrast to the customs revenues, the revenues from the salt gabelle had never been an assured source of income for the central government. Traditionally, the actual collection was done by the provinces, and some portion was then remitted to the imperial government. The lack of serious foreign interest in salt taxes and the difficulties of combating smuggling and tax evasion made the salt revenues fair game for either Peking or the local governments, depending on their relative power positions in a particular area.

This rivalry for salt revenues started at the very beginning of the period.[8] As the tempo of the civil wars increased and the need for funds became more pressing, many militarists came to view the salt taxes collected in their areas as a natural means of increasing their own income.* After 1924, acts of interference and expropriation by militarists affected a large area, including the provinces of Kwangtung, Kwangsi, Szechwan, Yunnan, Hunan, Chekiang, Anhwei, Kiangsu, Hupeh, Shantung, Shansi, Fukien, and the three Manchurian provinces.[9] As Table 10 shows, the revenues from the salt gabelle increased up to 1922, after which they began to fall steadily, and then more precipitously after 1925. But even more precipitous was the decline in the central government's share. The year 1924 marked the first time that local retention outweighed Peking's share; by 1928 Peking's share had dwindled to nothing.

While the table shows a decline in the total net receipts after 1923, the amount of revenue various militarist regimes extracted

---

* Their interference with the salt revenues might take one of several forms: they could refuse to permit the establishment of the salt inspectorate; they could insist that the revenues be paid to them rather than to the Peking government; they could force salt merchants to make loans to them; they could loot banks and intimidate inspectorate personnel; and they could impose additional taxes on salt illegally and independently. See Adshead, p. 197.

TABLE 10
Distribution of Salt Gabelle Revenues, 1918–1928
(Thousand dollars)

Year	(1) Central government share	(2) Local share	(3) Total
1918	$56,600	$15,000	$71,600
1919	49,100	26,000	75,100
1920	40,000	24,000	64,000
1921	52,400	18,000	70,400
1922	47,862	30,000	78,862
1923	unknown	unknown	unknown
1924	31,700	33,000	64,700
1925	32,900	33,000	65,900
1926	8,868	47,672	56,540
1927	2,750	52,557	55,307
1928	0	39,642	39,642

SOURCE: *China Year Book*, 1926–27, pp. 507–10; 1928, p. 641; 1929–30, pp. 672, 674. *North-China Herald*, February 3, 1923.

from the production and sale of salt had not declined. Most probably, the producers and distributors of salt had to pay higher taxes than ever. There were cases where the militarists simply collected their own taxes.[10] After 1925, it became increasingly common for militarists in control of some territories not only to collect their own revenues but even to manage the production and sale of salt, thereby making it impossible for the Salt Gabelle even to calculate its revenue losses.[11] There is no doubt that during these later years salt revenues became an important source of income for local and regional militarists everywhere in China, while their importance to the Peking government diminished to the vanishing point.

The *likin*, or tax collected on domestic goods in transit, was another important source of revenue. Even during the Ch'ing period, the collection of the likin was lodged in the hands of provincial officials.[12] During the 1910's and 1920's, the local militarists obtained full control over the likin. The fragmentation of territorial control among the militarists brought about the collapse of the rather well-established likin system which had existed under the empire. In many cases, where the provincial military or civil governor's position was weak, the revenues would be collected by whoever was in firm control of the territory, be it a district or a county. The result was a drastic increase in rates and a proliferation of new likin taxes. For example, although the number of recognized likin stations (735) in 1921 was about the same as in the late Ch'ing period, the number of substations and barriers where taxes were actually collected had increased significantly.[13] The stations and barriers were usually set up at railway stops, by waterways, or upon main highways, where most commerce and travel had to pass. On the government-owned railways, for example, in the 1920's there was a likin barrier every 60 or 70 miles.

Local variations and widespread corruption make it difficult to calculate the amount of revenue yielded by the likin, but there are some rough indications of the growing importance of the tax. In the 1890's, the total likin receipts amounted to about 13 million treasury taels, an amount about equal to the salt revenues.[14] Moser's estimates of the likin revenues in the 1916–28 period range from a very conservative figure of 64 million taels (or Mex. $96 million) to a more realistic figure of 160 million HK.Tls (or Mex. $240 million).[15] Despite the lack of precise information, there is no doubt that the likin revenues constituted a major source of regular income for many militarists. In some provinces, only the land tax was more productive.

Special Sources of Income

China's financial relations with the outside world changed in several ways after the beginning of the twentieth century. Previously, Western countries had been the chief providers of loans. But with the advent of World War I, these Western countries, including the United States, had no surplus funds to spare for China. Under these altered international conditions, Japan emerged as the most important lender.

There is little doubt that immediately following the collapse of the central government's authority in 1916, it was Japan that provided the principal source of foreign funds to Tuan Ch'i-jui and his Anfu political allies. Although the exact amount is unknown because many of the loans were made secretly, informed sources suggested that before Tuan's downfall in 1920, the Japanese government had extended to the Peking government alone loans that probably reached at least $350 million.[16] The data presented by the Financial Reorganization Conference of the Peking government shows that, by the end of 1925, China's indebtedness to

Economic Capabilities 157

Japan in the unsecured loan category was six times larger than its indebtedness to Great Britain.[17]

The most comprehensive research into China's borrowing in this period was done by Hsü I-sheng. According to his data, some 319 foreign loans were made to the Peking regimes and their northern militarist allies during 1916–27, totaling Ch. $742 million.[18] It is very likely that this figure underestimates the actual size of the debt. In order to assess the cumulative effect of China's foreign indebtedness, we need also to look at the amount of debt outstanding in a given year. In 1921, the budget released by the Finance Ministry stated that the foreign loans as of September 1921 amounted to Ch. $1,269 million. Then, in 1924–25, the Ministries of Finance and Communication of the Peking government were reported to owe foreign debts totaling Ch. $2,200 million. Finally, according to the *China Year Book*, on January 1, 1929, China's foreign debt still outstanding was Ch. $1,043,500,000.[19]

Of course, these figures should at best be regarded as rough estimates rather than precise accounts. It is also true that the total figure for any given year would include debts incurred long before 1916, such as the war indemnities. But over time, the size of these debts should be decreasing progressively. If the indebtedness actually increased, we can assume that there were new obligations. However, even if there is a certain margin of error in Hsü's figures (given in Table 11), they do show two things. First, the size of the debt was fairly large for a poor country like China. Second, foreign loan obligations remained high from 1920 to 1925, and then declined rather sharply from 1925 onward. Now, as most foreign loans were secured ones, the payments of principal and interest were made quite faithfully. Therefore, the actual increases in foreign indebtedness between 1916 and 1925 were considerably greater than the figures in Table 11, since old loans were being paid off and liquidated in the meantime. On the other hand, the decline after 1925 was certainly partly due to the continued amortization of previous debts. More important, it might have been due to the unavailability of new foreign loans. The Peking government's position had become so untenable that foreign powers simply refused to bet on its continued survival. The cutoff of foreign loans undoubtedly hastened the demise of that government.

It must not be assumed that foreign powers lent money only to

TABLE 11
Foreign Loans to China, 1916–1927
(Thousand dollars)

Year	No. of loans	Amount borrowed	Amount actually received
1916	15	Ch.$39,378	Ch.$36,195
1917	19	73,485	64,938
1918	50	149,585	127,900
1919	41	47,990	44,520
1920	58	71,224	57,820
1921	49	84,340	67,040
1922	22	52,892	51,050
1923	10	39,697	26,722
1924	20	28,157	15,357
1925	24	136,022	102,389
1926	5	4,651	3,551
1927	6	15,294	11,669
TOTAL	319	Ch.$742,115	Ch.$609,151

SOURCE: Hsü I-sheng, *Chung-kuo chin tai wai chai shih t'ung chi tzu liao, 1853–1927*, pp. 148–97, 240–41.

the Peking government. From time to time, they did lend money to individual militarists and local regimes as well. Local militarists could contract foreign loans so long as they were prepared to accept exorbitant terms. For instance, between 1916 and 1927, the Manchurian militarists contracted foreign loans totaling Ch. $23 million, mostly from the Japanese government or banks. Other provinces were also able to find willing lenders. Hsü's data show that some eighty foreign loans had been contracted by local governments and militarists, in the amount of Ch. $90 million, or roughly one-sixth of the national total for 1916–27.[20]

Domestic borrowing during the Republican period usually took one of three principal forms. The first was government bonds (*kung chai*). Bonds usually carried long-term obligations, sometimes from five to ten years, and occasionally as long as thirty years.[21] The second was treasury notes (*kuo k'u cheng chüan*). These notes were usually issued to meet certain specific financial needs in an emergency situation and were redeemable within a shorter period of time.[22] The amount of the notes might vary from a million dollars to more than ten million dollars, depending on the nature of the project. The bonds and treasury notes could be either secured or unsecured. The third form was short-term loans

TABLE 12
Revenue Received from Government Bonds,
1912–1926

Year	Revenue	Year	Revenue
1912	Ch.$6,248,460	1920	121,960,450
1913	6,842,200	1921	115,362,248
1914	24,970,520	1922	83,234,910
1915	25,834,155	1923	5,000,000
1916	8,770,515	1924	5,200,000
1917	10,516,790	1925	15,000,000
1918	139,363,760	1926	15,400,000
1919	28,358,700	TOTAL	Ch.$612,062,708

SOURCE: Ch'ien Chia-chü, "Chiu chung kuo fa hsin kung chia shih ti yen chiu," *Li shih yen chiu*, no. 2 (April 1955), pp. 112–13.

from domestic banks. This borrowing usually fell into one of three categories: loans secured by the salt surplus, short-term loans, or advances.[23]

During these years, the most important source of the government's domestic borrowing was the urban commercial sector, composed of wealthy individuals, chambers of commerce, and particularly the modern-style banks. Many banks regularly subscribed to governmental bonds and notes as their major or only business operation. Bonds and notes of this kind were profitable, because they were usually obtained at a fraction of their face value and carried interest rates much higher than the market rates, and because their market value fluctuated violently according to the political fortunes of the militarist group ruling Peking. By the same token, of course, they might become totally worthless, if the government defaulted in redemption.

With respect to government bonds, it is estimated that between 1912 and 1926 some 27 domestic bond issues were floated by the Ministry of Finance, with a combined face value of Ch. $876,792,-228. The actual amount received was only Ch. $612,062,708, probably because some bonds went unsold.[24] As the figures in Table 12 show, nearly 90 percent of the bonds (Ch. $548,167,373 worth) were floated between 1916 and 1926. The figures include only the formally declared bond issues of the various regimes in Peking. There may have been some unannounced issues, but there is no way to ascertain their amount.

It is even more difficult to ascertain the amount of money obtained through treasury notes or short-term loans from the commercial banks. According to the report of the Committee on Financial Reorganization, under the auspices of the Peking government, 73 different kinds of treasury notes were issued between 1912 and 1925, most of them after 1916. These, together with other short-term borrowing, had amounted to an outstanding debt of Ch. $172,464,454 at the end of 1925.[25]

Of course, the Peking government was not alone in tapping the domestic sources of loans; local militarists and provincial authorities often floated their own bonds and notes. The position of the central government vis-à-vis the local militarists with respect to domestic borrowing was weakened by several factors. First, internal political realities contradicted the legal fiction that the Peking government was the only legitimate government in China. The militarists were recognized as the de facto supreme political authority in their areas. Second, the profit incentive worked as strongly on the local level as on the national level. When the opportunity for making a quick profit through speculation presented itself, some local bankers and wealthy individuals were bound to take it. Furthermore, the threat of coercion was more likely to be used on the local level than on the national level. The national government floated its bonds primarily by peaceful means; the presence of the international concessions provided a shield for the banks against high-handed treatment by the government. In the provinces, little legal protection existed; the local chambers of commerce, the old-style community banks, and the landed gentry and professional people could not escape the various forms of extortion backed by threats of physical force.

At one time or another, almost all the provincial regimes floated their own bonds during this period.[26] The most serious competitor of the central government in domestic borrowing was the military government at Canton, which had its own Ministry of Finance and claimed to be the only legitimate government in China. As early as October 1917, this government announced that it would issue military bonds in the amount of Ch. $50 million.[27] Smaller amounts were issued in subsequent years. After the advent of the Northern Expedition, the Nationalist government also turned to domestic borrowing to meet its mounting expenses. Between 1926 and 1927, the KMT governments at Canton and Wuhan probably issued Ch.

Economic Capabilities

$36 million worth of bonds. After the KMT government was formally installed in Nanking, it floated two more bond issues, totaling Ch. $70 million before the end of 1927, and another Ch. $110 million worth were issued in 1928.[28] If these figures are correct, then the KMT had issued about Ch. $216 million worth of government bonds in less than three years.

The manipulation of currency was another source of revenue for the militarists. This device had several advantages. In the first place, the people usually had no access to information on the quantity of paper currency in circulation, and the impact of the currency on their cost of daily living was not as immediately obvious as the impact of taxes. By the time they realized the unsoundness of the currency, considerable damage had already been done. These factors tended to mitigate the people's dissatisfaction and resistance. Second, even when resistance to the currency occurred, it often took the form of isolated individual acts. Since currency was usually first paid out to armies to buy provisions, in most cases it was the soldiers who introduced the currency into the market. The small shopkeepers and peddlers could refuse to accept it only at their own risk. Moreover, unlike taxes or bonds, currency was a medium of everyday exchange, and the demand for some form of currency was both constant and enormous. When a currency was backed by rifles and bayonets, the average person had little recourse but to accept it as payment for goods and services.

Thus, it is no surprise that during the 1920's virtually every province issued its own currency. The mint was considered as important a military objective as the arsenal. Provincial military governors and lesser militarists vied for the control of facilities to issue paper currency. During the period 1916–28, at least nineteen provincial banks were in existence at different times, and seventeen of them issued their own currency, usually of several different kinds.[29] However, the provincial banks were not the only agencies that issued currency. On numerous occasions, a so-called *chünyung p'iao* (or military notes) was issued by militarists without using the banks at all.[30]

The militarists who issued their own currency almost never had enough credit to back it up. For instance, Hunan printed $22 million worth of paper currency backed by a reserve of less than $1 million.[31] In 1927, Chang Tsung-ch'ang's Shantung provincial bank printed and circulated about $55 million in paper currency with a silver reserve of only $1.5 million.[32] Militarists who lacked a stable territorial base usually had greater difficulty issuing paper currency, because it was obvious that they had no capital reserves and because their lack of established channels of economic control made it easier for the people to avoid their currency. On the other hand, these were the militarists who tended to have the greatest need to resort to printing paper currency, since they lacked other regular sources of income. In this respect, Feng Yü-hsiang provides one of the most illuminating examples. In 1927, when his troops were hard-pressed for money, Feng bought $400 silver worth of printing paper and used stone blocks to hand-print one million dollars' worth of military notes. These notes were then paid to the troops to buy goods and services from the people.[33]

Such irresponsible methods eventually led to the collapse of the currency's credibility and thus to its rapid devaluation. In Feng's case, his military notes could circulate only in the area under his tight control, and even there its value gradually dropped to nothing.[34] Almost none of the banks were capable of fully redeeming their own currency at par. Even the soundest currency was redeemed at a considerable discount, and at times the discount was so great as to make the currency practically worthless.

The circulation of currency followed closely the shifts in the political arena. Most frequently, militarists inundated the market with new paper currency when they suddenly needed a large amount of money to prepare for or to conduct civil wars. This close relation between the volume of paper currency and the need for arms, and the harm such a relation could do to the economy, was most graphically demonstrated by the steady deterioration of the Manchurian currency, *feng-p'iao*. By all economic yardsticks, Manchuria was unquestionably the most prosperous region in the whole country. As Table 13 shows, prior to 1922, when Chang Tso-lin had contented himself with a regional role, the volume of feng-p'iao in circulation was not great, and its value fluctuated within a limited range. After 1922, however, a conspicuous increase in volume took place. The increase became phenomenal between January and November 1924, during which time Chang not only had engaged in a very costly war against the Chihli faction, but had extended his territorial domain into the Yangtze area. After 1924,

TABLE 13
Volume and Value of Feng-p'iao, 1916–1927

Year	Volume in circulation (*Thousand dollars*)	Value (no. of *feng-p'iao* equal to one silver dollar)
1916 (Dec.)	$15,800	
1917 (Dec.)	16,935	1.27
1918		1.61
1919		1.58
1920		1.67
1921		1.51
1922 (Dec.)	36,000	1.66
1923		1.48
1924 (Feb.)	51,000	1.59
(Nov.)	223,284	
1925 (Jan.)	511,723	2.21
1926	570,000	4.81
1927		10.61

SOURCE: Chin kuo-pao, *op. cit.*, pp. 145–48. Ch'ao Lin, "Feng p'iao tieh chia yu Feng hsi chun fa chih ch'ien t'u," *Hsiang tao*, no. 170, September 10, 1926. *China Year Book*, 1928, p. 658.

the suppression of the internal rebellion of Kuo Sung-lin, the necessity to maintain a sprawling military establishment and territorial control, and the increasing cost of fighting external enemies (like the Kuominchün) caused the volume of the feng-p'iao to skyrocket and its value to plummet. The value continued to deteriorate until in May 1927 one feng-p'iao was quoted as worth only 9 cents to the silver dollar. The rapid depreciation of the Manchurian currency not only made the military presence of the Fengtien faction in North China shaky, but also caused considerable hardship in its home provinces.[35]

Opium was another important source of revenue for the militarists. During the last year of Yüan's reign the official opium ban broke down completely, and opium profits became an important source of income to finance political activities. After Yüan's death, even the central government could not resist the lucrative profits of the opium trade.[36] After 1920, opium became an increasingly important source of income for many militarists, and, indeed, for some the most important source of income. Rough estimates of the opium revenues received by militarists in eleven provinces in the two years for which we have information are given in Table 14.

Usually, the militarists' exploitation of the opium trade took

TABLE 14
Opium Revenues Paid to Militarists in Eleven Provinces,
1924 and 1927
(Thousand dollars)

Province	1924	1927
Szechwan		Ch.$10–30,000
Shensi	Ch.$10–24,000	
Fukien	20,000	
Kwangtung		12,000
Yunnan		50,000
Hupeh	15–20,000	
Kwangsi		10,000
Kansu	20,000	
Anhwei	3,000	
Honan		3,000
Kiangsi		3,000

SOURCE: *Chung kuo ching chi lun wen chi*, 2: 34–37. *China Year Book*, 1924, pp. 572–85; 1928, pp. 528–35. Chou Hsien-wen, "Chung Kuo chih yen ho chi ch'i chiu chi ts'e," *Tung fang tsa chih*, 23, 20 (October 25, 1926): 33–34. Lai Hsin-hsia, "Pei yang chün fa tui nei shou kua ti chi chung fang shih," *Shih hsüeh yüeh k'an*, no. 3 (March 1957), pp. 8–11. Wu Ling, "Fan Feng chan cheng ch'i chien Shen-hsi ko fang mien chih ch'ing k'uang," *Hsiao tao*, no. 145 (February 10, 1926).

NOTE: The figures in this table are crude estimates based on the scanty evidence available.

one of several forms. The most basic form was taxation on production. Many militarists forced the peasants to grow poppies and then confiscated the crop under the pretext of the official ban and sold it for personal profit. Or they might impose fines that were in reality regular taxes in disguise.

According to the reports published by the International Anti-Opium Association (Peking), the provinces of Fukien, Anhwei, Kweichow, Yunnan, Honan, Shensi, Kansu, Suiyuan, and Shantung were identified as places where opium was "cultivated extensively."[37] The total national production, according to one source, was 15,000 tons in 1921.[38] By the mid-1920's, possibly more than 5 million *mou* of land were used to cultivate poppies.[39]

When the opium was shipped to domestic and international markets, the provinces that controlled the main trading routes could also levy exorbitant transit taxes. As most of the opium from Szechwan, Shensi, and Kweichow had to be shipped on the Yangtze River, the province of Hupeh became a pivotal point for its distribution to other provinces down the river. In fact, the opium traffic became a monopoly under the military authorities in Hupeh.⁴⁰ A similar situation existed in Kwangsi, through which most opium from Yunnan (and to a lesser extent from Kweichow and Szechwan as well) had to pass to reach Kwangtung, Hong Kong, and eventually Southeast Asia. Consequently, opium taxes constituted the single most important source of revenue for the Kwangsi militarists; the amount usually exceeded $10 million a year.⁴¹

Finally, the provinces could tax the consumers. During the 1920's, opium was smoked extensively. Public opium dens were taxed; opium lamps were taxed; and opium smokers sometimes were required to pay a monthly tax. Consequently, militarists in almost every province, with the exception of Shansi, could count on the opium consumption taxes as regular income. Opium smoking was in fact so pervasive that even the Nationalists could not resist taking advantage of it. In 1927, the Nationalist opium monopoly in Kwangtung was reported to be raising about a million dollars a month through opium taxes.⁴²

There were several other sources of revenue that militarists could tap when their territorial bases were conveniently located. Chief among these was the railways. For instance, during the first six months of 1924, Wu P'ei-fu confiscated Ch. $6 million from the Peking–Hankow railway (out of its gross income of Ch. $14 million).⁴³ According to an official report issued by the Ministry of Communications in September 1925, some $180 million had been plundered by the militarists from China's railways up to the end of 1924.⁴⁴

The exploitation of the railways by the militarists went beyond the confiscation of funds. Soldiers seldom had to pay for rides, and militarists regularly commandeered the rolling stock to move troops and supplies free of charge. The military use of railway service (which represented a net loss of revenue for the railways) was always substantial, and became particularly heavy when political tensions rose.*

Another important form of raising revenue was gambling taxes, in areas where gambling was a popular pastime. The usual practice was to set up a monopoly over gambling dens. A typical example is found in Kwangsi, where in 1915 the civil governor and

---

* In 1925, for example, the percentage of total freight and passenger volume used by the military was 34 percent on the Peking–Hankow line and 25.8 percent on the Peking–Fengtien line. Yen Chung-p'ing et al., p. 210.

his finance commissioner granted gambling licenses to syndicates in return for a fee of nearly $2.5 million.⁴⁵ Gambling taxes continued to be important to Kwangsi militarists throughout the entire period regardless of their political orientation.* In Kwangtung, although gambling was nominally banned for some time, when Sun Yat-sen was elected president of the Canton government in April 1923, he immediately lifted the ban and devoted the revenues from this source to military expenses.⁴⁶

The last major source of irregular income was the so-called *ping ch'ai* or *t'an k'uan*. While ping-ch'ai could assume many different forms under different names, they were all associated with a supposed emergency situation. When the militarists found their normal tax revenues insufficient to meet the emergency, they would turn to the population for additional funds or services. Most frequently, money was demanded, but sometimes carts, draft animals, food and fuel, and even human labor were commandeered. Many villages and hsien were required to make large payments for being "protected" from enemy troops, or for being "saved" from the troops driven out by the new conquerors.

When provincial or local administrators were presented with such demands, they apportioned the burden among the hsien and villages. If an area was hit by a number of such emergencies, the financial burden could be extraordinarily heavy. This was especially true in areas (such as North China) where the militarists' regimes were unstable and were under the constant threat of being overthrown by neighboring militarists.†

When a large sum of money had to be raised quickly, the militarist usually turned to the local chamber of commerce as an easy prey, because the business community was especially vulnerable to extortion. During the 1920's, it was common practice for militarists to assess cities sums of money. If the full amount was not raised in time, then the militarists would allow the soldiers to loot.

---

* Although Li Tsung-jen was considered a "progressive" militarist, gambling proceeds made up about one-third of his income in 1922. See Huang Hsü-ch'u, "I Kuang-hsi tzu chih chün yü ch'ün hsiung ko chü chih chu," *Ch'un ch'iu*, no. 244 (Sept. 1, 1967), p. 19; Huang Shao-hung, I: 77–78.

† For instance, in 1925, when Shantung was engaged in war with Feng Yü-hsiang, Chang Tsung-ch'ang added four new kinds of taxes in connection with the land taxes. These amounted to about four times the original land tax. S-sheng, "Chang Tsung-ch'ang t'ung chih hsia ti Shan-tung," *Hsiang tao*, no. 131 (Sept. 25, 1925).

Defeated troops refused to depart until they had obtained their traveling expenses. New conquerors professed their inability to restrain their soldiers unless a "welcome fee" was presented. And the helpless small businessmen and residents had no alternative but to comply.

Evaluating the Financial Policies of the Militarists

It is clear that the financial resources at the disposal of the local militarist regimes far exceeded those of the central government at Peking. The crux of the matter was territorial control. With the exception of the surplus from the customs service, and to a lesser extent the salt gabelle, the central government held no visible advantage over the local regimes.

The central government's financial position was never very strong after the 1911 revolution, partly because of increased expenditures and partly because of suspended contributions from some provinces, but the critical point was probably not reached until Yüan's death. According to Finance Minister Ts'ao Ju-lin, the annual receipts of the central government in 1917 amounted to merely Ch. $144 million. Consequently, the government was forced to resort to large-scale borrowing to meet the deficit of some Ch. $250 million.[47]

After 1920, the Chihli faction became the new master of a government in financial crisis. Although Chihli's military power overshadowed all other rivals for nearly four years, the financial position of the Peking government was never improved. Chihli militarists continued to run their territories as financially independent satrapies. Not only did they not surrender fiscal control to Peking; they even asked Peking for subsidies.*

Thus, even when the Peking government was controlled by a fairly strong military faction, its financial position remained shaky. The militarists had accepted financial decentralization as a way of life and were reluctant to reverse it at the risk of antagonizing their friends and followers. They wanted to use the Peking government as an additional source of income, but they could hardly conceive

---

* For instance, although Wu P'ei-fu already controlled the revenue from Honan and the Peking–Hankow railway, he still asked the Peking government in December 1923 for $5,540,000 to meet fifteen months' pay in arrears to his troops. As usual, the Finance Minister had no way of meeting this demand, and Wu had to settle for the meager sum of $200,000. *CWR*, Dec. 15, 1923.

giving up their own authority in order to strengthen Peking's position. So long as this mentality prevailed, the Peking government was doomed. Thus, during Chihli's reign, no serious attempt was ever made to reassert the central government's authority to collect and dispose of the taxes in the Chihli-controlled territories. Rather, whenever a finanical crisis surfaced, a new finance minister was installed to search for some yet unexplored sources of funds.[48] Once these funds were exhausted, as they always quickly were, another financial crisis, another finance minister, and another set of stop-gap solutions followed. After Chihli's downfall in 1924, the subsequent regimes in Peking were even less able to make the necessary changes. Given such political realities, the financial position of the central government was destined to remain precarious to the end.

Although the militarists were in a stronger position than the central government, they faced the problem of rising demands for revenue. After 1916, there was a sharp increase in expenditures in all the provinces; the sharpest increase was in military expenses. More soldiers were being mobilized and more arms and ammunition were being deployed and consumed.

It is unfortunate that most militarists did not leave records of their war costs. Our available data, though incomplete, seem to show a clear trend of escalation. According to Ts'ao Ju-lin's testimony, Tuan Ch'i-jui's Anfu government borrowed 105 million yen (or Ch. $84 million) from Japan to finance the Hunan campaign during a ten-month period. Thus, the Peking government was spending an average of about $8 million a month for the war in 1918.[49]

The first Chihli-Fengtien war lasted one week. After his defeat, Chang Tso-lin conceded that the war had cost him about $24 million.[50] In other words, one day's fighting in 1922 cost about as much as one month's fighting in 1918. In the 1924 rematch between the same factions, the cost of war increased further. That war cost Fengtien some $50–60 million.[51] When the Rehabilitation Conference convened in 1924, it reported that the total military expenditures of the major conflicts of 1924 had been a staggering $350 million.[52]

The year 1924 marked a watershed in war costs, as it did in many other respects. Before 1924, a war was more easily defined. At least in the major wars, there was a small number of participants

Economic Capabilities 169

and hostilities were usually concluded within a relatively short period of time. Furthermore, a long period of peace followed before the next war began. But after 1924, it would be accurate to say that wars were taking place continuously, with only occasional brief intermissions. Therefore, the calculation of war costs becomes more difficult.

One thing, however, is clear: the cost of war continued to soar with each passing year between 1925 and 1928. The established factions like Fengtien, Chihli, and Feng Yü-hsiang's Kuominchün continued to spend millions of dollars every month in fighting each other. After mid-1926, even the previously dormant KMT began to demonstrate its prowess, which forced a further increase in the pace as well as the cost of war. The KMT's Finance Minister, T. V. Soong, reported in 1928 that he had been required to provide $1,600,000 to the military every five days during the entire duration of the Northern Expedition.[53] Soong's figures would indicate that the KMT's military expenditures amounted to about $115 million per year. This is indeed astounding, especially in view of the fact that only a few National Revolutionary Armies were directly financed by the party.

Thus there had been an unmistakable trend. During the late Manchu years, the annual military expenditures for the whole empire were usually under $100 million.[54] In 1916, when the anti-Yüan rebellion broke out, the total military expenditures were about $142 million. By 1928 military costs had soared to $800 million.[55]

Since the traditional fiscal system was incapable of absorbing the mounting costs, militarists everywhere were forced to resort to deficit spending.[56] The situation in the wealthier provinces was no better, even though their revenues were larger. On the contrary, the militarists in these provinces usually took advantage of the provincial wealth to build larger armies. Szechwan, for example, was a wealthy province, and its military expenditures were also among the largest of all provinces.*

The militarists thus overextended themselves financially. Their military expenditures kept rising, but the fiscal system they in-

---

* According to the Committee on Local Financial Reorganization of the Ministry of Finance of the Peking government, the budgeted gross tax receipts of Szechwan in 1924 were $12,540,000, but the military expenditures were $26,510,000. Chang Hsiao-mei, C17–18.

herited was too loosely structured to respond to measures of rapid expansion. Consequently, most militarists found it necessary to go beyond the traditional tax structure in search of additional funds. We have described how these additional funds were acquired. Our task now is to analyze the rationality of the militarists' entire financial process.

As a rule, militarists gave the highest priority to the preservation of their power and position in the national political system. This goal required control of a definite piece of territory. A territorial base meant not only a better defense position but also a guaranteed source of financial support. Yet it was precisely this goal of controlling territory that engaged the typical militarist in a vicious circle. To protect the newly acquired territory, the militarist needed to increase the size of his army. But he also had to reward the subordinates who had contributed to his acquisition of the territory. He usually rewarded the subordinates with a portion of the territory, or money, or permission to expand their own units. To meet these needs, the militarist needed new resources.

Thus, the militarists were usually driven to pursue expansionist policies. The stronger their forces became, the more assured they were of their place in the political system. But the stronger they became, the greater the rewards they had to give out to satisfy their subordinates' rising expectations. Therefore, defense requirements always begot new demands for more resources and more territory, which in turn begot more defense requirements.

The rational course for the militarists would have been to strive for economic self-sufficiency. To achieve such a goal, the least they needed to do was to erect an economic wall to shield them from any adverse influence from their competitors. But more fundamentally, to develop their political and military power on a sound basis, they needed to enhance the economic well-being of their own territory, to explore new resources, to institute more efficient ways of mobilizing and utilizing existing resources so as to strengthen the general economy in the long run. In fact, however, the militarists' economic policies hindered the realization of these goals.

Upon examining the economic policies of the militarists' regimes, we are struck by the fact that land taxes constituted the major source of regular revenue for most of them. The major tax

Economic Capabilities

burden was inescapably placed on the shoulders of the peasants. High taxes, high rent, high interest rates, together with mounting population pressures on land and the flight of the rural leadership—the scholars and gentry—into urban centers, conspired to disrupt beyond repair the social fabric and economic equilibrium of traditional agrarian China. Under these adverse conditions, the deterioration of the rural economy was bound to be severe. As Myers points out, if high taxes were continued and further increased, "the peasants might be discouraged from investing and replacing their farm capital," which would bring about a decline in productivity and output.[57] This seems to have been the case in the areas hardest hit by militarism.

In addition to basic land taxes, the other revenue-raising devices used by the militarists also had an adverse impact on the economy. The likin created numerous barriers to commerce. It also created disincentives for peasants, because agricultural products, usually bulky and heavy, were the best targets for extortion. Delays at the checkpoints could be disastrous for perishable goods.

The adverse effects of the exploitative tax system were compounded by the inadequate and expensive transportation system. And the limited railway facilities were frequently disrupted or damaged by civil wars. When a military crisis approached, much of the rolling stock was mobilized for military use, while the agricultural products were left on the landings to rot. As Myers describes it, "The rural staples such as cotton, wheat, and peanuts which normally flowed from villages into the main markets... declined. This forced manufacturing enterprises to operate at only one third or half capacity. Employment declined, and many villages which depended upon this wage income suffered."[58]

The unscrupulous currency policies of the militarists further reduced the credibility of the money economy and pauperized the common people, among whom the bulk of the currency circulated. The effects on commerce and industry were equally devastating. Since each territory had its own currency with unpredictable stability, the exchange of goods between territories was naturally impeded. In Manchuria, for instance, all transactions were conducted in feng-p'iao. But when Manchuria traded with Shanghai, they had to use bullion or a reputable foreign currency.[59]

But more fundamentally, political unrest and civil wars made any long-range investment extremely precarious. The lack of guarantee of property rights discouraged even the most enterprising investors. Industries owned by Chinese on Chinese soil not infrequently became the hapless victims of militarists' extortion.* And even when the industrialists were able to cope with the militarists' exactions and survive the many "bureaucratic corruptions," they were still vulnerable to the chaotic monetary system, which made long-range industrial investment on Chinese soil inadvisable. Such policies inevitably caused the flight of Chinese capital and investment into the International Settlement in the treaty ports, beyond the militarists' jurisdiction.†

Considering China as a whole, our discussion should have made clear that the financial policies of most militarists were by no means conducive to strengthening their territorial regimes in the long run. As a matter of fact, eventually they could only lead to bankruptcy.

How can we explain the apparent contradictions between the ends and the means of the militarists' economic policies? Were they oblivious to these contradictions? In order to answer these questions, we need to probe a little deeper into the political characteristics of the militarists' regimes.

The essential reason for the militarists' economic policies lay in their exclusive preoccupation with their physical force in being. The militarists were compelled to adopt a war-oriented policy that required maximum effort to keep their force at the highest state of combat readiness and efficiency. Emotional attachment to

* The Chung-hsin Coal Mine could be considered a typical case. Chung-hsin was the third largest Chinese-owned and Chinese-managed coal mine in the country and before 1925 showed an annual profit of Ch. $2 million. In 1926, when Chang Tsung-ch'ang ruled over Shantung, where the mine was located, he demanded a large contribution from the mine, and the net profit plummeted to Ch. $5,000. After Chang was driven out by the KMT, the latter also demanded about Ch. $1 million from the management. Consequently, in 1927–28, the industry suffered a net loss of over Ch. $1.5 million annually, which nearly brought it to the brink of bankruptcy. Chu Ch'i-hua, pp. 340–41; Yen Chung-p'ing et al., p. 155.

† In Shanghai, for example, there were 3,421 factories located in the International Settlement employing 170,704 workers, as contrasted with 2,676 factories in the Chinese municipality employing 245,664 workers. This certainly represented an inordinately large concentration of capital investment in the foreign section of the city. Murphey, pp. 168–69.

the territorial base was unrealistic, since their jurisdiction could be terminated at any time. Furthermore, since there were limits on the resources that could be extracted from a given territory, civilian economic development programs had to compete for funds with military uses. A more rational and balanced development of the general economy might produce both more guns and more butter in the long run. But time was a luxury these militarists could not afford. The militarists had to be perpetually wary about the slightest portent of alteration in their relative power relationship and to exert full effort to make up any discrepancy. If they engaged in long-term economic construction, there was a genuine possibility that they might be outdistanced by their opponents in the immediate military build-up, and thus be prevented from reaping the fruits of their labor. The ever-shifting constellation of power made it hazardous to become too tied to long-term objectives.

Thus, instead of devoting energies and resources to the creation of real capital gains and accumulation through providing conditions favorable to industrialization, commerce, educational improvement, and agricultural development, which in the long run would yield more liquid capital to finance their armies, the militarists in general resorted to exploitative policies that would yield the largest sums in the short run but which would exhaust the general economy before long. After a war was over, the matériel that had been so painstakingly acquired was either demolished or greatly diminished, even in the case of the victors. War-making was a luxury item of direct and compulsory consumption for a reluctant people, who were so squeezed of their last resources that they had no more to spare for economically constructive purposes. And eventually, even their ability to support the civil wars diminished.

There was yet another politically significant consequence of these economic facts. We described how political disintegration had caused economic disintegration in the first place. As time went by, however, economic disintegration in turn retarded political reintegration. Attempts by leading militarists to consolidate the internal organization of their factions often met insurmountable economic obstacles. The faction was composed of smaller military units which controlled their own territories. Under normal circumstances, these smaller units had virtual control over the local taxing agencies, the communication routes, or the banks. When their territory grew large enough to have a fairly comprehensive economic system, they were quite capable of going their own way. Probably the only plausible threat was the use of physical coercion. But this went against the law of expansion. For in order to expand, a militarist had to delegate authority and divide labor. But once victory was achieved and old enemies were eliminated, new enemies would be created within one's own ranks as one's subordinates were rewarded, often with territories. In this case, the old pattern of rivalry was simply replaced by a new one, while the economic power inherent in the respective territories was hardly diminished.

This is not to argue, however, that economic integration was impossible. There were several occasions in which strong centralized economic control was exercised by the factions over their components. These cases tended to occur at the height of military success and tended to be short-lived. Force was the necessary ingredient of successful economic integration, but force alone was not sufficient. The economic relationship between the faction and the components could change only if the economic position of the latter was undercut. Component units were loyal to the faction only when they were stripped of their independent sources of income and had to rely on the faction for pay, provisions, arms, and ammunition. In this sense, economic problems could not be solved in isolation; they could be solved only in conjunction with other military and political problems.

The KMT presents a unique and fascinating case of how economic integration could be achieved through a combination of ingenious military and administrative devices.

Prior to 1923, the KMT government existed in name only. The local revenues were jealously guarded by the local militarists. Nor did the KMT dare to send its own tax collectors into the countryside, for they would have been driven away, imprisoned, or killed.*

The establishment of the Whampoa Military Academy and the suppression of the Canton Chamber of Commerce revolt marked the starting point in eliminating the economic barriers. In the next two years this new military force succeeded in overthrowing

---

* *KMWH*, 7: 18–19. For a while the main source of the KMT's income came from contributions by overseas Chinese. During this time, the government was so poor that all bureaucrats from ministerial rank down to desk clerks got a flat salary of Ch. $20 a month.

Economic Capabilities 175

the local militarists and in extending direct rule from above. Among the many novel features introduced by this party force was the strict separation of military and administrative functions in local affairs. The management of administrative and economic affairs of a conquered territory was immediately turned over to the party functionaries.[60] The military was thus deprived of the chance to acquire a territorial base and was compelled to rely on the party for supplies. This was indeed a revolutionary change in the relationship between the military government and its armies.

The KMT instituted a few other economic measures that merit special attention. First, the Ministry of Finance became the only government department responsible for handling economic matters and the sole recipient of income after the suppression of the Yunnan and Kwangsi forces in June 1925.

Second, the government tried to cut drastically the number of extra taxes and to reduce waste and corruption. A system of checks and an anti-smuggling bureau were established. The tax-farm system was abolished. A budget system was instituted in which it was necessary for all appropriations to be cleared through a budget committee.[61]

Third, the government simplified the transit tax by taxing commodities only once instead of many times at different stations.

Fourth, supported initially by a Soviet loan, the KMT bank issued a unified currency with no reservations on redemption. The bank honored its pledges and firmly established its credit. Its notes were even accepted by the Customs, a rare sign of trust denied to all other currencies. The demand for the KMT's currency increased with the success of its military expansion, and the money even circulated in territories beyond the KMT's effective control, by voluntary acceptance. The bank's credit was so good that private savings deposited in the bank increased six times by 1926.[62]

These measures represented the first attempt to pursue a coherent policy of economic integration on a provincial basis. Although military expenditures were still the top priority—about 80 percent of the total expenditures—the KMT government was beginning to show an awareness of the connection between military objectives and the civilian economic structure.

The results achieved by these measures were quite encouraging. The most conspicuous gain was the rapid increase in income, which rose ten times within two years, from Ch. $8 million in 1924 to

Ch. $80 million in 1926.⁶³ Equally important was the redistribution of the various taxes. Land taxes, previously the most important source of income, had fallen to seventh place by 1926, bringing in a mere Ch. $3 million, or about 4 percent of the total income. Transit taxes moved to first place among the taxes, constituting a little less than 15 percent of total income. The largest proportion of income came from government bonds and bank stocks; together they constituted about 30 percent of the total income.⁶⁴ These figures indicate a more equitable redistribution of the financial burden among the different classes. The burden on the peasants was apparently lessened. The burden upon the ordinary consumers remained roughly unchanged, while that on the wealthier class was greatly increased in both proportional and absolute terms.

An important factor that made possible the remarkable resurgence of the KMT was Soviet aid. Although the existence of close economic ties between the two countries has been common knowledge for a long time, details have been shrouded in great secrecy because both sides are reluctant to talk about it. Evidence indicates that the Soviet Union gave more than Ch. $2.5 million to finance the Whampoa program and another $10 million to put the KMT Central Bank in business.⁶⁵ At the time, when the KMT was struggling to stand on its own feet, these funds were important contributions.

From our description of the economic conditions that prevailed in the factions, it is easy to see that, with the exception of the KMT, most factions were pursuing self-defeating policies. If regional self-sufficiency was the objective, then logic required that militarists should spare no effort in developing a healthy economic structure by promoting commerce, building up industries, and establishing a sound fiscal policy; that is, they should create wealth instead of draining it. Yet, in general, the militarists engaged in acts that would produce precisely the opposite effect.

This contradiction cannot be explained away simply by saying that the militarists acted contrary to common sense. The problem was not that they failed to see the contradiction in logic, but rather that they were powerless to pursue any other alternative. They were under the perennial threat of being overthrown, either by subordinates or by hostile neighbors. This being the case, it is easy to see why militarists allocated such a large portion of their available resources to defense requirements. Furthermore, the precariousness of their territorial bases made it seem futile to plan long-range economic development. Without territorial stability, there was no incentive to develop a bureaucracy. Without a clean and efficient bureaucracy, there was no machinery for the management of the economy and utilization of resources. Without a sound economy, militarists could not successfully defend their territories. Thus, even though the contradiction between the need for self-sufficiency and an exploitative policy probably did not escape the scrutiny of the more thoughtful militarists, the vicious circle was not easy to break. As soon as they acquired a piece of new territory, they had to exact all they could from it in order to consolidate their military position and to be prepared to cope with the external dangers that were never slow in coming.

Thus, the economic problems that most militarists faced were not solvable by economic means; they were fundamentally political problems. Only a few militarists were fortunate enough to control a definite piece of territory for a long period of time: Yen Hsi-shan in Shansi, Chang Tso-lin in Manchuria, and the KMT in the south. (Other areas, like Hunan, Yunnan, Szechwan, and Kweichow, were more or less free from external aggression, but they were not free from constant shifts of power among internal groups and therefore were no less precarious than their northern counterparts.) Only the territorially secure regimes had any incentive to devote a significant portion of their resources to economic development. For only these regimes could feel confident that their efforts would not be cut short by the loss of the territory and could enhance their security by building a strong economy capable of absorbing the mounting costs of war. It is not surprising, then, that of all the northern militarist regimes, only Shansi and the Fengtien faction survived to the last days of the system.

Among the northern militarists, an instructive point is provided by comparing Feng Yü-hsiang and Yen Hsi-shan, both of whom were enthusiastic supporters of economic construction. On many practical matters, Feng's approaches were quite similar to Yen's. The fundamental factor that contributed to Yen's success and Feng's failure was Feng's lack of territorial security. By 1926–27, when Yen was about to plunge into action, Feng was already battered, exhausted, and on the verge of collapse, and was only saved by his decision to collaborate with the KMT and the injection of a considerable amount of external aid. The simple fact was that Feng, having been without a base he could call his own for so long, simply could not afford to play a big role any longer.

Feng's plight was of course shared by most other militarists. The wars of annihilation and attrition could only be sustained by a sound economy achieved through either self-development or massive foreign aid. The territorially and economically vulnerable militarists were eliminated early in the game. Even the territorially secure militarists were quite exhausted after twelve years of fighting, during which every thinkable (and unthinkable) way of milking the people had been tried. Yet, in 1927–28, they were forced to do battle on an increasing scale with an enemy (the KMT) that had hitherto been spared deep involvement in the system and that was just beginning to flex its muscles. That they should suffer in such a confrontation is simple to understand in view of their comparative economic conditions.

Thus, there seems to have been a direct relationship between the cost of war and the stability of the system. When the cost of war was low, and when war damage could be repaired within a short period of recuperation, the system was favorable to the existence of a larger number of participants. When the costs and damage of war became too high, many participants either were eliminated or surrendered.

The example of the KMT suggests a more rational alternative to the other militarists' economic policies. The KMT started with far less favorable conditions. Its success was largely the result of its ability to strike a reasonable balance between long-range objectives and immediate needs. In assessing its success, however, we must not neglect the peculiar circumstances under which it occurred. That success might well have been impossible had not the northern militarists given the KMT a relatively long period of isolation. This isolation enabled the KMT to eliminate internal obstacles one by one and to institute a series of policies that eventually strengthened its economic position while the economic resources of other militarists were being exhausted.

CHAPTER 8

Normative Aspects of Military Politics

Up to this point, our effort has been to describe the major institutional aspects of military regimes. Inevitably, we have to come to grips with the sources and basic structure of the average militarist's value system, because a man's political behavior is ultimately guided by his values. In any political system there must be a basic body of norms and principles that the actors share, if only to provide a minimal measure of orderliness in their political transactions. In this chapter we will inquire into the norms, values, and principles that shaped the militarists' political behavior. We will begin with a description of the militarists' personal values and characteristics and then outline their code of behavior, the rules that governed the militarists' interactions with each other. Finally, we will analyze the basic political values that shaped the militarists' behavior in their attempts to establish their political legitimacy.

Although there have been a few recent studies of the political culture of the Chinese people, they have all been concerned with the general political attributes of the people as a whole. So far there has been no systematic effort to investigate whether these attributes are shared by all political elites and to what extent they can explain the political conduct of any particular elite. Needless to say, we do not yet have the resources to undertake a study of such depth. What we can do here is make a preliminary effort to identify a few of the shared values that exerted a strong influence in shaping the militarists' political perceptions and in guiding their political behavior.

Personal Values and Characteristics

On the question of the value system of the militarists, current opinion is divided. One group holds the view that the militarists were generally unprincipled, whimsical, and arbitrary. Others hold that the militarists did observe certain codes of behavior.[1] My own view is that the militarists could not and did not act in the way they wished. Our analysis later in this chapter will demonstrate that the militarists had to act under certain constraints and that they were quite aware of the consequences of their actions. To this extent, we must say that the militarists were principled people.

There is little doubt that the ideological influence of Confucianism was pervasive in traditional, or even early Republican, China. It became deeply imbedded in the Chinese mind, both conscious and unconscious, through a number of devices such as the civil service examination system, the penal code, the clan system, and the popular ideological campaigns launched from time to time. However, it is important to note that there always existed a distinction between orthodox Confucianism and its vulgarized version, the distinction between the "classic" and "folk" cultures, or the "great" and "little" traditions. As Redfield once stated, "The great tradition is cultivated in schools or temples; the little tradition works itself out and keeps itself going in the lives of the unlettered in their village communities."[2]

China has long been regarded as having a homogeneous culture, and the little tradition contained few sharp departures from the great tradition. My personal view is that, in addition to the family and clan system and the religious practices which are believed by many people to have left a great impact on the members of the peasant community, the content of mass communication and popular forms of entertainment must also have had enormous influence on the social personality of the people in the "little" tradition. In other words, traditional stories, folk songs, and operas were probably more influential than classical Confucian writings in shaping the values and attitudes of the majority of people.

This distinction can help us understand better the source and content of the value system of the militarists, very few of whom were steeped in classical Confucian training and some of whom were actually illiterate. It is my contention that the overwhelming

Normative Aspects of Military Politics 181

majority of the militarists in this period acquired their value system through the "little" tradition, through folklore and the vulgarized interpretation of the "great" tradition. Therefore, it is pertinent for us to investigate the values that were most widely propagated in the "little" tradition and to see to what extent they shaped the thinking and behavior of the average militarist.

The most influential cultural forms among the Chinese masses were undoubtedly the traditional stories and operas. Among the stories, the all-time best-sellers amounted to probably no more than a dozen, most of them written in the vernacular so that anyone with a minimal reading ability could understand them.* Those who could not read at all eventually learned about their contents through the ubiquitous storytellers.† Out of these novels came the materials for the Peking operas and their local variations. Although the limited repertoire remained unchanged for long periods of time, country people still flocked to them. Stage plays were important not only because they were the only form of organized entertainment for most villagers, but also because they were taken seriously as a method of imparting moral values and of pointing out the goals to which men should aspire.‡

In these novels and legends, a man interested in military affairs could find an ample supply of heroes and exemplary behavior.

---

* They invariably included *San kuo yen i* (The Romance of the Three Kingdoms), *Shui hu chuan* (By the Water Margin), Hsi yu chi (The Monkey), *Shih kung an* (The Investigation of Inspector Shih), *P'eng kung an* (The Investigation of Inspector P'eng), *Ch'i hsia wu i* (Seven Knights and Five Righteous Men), *Yüeh chuan* (The Story of Yüeh Fei), *Hung lou meng* (The Dream of the Red Chamber), *Hsi hsiang chi* (The Story of the Western Chamber).

† In fact, storytelling became so popular that it developed into an important art form itself, called the *shuo-shu*. The popularity of storytelling is shown in this passage from Feng Yü-hsiang's autobiography: "Our squad leader Li Hou-t'ang was particularly fond of telling stories from the *San kuo yen i*. Whenever he started the storytelling session, a large crowd would soon gather. The audience was usually so intent on listening that nobody would even dare to cough aloud." *Wo ti sheng ho*, 1: 38.

‡ Feng Yü-hsiang's autobiography provides vivid accounts of how these plays left an indelible impact on his adolescent mind and shaped his personality for the rest of his life. *Wo ti sheng ho*, 1: 23–24. The influence of the novel *San kuo yen i* on the militarists was probably tremendous, not only because it was the most popular work but also because the period depicted in the story bore a striking resemblance to the political situation in the early twentieth century. The *San kuo* abounded in characters who embodied the best of the martial virtues. In fact, one of its main characters, Kuan Yü, was accorded the status of deity by people all over the country. Gamble, *Ting Hsien*, pp. 398–401.

There has always been a relatively strong tendency among the Chinese to choose a model personality very early in life and to orient their lifetime efforts toward approximating that model.³ Once a choice had been made, a man was likely to structure his life to resemble that of his model as closely as possible. He would try to acquire an exhaustive knowledge of his hero and to interpret his own problems in terms analogous to those faced by his hero. In this process, he developed a particular frame of reference and proceeded to impose it on contemporary political realities. The Chinese militarists naturally chose military men of previous generations as their model. Thus, analogies from *San kuo yen i* and other popular works exerted extremely persuasive power over the militarists.

The novels, storytelling, and stage performances contained a few common themes that left a strong imprint upon people in the lower socioeconomic classes from which the early twentieth-century militarists came. First, anyone familiar with militarists' behavior can easily see that the traditional forces of familism operated strongly upon them. Even though they lived in an age when traditional familism had already come under scathing attack by the Western-oriented intellectuals, the militarists as a group were little affected. Even some of the most notorious generals had the reputation of being faithful and obedient sons.

Equally as important as filial piety were the reliance on particularistic ties in structuring political relations and the belief that one was morally bound to help one's less fortunate kinsmen. In our earlier discussion of the internal composition of the factions, we presented abundant evidence that primary and secondary associations constituted important criteria for membership. In fact, some military units were literally family enterprises. In the wake of the disintegration of the traditional political order, the corruptive force of nepotism became totally unrestrained.*

---

* Even a man like Wu P'ei-fu, who had a reputation for being upright and uncorrupt, was no exception. When Wu was the High Commissioner of Chihli-Shantung-Honan, he appointed his wife's brother director of both the bureau of transportation and an automobile company in Loyang. He also appointed one of her brothers-in-law director of the bureau of military procurement and another brother-in-law the deputy director of the bureau of overseas Chinese affairs of the Peking government. Chang Chün-ku, *Wu P'ei-fu chuan*, 2: 440–45.

Normative Aspects of Military Politics

A second characteristic of the militarists was their separation of personal loyalty from political loyalty, which is a reflection of the little tradition of a people who had remained politically apathetic over a long period of time. Generally, the militarists took personal loyalty seriously but treated political loyalty rather indifferently. They appeared to acknowledge that political interests might produce transient alliance or opposition but that these should in no way be allowed to poison a strictly personal relationship. This explains the situation where two militarists would have their soldiers engage in fierce fighting but would refrain from doing any physical harm to each other's person.*

Another characteristic of the militarists was a high sense of drama and personal charisma. Many of them tried to cultivate a legendary past, with the knowledge that this would help enhance their legitimacy among the people. The militarists in general loved having the reputation of possessing special physical features, because according to Chinese folklore only extraordinary men had extraordinary features. That physical uniqueness or eccentric behavior was of some importance to the people can be demonstrated by the fact that many militarists acquired nicknames that magnified these points. Thus, we have "long-legged general," "dog-eating general," "red-bearded bandit," "dragon," "tiger," "dog," "fast rider," "big tongue," and "blue sky," all expressions reminiscent of characters who appeared in novels about Chinese knights-errant. Pearl Buck, who had abundant opportunity to observe the militarists at close range, was once moved to remark:[4]

---

* This dualistic approach toward loyalty was best demonstrated by the militarists' attitude toward the deposed Manchu emperor and his court officials. The emperor continued to be accorded the respect usually reserved for a head of state; he was allowed to maintain his own court and to exercise jurisdiction within the Forbidden City. The relations between the Republican government and the Manchu court were conducted as if between two sovereign states, and the militarists still eagerly flocked to the court on holidays and other propitious occasions to pay their homage to the child-emperor in accordance with the traditional court etiquette, which included the kowtow. They also pressed the Republican government to extend favorable treatment to the Manchu court; as a result, during the Hung-hsien reign and the anti-restoration campaign, the court escaped serious damage to its position. The militarists gladly did these things, regarding loyalty to one's old master as a virtue, even though they themselves had been instrumental in bringing down the empire. Other instances of scrupulous adherence to personal loyalty abounded, and the violation of this principle could bring about extremly unpleasant results.

Without exception, the war lords I have known have been men of unusual native ability, gifted with peculiar personal charm, with imagination and strength, and often with a rude poetic quality. Above all, they carry about with them, in them, a sense of high drama. The war lord sees himself great—and great in the traditional manner of heroes of ancient fiction and history who are so inextricably mingled in the old Chinese novels. He is, in effect, an actor by nature.

Ostentatious living was another important device to mark one's superiority. The scholar-officials of the traditional society followed a life of conspicuous consumption, as much to impress their inferiors as to amuse themselves. The militarists, in general, followed in their footsteps. This was particularly noteworthy in view of the fact that many militarists had come from very humble social backgrounds and had been brought up to value hard work and frugality. Upon becoming powerful, however, they squandered money, not only because they obviously enjoyed more luxurious living, but also because they believed they had to live ostentatiously in order to command respect. Thus they maintained palatial residences, kept a large number of personal servants, indulged in excessive gambling, drinking, and other forms of debauchery, and frequently threw extravagant parties. A militarist who attempted to cut corners on these expenses would be considered cheap and would find it difficult to make friends or exercise authority.

This concern with appearances, or *p'ai-ch'ang*, also constituted an important part of the etiquette that guided the militarists' official conduct.* In conducting diplomatic relations, their behavior had to be appropriate to their official position, and most important, they were not to do anything that might be interpreted as loss of face.

Such excessive concern with pride and image often made it difficult to achieve constructive results through face-to-face negotia-

* For instance, when the victorious Chang Tso-lin entered Peking in 1926, ordinary traffic was halted, people were cleared from the strets, 15,000 policemen and soldiers stood guard, and the route was covered with a layer of yellow sand. "Shih-shih jih chih—Chung-kuo chih pu," *TFTC*, 23, 14 (June 25, 1926): 142. These were all honors accorded only to the emperor in the imperial days. Although Chang was small, he had in his reception hall a huge thronelike chair, decorated with a menacing tiger's head mounted on each side.

tion between leaders. Neither side could afford to yield without incurring loss of face. The usual give-and-take and the probing for intentions and resolve necessary for fruitful negotiation became more difficult. Diplomacy on the summit level had a tendency to become rigid because of the militarists' social expectations. Harmony and friendship were considered so important that militarists were often reluctant to disagree openly with each other. Therefore, either difficult problems were evaded or some abstract solution was agreed upon that in fact left the real problems very much unresolved. Most Chinese militarists much preferred to delegate diplomatic responsibilities to their subordinates.

Code of Behavior Toward Other Militarists

In this highly volatile period, during which the issues of war and peace were constantly in the forefront of any militarist's mind, the existence of some "rules of the game" assumed added importance. Every actor needed some criteria for assessing the behavior of others as well as for his own conduct. Although the rules could be modified or become obsolete when external conditions were altered, during much of the period from 1916 to 1928 the behavioral system was largely self-contained and subject to little alteration.

The following are evidence of a regular, discernible pattern of militarist behavior. When a militarist acted, his alternatives were constrained. Adherence to the major rules was necessary for a successful political career; violations entailed major costs, which might include frustration in one's career or physical sanctions by other militarists. There was no central institution to enforce these rules; they derived their force mainly from adverse consequences that followed their violation. In this respect, the system resembled an international system in which laws were enforced by individual members.

In this behavioral system, diplomacy occupied a prominent place in the militarists' relationships during peacetime. Almost all the important militarists stationed personal representatives at one another's headquarters, to perform such routine tasks as gathering information, channeling correspondence between the militarists, participating in ceremonies, and socializing. When a matter of grave importance was involved, a special envoy with greater authority might be sent. The principle of the inviolability of the envoy was scrupulously observed.*

On still other occasions, the militarists held conferences among themselves. The Nanking conference of 1916, the Tientsin conference of 1921, and the conference of Tuan Ch'i-jui, Chang Tso-lin, and Feng Yü-hsiang in 1925 all involved the most powerful militarists in the system. Other conferences involving lesser militarists abounded. No participants in these important conferences were ever threatened with arrest, detention, or bodily harm by the host militarists, even when such action had apparent immediate advantage.†

There are two possible explanations for the nearly universal respect for the immunity of diplomatic personnel and the leaders of other factions. First of all, the militarists shared a particular political subculture, a spirit of political sportsmanship, because of the intricate network of diversified personal ties among them; an act of treachery would be censured by fellow militarists. The immediate advantage to the offender might be offset by almost certain social ostracism, public denunciation, and retaliation. Second and equally important, personal diplomacy was the major means of communication among the militarists, and everyone had an active interest in keeping the channels as open as possible. Thus restraint can be traced to both moral values and fear of physical retaliation.

Additional rules governed conduct in wartime. In the first place, wars were usually preceded by formal declarations; it was generally regarded as a matter of martial honor not to attack without warning. An open challenge followed by a clean fight was considered to be the minimum standard of behavior befitting a militarist. Typically, a barrage of circular telegrams of mutual denunciation would be launched by the principal opponents for quite some time

---

* For instance, prior to the second Chihli-Fengtien war of 1924, Ts'ao K'un thrice dispatched his younger brother to Fengtien to negotiate for peace. To reciprocate, Chang Tso-lin sent one of his in-laws. Had there been any doubt about the envoys' safety, neither militarist would have risked sending a close relative.

† For instance, Chang Tso-lin visited Tuan Ch'i-jui a few days before the 1920 war, when it was already clear that he would join Tuan's enemies. But Tuan made no attempt to kidnap or kill Chang, who went back and declared war against Anhwei.

before actual hostilities began. The war of words was, of course, primarily a psychological war intended to isolate one's opponents and to win over neutrals and waiverers. In this light it is of interest to note that most denunciations gave more weight to the opponent's alleged violation of traditionally defined personal virtues than to the merits or faults of his political stance. Filial impiety, betrayal of friendship, disrespect for seniors, or violation of kinship norms provided much ammunition for such denunciations.[5]

From a practical point of view, the backward state of military technology and severely restricted mobility greatly reduced any prospect of achieving drastic results by surprise attack. Besides, all the militarists kept their armies in a state of maximum mobilization at all times, and a defender could respond at almost the instant he was attacked. Thus while a militarist might have little or nothing to gain by launching an unannounced attack, he might have much to lose by omitting the formal declaration of war.

The militarists were generally rational and pragmatic politicians; they were probably the least ideologically oriented group in modern Chinese politics. They made their political calculations and decided on the important issues of war and peace, not on the basis of personal sentiments but on the basis of relative capabilities. Their behavior suggested an acute awareness that they were playing a kind of "game," that they were drawn into relationships because their respective power positions required it. It is fair to say that militarists were professionally opposed, but not necessarily personally hostile, to each other.* Since the distinction between official and private relationships was fairly clearly demarcated, con-

---

* Probably the most extreme manifestation of the lack of personal animosity was reported to have taken place in Szechwan. According to Chang Jen-min, "The Szechwanese generals were most civilized in their civil wars. For instance, while two opposing armies might be fighting to the death outside Chengtu or Chung-king, their leading generals could be playing mah-jong at the same table. The subordinates from both sides would come to the table and report on the war's progress. After the mah-jong was over, they would still part as friends. The victorious side would immediately provide protection for the families of the defeated generals. If the defeated generals had parents or other senior family members residing in the city, the victorious general would make a personal visit to console them, and to see that they would receive money and gifts every month. Therefore, although civil wars occurred in Szechwan frequently, there was never any personal hatred or cruelty involved." Chang Jen-min, "T'se tung Ch'uan Ch'ien liang sheng t'san chia pei fa chih hui i," *Ch'un ch'iu*, no. 98 (Aug. 1, 1961), p. 3.

flict could be restricted within the official arena. Thus there were two other important rules of behavior: militarists did not kill each other in battle, and the victors did not kill or imprison the defeated opponents.

Consequently, one finds that although numerous big and small wars were fought, the human cost among the militarists remained exceedingly low. An exhaustive review of official records shows that as a result of the four wars fought between 1916 and 1922 (anti-Yüan, anti-restoration, Chihli-Anhwei, Chihli-Fengtien), a total of only 41 persons were accused of war crimes. Of these, only ten were military professionals; the other 31 were party hacks or personal advisers to militarists. Only three of these men were actually arrested, and they were inadvertently caught in the midst of confusion by soldiers rather than by the police or court personnel. These facts leave no doubt that most militarists tried not to be vindictive; they did not want to foreclose any possibility of cooperation in the future.

In spite of the fact that war was almost a daily occurrence, there were only a few significant cases in which a leading northern militarist deliberately eliminated another militarist by murder.* Indeed, when one tabulates cases of violence among militarists between 1916 and 1928, one can find no more than a dozen. And if violence were committed, the pressure from the militarists' subculture could be so great that the violator would soon find that the immediate advantage was more than neutralized by the long-range disadvantages.†

In order to survive in a highly volatile political system in which

---

* These included the execution of Pao Te-ch'üan in 1922 and the assassination of Kuo Chien in 1921 by Feng Yü-hsiang, the execution of Chiang Teng-hsüan by Kuo Sung-lin, and the execution of Kuo Sung-lin by Chang Tso-lin. Feng's action greatly angered Wu P'ei-fu and caused himself a lot of trouble in the Chihli faction. Feng Yü-hsiang, *Wo ti sheng ho*, 2: 167. Kuo Sung-lin's action so infuriated other Fengtien generals that his rebellion collapsed in less than two months from lack of support. Shen I-yün, p. 236.

† This can be shown by the case of the execution of Lu Chien-chang, an important member of the Peiyang Army and a former military governor of Shensi. In 1917–18, Lu waged a personal campaign to persuade other militarists to oppose Tuan Ch'i-jui's military adventures. His crusade produced such a serious divisive effect within the Peiyang ranks that in mid-June 1918 Hsü Shu-cheng, Tuan's protégé, set a trap and executed Lu in his own garden, claiming that Lu had committed treasonous acts. The entire military community was outraged by this act, and neutrals as well as adversaries joined in denouncing Hsü's action as unbecoming to a Peiyang member. Although Tuan had had no prior

Normative Aspects of Military Politics 189

their political interests might complement or conflict with each other rather unpredictably, the militarists had a common interest in minimizing the harshness of the political consequences of conflict. But the definition of common interest was accepted only because most militarists knew each other personally and shared certain basic values and other subcultural traits.

If this hypothesis is plausible, then its opposite should be equally plausible; that is, in the absence of these personal ties and implicit consensus, we would expect a marked increase in personal violence among the militarists.

Our preliminary examination reveals that, between 1916 and 1925, personal violence among southern militarists far exceeded that among northern militarists. Although my research was not exhaustive, it uncovered nineteen important cases of militarists who were killed by other militarists, either through execution or by hired assassins, in addition to many other cases of attempted killings.* Overall, then, militarists in the south seemed to be more inclined to view the physical liquidation of rivals as the most effective way of removing them from the political arena.

The significant differences between the northern and southern militarists in the use of violence may be explained, at least in part, by the basic subcultural and organizational differences between the two groups. The subcultural differences among the provinces in the south were more pronounced than in the north; in the south, physical mobility was more hampered by the mountainous terrain, and differences in dialects and customs were sharper. Therefore, a feeling of mutual trust and common interest was much harder to generate among southern militarists.

There was also greater diversity in the professional backgrounds

---

knowledge, the execution cost the Anhwei faction a great deal of support and contributed significantly to its defeat in the war of 1920. In subsequent years, many militarists felt reluctant to cooperate with Anhwei because Hsü continued to enjoy Tuan's confidence. Finally, in 1925, Hsü himself was kidnapped and summarily executed by Lu's relatives.

* In 1924, for example, when the Kwangsi General Huang Shao-hung was visiting Canton, his residence was attacked by assassins hired by rival Kwangsi militarists. Although Huang managed to escape personally, many of his guards were killed. Huang Shao-hung, 1: 78–80. In Hunan, T'ang Sheng-chih once tried to lay a trap to catch rival militarists by inviting them to a Buddhist retreat at Heng-yang. Most militarists realized his design and declined to attend. One brigade commander from the Hunan 3d Division went and was executed. This incident touched off a civil war in Hunan. Kung Te-po, *Kung Te-po hui i lu*, 1: 149.

of the southern militarists. There was no southern counterpart to the Peiyang establishment, and as a result southern militarists did not undergo the same schooling, training, or work experience. This diversity in subcultural and professional backgrounds made it difficult for them to reach agreement upon a set of common rules of behavior. There was less stability in their expectations; they could not confidently predict what other militarists might do under given conditions. The absence of an implicit consensus on behavioral rules created an atmosphere unfavorable to restraint, hence the propensity toward the use of violence against each other.

One may argue that the diplomatic flexibility exhibited by most militarists in this period was directly attributable to the scrupulous observance of basic rules. That the scrupulous adherence to a nonvindictive policy in dealing with defeated militarists indeed contributed much to diplomatic flexibility was apparent in the coalition patterns among the northerners.*

However, this was not the case in the relations between the KMT and the northern militarists, especially after 1925, when the KMT had grown to be a serious power. The lack of personal ties or similarity of subculture between these two groups removed the incentive to avoid violence. A typical example of the outbreak of violence took place in December 1925, when Chiang Kai-shek sent two regiment commanders on a mission to persuade Sun Ch'uan-fang to cooperate with the KMT. In order to demonstrate to his own northern subordinates his resolve to fight to the bitter end, Sun ordered Chiang's emissaries executed. In retaliation, Chiang executed two of Sun's corps commanders who had been taken prisoner. At approximately the same time, Chiang also accused Sun of deliberately murdering three hundred KMT officers and soldiers who had been captured.[6] These incidents rendered it impossible for the two sides to come to a negotiated settlement and forced them to settle their differences through battle.

Values Affecting Political Legitimacy

One of the most deeply ingrained Chinese beliefs is that their country should be unified. They view their history as an essentially

---

* In 1920, Chihli and Fengtien against Anhwei; in 1922 and 1924, Fengtien and Anhwei against Chihli; and in 1925, Fengtien and Chihli against Kuominchün.

Normative Aspects of Military Politics 191

cyclical pattern, as expressed in the saying, "The land under Heaven will disintegrate after a long period of integration, and will reintegrate after a long period of disintegration." Most Chinese are quite convinced that this is the *only* explanation for China's history, and they cite numerous instances from the vast expanse of their past to prove the point. The principle of national unity has acquired the status of a national consensus, for scholars and peasants alike, and has become an item of unquestioned faith. It forms the frame of reference within which the Chinese mind and behavior find meaning, and no political organization would expect the people to view its authority as legitimate if it dared to challenge this national consensus.

This universal commitment to national unity created a legitimacy crisis for all militarists. They were caught between their desire to preserve their political independence and their inability to repudiate the principle of national reunification.

One way to legitimize authority was to preserve the institutional façade of a centralized national government and profess to exercise authority on its behalf. This explains why the militarists fought so zealously to preserve the sham government in Peking. During the twelve-year period, there were six changes of the head of state and 25 cabinet reshuffles, but the governmental structure was kept intact until 1927. All the powerful factions aspired to control the central government and fully realized the advantages to be gained from such control.

Since Peking had been the capital of China for centuries, it came to be the symbol of political unification and conferred legitimacy on those who occupied it. The control of the central government machinery with all its trappings enabled the ruling militarist faction to denounce other factions as perpetrators of political disorder. Hence, all the militarists who controlled the central government insisted, with a rare and sometimes comical tenacity, on issuing directives to other provinces even though they knew well that the directives would be defied. From time to time, they deliberately provoked the local militarists into defying them and then interpreted the defiance as unpatriotic. Another tactic was that of issuing directives with which other militarists would willingly comply. Hence, after each change of government, the new masters in Peking would renew the appointments of all important incumbent military and civil leaders, which usually amounted to nothing more than acknowledging the positions already held. The ritual of making these appointments was believed to give the militarists an aura of legitimacy and was always scrupulously observed.

The need to enhance legitimacy compelled all militarists with sufficient power and aspiration to strive for national unification. The existence of such a universal value made it impossible for the militarists to be satisfied with limited goals and forced them to compete until one of them achieved the absolute goal of reunification. This provides one major explanation for the great frequency of fighting in the 1920's.

Since there was only one national government and it could be controlled by only one faction at a time, the other militarists still had to face the legitimacy crisis and to find a rationalization for their autonomous status. In some cases, regional support was sought to bolster the legitimacy of their regimes. The militarists very early recognized the utility of regional sentiments and tried to use them to advantage. In so doing, some succeeded in sidetracking the issue of national unity by asserting that they were not at all opposed to national unity but that since political fragmentation was a fact, the second-best policy was to protect the region under their control.*

Those who tried to build a political regime on regional support usually wanted to pursue two goals. Internally, they wanted to achieve autonomy for their territory, and externally they wanted to follow a policy of isolationism.† Whether these two goals could be realized depended on a number of factors. Other things being equal, it seems that regional sentiments were usually heightend

---

* Reflective of this assertion was the so-called federalist movement (*lien-sheng tzu-chih*), or movement for provincial self-government, sponsored by Hunan in the 1920's. Hunan actually drew up a provincial constitution and elected its officials by popular vote. Several other provinces proclaimed their intention to follow suit. It goes without saying that all these acts were the results of manipulation by the governing militarists of each province, who acted to enhance their claims to legitimacy without a genuine commitment to improve the rights and welfare of the people.

† For instance, the Hunan constitution contained an article specifically forbidding outside armies to pass through or be stationed on Hunan soil. Freedom from external intervention was the main feature of the constitution. Li Chien-nung, 2: 547–51.

by the presence of danger—the threat of war with a neighboring power or the existence of outside troops in one's home territory.

But regional sentiments could become a liability when the militarists and their armies were foreign to the region they ruled. A survey of the geographical origins of the ruling militarists during the 1916–28 period shows that the overwhelming majority of them were northerners, especially from the provinces of Chihli, Shantung, and Honan.[7] While North China was always controlled by northerners, southern provinces were also often controlled by northerners. There was a sharp contrast between northern and southern militarists in area controlled: whereas individual southern militarists' territorial control seldom extended beyond one province, northern militarists' territories often extended over several provinces. Thus, of the 25 provinces, only five (Shansi, Kwangsi, Szechwan, Kweichow, Yunnan), plus Manchuria, ever had indigenous regimes; the rest were under the control of northern militarists for most or all of the time.

Two contradictory positions on the question of regional sentiments thus arose. Those consistently invoking these sentiments were all indigenous regimes whose rulers were weak and threatened by powerful neighbors and saw no realistic hope of outward expansion. In these areas, regional support was actively courted to ward off external encroachments. On the other hand, those who condemned regionalism were invariably powerful and ambitious militarists who presided over a carpetbagger regime and wanted to expand into new territories.

We need also to ask whether regionalism was indeed a viable alternative for most militarists. In this connection, one must not confuse the existence of "regional sentiments" with "regionalism" itself. Regional differences and sentiments certainly were quite pronounced in China. But it is also true that the great progress in social, economic, and cultural integration that had been accomplished in the past several centuries was, by the early twentieth century, reinforced by an emerging anti-foreign and anti-imperialist feeling.[8] The people's greatest desire was for nationalism through power and unity, not regionalism through continued division. Regionalism was acceptable only as a temporary device to escape the oppression of civil wars. Where the people were not responsive, regionalism could not strike root. Thus, only in a few cases, such as Shansi and Manchuria, did the military regimes register some success in presenting a clear-cut regional character.*

To sum up, then, the national consensus in favor of unification made the legitimacy of all the militarists' independent regimes vulnerable. The international system is far more stable in this respect, because the principle of territorial integrity and political sovereignty of the actors is universally accepted and honored. In China, however, the entire system of military regimes was regarded as illegitimate. The only system recognized as fully legitimate was a unified nation with a central government in Peking. Since the militarist system itself was illegitimate, the militarists had no right to preserve either their territorial integrity or their political independence. While the smaller military units were able to command loyalty on personal grounds (because national issues were too remote), the powerful ones could not conveniently evade the issue and had to explain why they had a right to exist.

Almost all the prominent militarists at one time or another engaged in sweeping attacks on militarism, advocated disarmament, and condemned the very nature of military regimes—criticisms invariably applied to others but never to themselves. But this type of hypocrisy could not long be sustained; by denigrating others, they also denigrated themselves. In the end, therefore, everyone's legitimacy was undermined.

A direct consequence of the weak legitimacy of the military re-

* That the militarists had no firm ideological commitment to regionalism but rather used it merely as a tactical device to strengthen their legitimacy is best illustrated by the changing attitudes of the leaders of Manchuria on this question. In terms of internal structure, Manchuria undoubtedly constituted a well-defined region. Prior to 1920, the theme that Manchuria constituted a geographically distinct entity was constantly underlined in order to protect its autonomy. Between 1920 and 1922, however, when Fengtien shared control over the Peking government with Chihli, it said little about regionalism. Between 1922 and 1924, when Fengtien was defeated by Chihli and forced to withdraw to its home base, it again declared itself an autonomous regional government and warned others not to interfere with its domestic affairs. After its victory over Chihli in 1924, Fengtien's power swept into Peking and eventually extended to the northern edge of the Yangtze valley. During this period, regionalism was again deemphasized, and the principle of national reunification was used to justify Fengtien's interventionist policy toward other militarists. But when defeated by the KMT in 1927, it once again invoked the sanctity of regional self-government, which it maintained in effect until the Japanese invasion of 1931.

gimes was that dramatic territorial changes were relatively easy. The militarists were identified with their troops more than with territories or populations. But in an age in which prolonged warfare could not be sustained without a solid territorial base, this fact necessarily had the most disturbing effect on the stability of the system.

Another consequence of the weak legitimacy of the military regimes was that of lack of respect for their political control. The weak link between the militarists and their territories, the lack of identity between their regimes and the people they ruled, made it relatively easy to destroy and eliminate them and to impose new regimes.

CHAPTER 9

The Chinese Political System

ONE OF THE primary interests of students of this period is the question of why the KMT succeeded in its Northern Expedition in 1928. From our discussion of organization, recruitment, training, weaponry, and finances, the KMT emerged as the superior force in the Chinese political system. In fact, these are among the reasons most often cited by historians to account for the KMT's final victory over the militarists. If this analysis were sufficient, we would expect to be able to explain the KMT success in 1928 by its clear superiority in some of the attributes previously discussed. Yet, as we will show in a brief examination of the financial and military attributes below, this was not quite the case. It is not enough to make a simple comparison between the KMT, on the one hand, and the militarists, on the other, to explain the reasons behind the KMT's success. It is also necessary to take into account the total political environment and to see what environmental factors helped the KMT.

Thus, we need to analyze Chinese politics in the early Republican era by looking at the total environment, that is, through a systemic view of politics. Our previous analysis of each individual variable or attribute could only provide us with an understanding of the military regimes in their static state. It had little to say about the political process—the interaction among the military factions —and it could not explain the transformation of the political system. Thus it is submitted here that neither the political process nor the causes of political transformation can be adequately understood without an analysis of the politics of militarism in its dynamic form. Only when we study these attributes in terms of

The Chinese Political System

active events—and actors involved in those events—can we appreciate the dynamic characteristics of the politics of militarism and move toward an understanding of the general behavioral patterns of the militarists in systemic terms. The purpose of this chapter, then, is to synthesize the materials presented in the previous chapters into a coherent interpretation of the system and process of the politics of militarism in the form of macroanalysis.

Limitations of a Static Analysis

In our previous discussion of finance (see Chapter 7), the KMT was shown to have been unquestionably superior to most other militarist regimes in the mobilization and rational utilization of physical resources. However, efficient utilization alone was not sufficient; another important variable was scale. In this respect, the KMT was less strong. One can easily think of several regimes that commanded a much larger resource base than the KMT: Chang Tso-lin's Fengtien faction, Sun Ch'uan-fang's five provinces in the Yangtze valley, and possibly even Chang Tsung-ch'ang's Shantung-Chihli territory.

To retain perspective, we must keep in mind that financial reforms were carried out first only in the province of Kwangtung, and then later in Kwangsi. As the KMT's spearhead units moved into enemy territory, the party was not able to swiftly implement a policy of financial integration. In addition, the conditions in these newly conquered territories were so chaotic that occasionally the KMT was forced to rely on the old financial system, which was rife with corruption and inefficiency.

The KMT's financial position improved when its armies gained possession of territories in Chekiang and Kiangsu, especially the city of Shanghai. On the other hand, its expenditures also increased enormously because of stiffer enemy resistance. In the spring of 1927, as military activities intensified, Chiang Kai-shek called for $20 million a month. Yet when all sources of income were tapped, the KMT government found that it could expect a net annual income of about $81 million, sufficient to sustain four months of campaigning at the rate of $20 million a month.

Thus, although the KMT's financial reforms aided in the launching of the Northern Expedition at a time when the resources of many other military regimes had been badly depleted through reckless exploitation, waste, and incompetence, the party was not able to fully mobilize the resources of the newly acquired territories to establish an absolute superiority. Therefore, it is dangerous to overemphasize the financial achievements of the KMT and identify them as the dominant factor in the success of the Northern Expedition. The KMT was never in a position of such overwhelming financial superiority as to make the result of the military contest a foregone conclusion.

On the military side, the picture was basically the same; the KMT's qualitative advantages were significantly offset by quantitative considerations.

On the tactical level, there is no doubt that the training program of the KMT forces was far superior to that of the average militarist and produced more highly motivated and skilled soldiers. On the other hand, we must not forget that the KMT's training program was still basically a crash program, producing a large number of officers and men rather hastily. Consequently, there were many minor weaknesses. For instance, during the very first campaign (the East River campaign) Chiang Kai-shek complained that his soldiers tended to waste ammunition, as if to compete with the enemies in a display of firepower rather than to shoot and kill enemies. On the eve of the decisive battle against Sun Ch'uan-fang, in October 1926, he complained that half the soldiers of the crack first and second divisions could not use their rifle sights properly and fired in all directions. Although the KMT armies generally had a much better reputation among the people and usually won their support, they were nevertheless susceptible to behavior characteristics of the old-fashioned armies.[1]

On the strategic level, great credit must be given to the services rendered by the Soviet advisers. They not only helped establish the Whampoa Academy and the military training program in general; they were responsible for introducing the political commissar system into the KMT fighting units and they assumed operational responsibilities in many of the combat-related departments of the KMT military hierarchy. These Soviet officers, with their experience in World War I, the Russian Revolution, and the subsequent civil war, furnished their Chinese trainees with knowledge in tactics, logistics, and organization. Furthermore, they even guided the KMT generals in mapping their strategy.[2] In the summer of 1925, at the zenith of their influence, over one thousand Soviet advisers were working in China. Within the KMT, Soviet General Blücher assumed the operational leadership of nearly all forces, sometimes issuing directives to the Chinese field commanders.[3]

However, in the fall of 1925, the influence of the Soviet advisers began to decline; during the second eastern expedition, the strategic and operational preparations were largely made by Chinese officers under the leadership of Chiang Kai-shek. On March 20, 1926, the Soviet advisers suffered another serious setback as the result of the Communist-inspired coup.[4] A few months later, the Northern Expedition was launched over the objection of the Soviet advisers. According to Harley F. MacNair, approximately fifteen Soviet advisers under the direction of General Blücher accompanied the KMT forces when the expedition got under way in July 1926.[5] This is a surprisingly small number of Soviet advisers compared with their previous numbers at peak strength and in view of the increasing need for expert advice in the most important expedition the KMT ever launched. One possible explanation is that by that time the Soviet advisers had already lost their influence and their functions were greatly reduced.*

With respect to the KMT's combat performance, we must not forget that its preparation for the expedition was hasty, and that

---

* On this point, there are conflicting positions. As Garthoff reports, Soviet writers in general insisted that Blücher played a very important role in developing the plans for the Northern Expedition, including supply of provisions, ammunition, clothing, communications, medical care, and combat coordination. F. F. Liu, on the other hand, contends that Blücher's contribution was limited mostly to offering criticism of the Chinese-drawn operation plans. He states, "Blücher seldom formulated or made any attempt to direct the expedition's course himself." (Garthoff, pp. 50–52.) The available evidence seems to support Liu's case. For instance, according to the memoirs of Huang Hsü-ch'u, a leading Kwangsi general, after Hunan was taken, a conference was called by Chiang Kai-shek at Changsha in August 1926 to decide the strategy for the second phase of the expedition. Huang did not mention Blücher's name among the participants in the conference. Furthermore, it was Li Tsung-jen's strategy that was finally adopted. Huang Hsü-ch'u, "Chiang Li ti erh tz'u chü wu ching kuo ch'iang ch'ing," *Ch'un ch'iu*, no. 235 (April 16, 1967), pp. 9–10. Finally, any claim that Soviet officers occupied strategic advisory positions in the KMT army corps must be doubted. Huang Shao-hung characterized the chief Soviet adviser assigned to the Kwangsi army in 1926 as "simpleminded" and said that he showed no expertise in military affairs and did not make any contribution to the Kwangsi army. Huang Shao-hung, 1: 124–26.

even in the course of fighting its enemies, the party was not entirely free from internal dissension. It was not until the end of 1925 that the remnants of the armies of Ch'en Chiung-ming, Liu Cheng-huan, and Yang Hsi-min were effectively annihilated; yet in less than six months the Northern Expedition had been launched.

Once the Northern Expedition was under way, continued Communist opposition and interference with its military efforts finally convinced Chiang that the Communists must be purged completely. In April 1927, the rift in the KMT ranks finally burst into the open to become a full-scale civil war within a civil war. The purge of the Communists in Shanghai led to the inevitable split not only between the KMT and the Chinese Communist party but also between the KMT right and the KMT left, and the split seriously undermined the Northern Expedition. In fact, it gave Sun Ch'uan-fang a respite that nearly brought disaster to the KMT forces.

However, the KMT was less than solid even without the Communists. Although the KMT launched the expedition on the strength of eight army corps, its real strength was considerably less impressive. The Second, Third, Fifth, and Sixth Army Corps consisted of a motley group of provincial armies that were stationed in Kwangtung and did not have great combat strength. The real fighting strength of the KMT consisted of the First, Fourth, and Seventh Army Corps. Yet, of these three crack fighting units, only the First Army Corps was fully trained and commanded by Whampoa officers and cadets. The Fourth Army Corps, mostly Cantonese, was affected by the Whampoa program to a lesser, though still important, extent. And the Seventh Army Corps was built independently by the militarists in Kwangsi.

Numerically speaking, the KMT started the Northern Expedition with decisive inferiority; the total strength the party ordered into combat could not have exceeded 60,000 men and 30,000 rifles. Of course, it is true that after some initial successes by the KMT forces in Hunan and Fukien, many provincial militarists in neighboring southern provinces decided to come under the KMT banner. But these new forces could hardly be relied upon to fight the major enemies of the party.

On the other hand, it was a fact that the Whampoa forces (First Army Corps) performed a rather limited role throughout the

The Chinese Political System

course of the Expedition. Much of the fighting during the Expedition was done by the forces of Feng Yü-hsiang, Yen Hsi-shan, Li Tsung-jen, and Li Chi-ch'en. The party's inability to sift these forces before they were incorporated into the National Revolutionary Army created serious problems for the Nationalists' rule in subsequent years.

For our present purpose, the important point is that the Northern Expedition cannot justifiably be presented as a case of the unequivocal military victory of the Whampoa army-building program over the traditional military establishment. It may be true that the contribution made by the Whampoa program was necessary for the victory of the KMT in 1928. The superior fighting ability, the iron-tight discipline, the painstaking political work, and the dedication to a political ideal helped the party forces to demolish their enemies and to win wide popular support wherever they went. Whenever these forces were pitted against the forces of other militarists, there was no doubt that their success could be attributed to their Whampoa background. But, on the other hand, many other militarists also joined the KMT and contributed to the fighting. Some of them were progressive forces (such as Feng Yü-hsiang and Yen Hsi-shan), but others were not qualitatively different from the KMT's enemies. These factors warn us that it would be erroneous to explain the KMT victory in 1928 exclusively in terms of its superiority in military organization or technology. A systemic analysis becomes necessary.

A Systemic Analysis of the Politics of Militarism

A systemic analysis, basically, involves the study of relationships between a number of variables. To apply such an analysis to Chinese politics is to search for a pattern of interactions among several actors and to specify the conditions under which this pattern may persist or change. Systems analysis lends itself most readily to the use of theoretical models, especially models that stress dynamic interaction patterns.

Of course, the Chinese system was an open historical case, not a closed model. The structural nature of the model inescapably places a severe limitation on its scope; it can take into account only the most salient characteristics in the actors' behavioral patterns and must treat any peculiarities of the individual actors as purely incidental from the systemic point of view. In the real world, however, the particular characteristics of individual actors must be given special attention, because they explain the divergent ways in which actors behaved within the system and thereby have profound, albeit indirect, systemic implications. This realization cautions us to avoid dogmatism in applying the model and counsels us to examine closely historic incidents and variables that are important for understanding the actual historical system but that may not be covered by the model.

A model serves an essentially heuristic purpose, after all; it is not a mirror image of reality. It is only a conceptual framework superimposed by us upon reality, a research guide that helps us to organize the mass of amorphous historical data into meaningful, coherent, and related categories. We use a model only because it enables us to understand a particular historical phenomenon from a distinctive perspective in a disciplined way. Concrete historical cases seldom conform completely to any model, and we must be careful not to fall into the trap of rigging facts to conform to the postulates of the model.

The Chinese political system of this period more closely resembled an international system than a national system. In several aspects, the Chinese political scene of 1916–28 is actually strikingly similar to an international system.[6]

Structurally, the Chinese system was composed of a number of independent and autonomous actors, the military factions. For practical purposes, these factions constituted the ultimate or "sovereign" political authority structures. Within each structure, decisions were made by a small group of militarists who were gathered around a leader on the basis of lasting personal ties. Within the hard core of each faction, a high degree of solidarity existed. But the relations of the factions toward each other and toward the entire system cannot be characterized by solidarity.

The number of actors was small enough and they interacted intimately enough for their decisions to be keenly felt by others and to have considerable impact upon the whole system. What happened to a particular actor could bring about fundamental changes in the stability of the entire system.

The relationships between factions were not formalized or institutionalized, nor was there any guarantee that these relationships would be durable. On the contrary, the actors' own behavior determined their relationships to other actors as well as their status in the system. Both were informal and subject to sudden change.

In addition, since each actor was the final guardian of its own preservation, its decisions had strategic connotations. The actors could not take their interrelationships or even their very existence for granted. Consequently, the Chinese factions had to employ diplomacy extensively; they attempted to bargain, using persuasion and threats; they tried to utilize alliances to win friends and warn enemies; and finally, they went to war when other means of achieving political objectives failed.

These features render the Chinese system appropriate for analysis as a "balance of power" system. But did the Chinese system operate as a balance-of-power system? Before we attempt to answer this question, we need to clarify briefly what we mean by a balance-of-power system.[7]

Generally speaking, there are two different views regarding the balance-of-power concept. The first, or "natural law," view maintains that balance will eventually be restored whenever there are several actors in the system, each struggling for the maintenance, and probably the improvement, of security. It implies the presence of an invisible hand that would adjust the balance whenever it is tipped toward one direction or another. The actors themselves do not have to be conscious of this balancing mechanism and are usually concerned with maximizing their immediate interests. The balancing process is automatic and requires no conscious human effort; it is deterministic and inevitable. This interpretation of balance of power is reflected in most traditional international political literature.[8]

The second view allows for parts to be consciously played by the actors. In this approach to the balance-of-power system, at least some actors must agree on the desirability of keeping the system in operation. Whenever they spot a tendency toward imbalance, they will act intelligently to correct the tendency, by diplomacy if possible, by force if necessary. According to this view, it is possible for an actor actively and conscientiously to pursue a balance-of-power policy.[9]

Neither of these views specifies the manner in which the mechanisms of the system function. Therefore, balance of power as traditionally used is a descriptive term devoid of precise meaning. It does not specify variables. When every situation involving the coexistence of several actors is characterized as a balance-of-power situation, the term fails to distinguish the prominent properties of one power situation from another. It does not allow for the possibility of non–balance-of-power situations, nor does it provide for transformation from one power relationship to another.

The balance-of-power concept can be used profitably in our inquiry only if we can make its definition more rigorous and more operational. In order to do this, we need to utilize a model with explicit and logically tight rules. The applicability of such a model is drastically limited in comparison with the general theories of balance of power. But limitation is precisely its dominant virtue, because it allows us to talk about balance of power in more concrete and precise terms.

The model that is most useful for our purpose is that proposed by Morton A. Kaplan in *System and Process in International Politics*. Kaplan's balance-of-power system is characterized by the existence of a number of actors (divided into two categories—essential and nonessential) and the absence of effective "supranational" institutions. The actors are free and independent agents, primarily concerned with their own preservation and other temporal interests. Aside from unforeseeable parametric changes such as technological breakthroughs or external aggression, the equilibrium of the system is maintained or disrupted by the actors only. The model contains six essential behavioral rules that the actors, or at least a significant number of them, must observe when they interact in order to maintain the equilibrium of the system: (1) Act to increase capabilities but negotiate rather than fight. (2) Fight rather than pass up an opportunity to increase capabilities. (3) Stop fighting rather than eliminate an essential national actor. (4) Act to oppose any coalition or single actor that tends to assume a position of predominance with respect to the rest of the system. (5) Act to constrain actors who subscribe to supranational organizing principles. (6) Permit defeated or constrained essential national actors to reenter the system as acceptable role partners or act to bring some previously unessential actor within the essential actor classification. Treat all essential actors as acceptable role partners.[10]

The Chinese Political System

These rules are couched in strategic terms and carry imperative implications. There is an inner equilibrium among these rules, which constitute the minimum requirements for the maintenance of a balance-of-power system. The rules are interdependent; the violation of one will lead to the violation of another, and may eventually undermine the system as a whole. Equilibrium must also be maintained between essential rules and other variables of the system as well as between the system and its environment or setting. Disruption of equilibrium in any of these areas may cause the system to undergo fundamental changes in its characteristic behavior and transform it into another system.[11]

Thus Kaplan's model allows for the possibility that the system may break down and political behavior may take other forms. The specification of the essential rules and other variables not only permits a more succinct analysis of the system itself, but also provides us with a basis on which to achieve some level of predictive power with reference to conditions under which the system will change its nature, i.e. transformation rules.

Furthermore, its six essential rules suggest that the model places more emphasis on the political process of attaining balance than on the point at which perfect balance exists. In this way, the model is dynamic instead of static. It arranges the political actors' behavior on a continuum ranging from balance to imbalance, rather than dichotomizing it into either balance or imbalance. Similarly, conflicts and their resolution by violence are not viewed as anomalies but as an integral part of the balancing process itself. Thus the occurrence of wars as a means of redressing balance can be viewed as a sign of the adaptability of the system.

It needs to be reemphasized here that the choosing of the Kaplan model does not mean that we are committed to viewing the Chinese case as a perfect historical balance-of-power situation; we are simply interested in using the model to specify a number of conditions conducive to stability in such a situation, and to demonstrate how the differences between the historical case and the model account for the instability of the former. The utility of the model extends only as far as it explains historical data meaningfully.

Obviously, the true historical actors did not conduct their behavior in order to satisfy the essential requirements of any intellectual model. We are faced with the problem of how to determine the extent to which the actors actually understood these conditions of stability. Apparently the stability of any system will be enhanced if most actors understand the system, although how much understanding is necessary for the maintenance of stability may vary from one historical case to another. In the Chinese case, it must be pointed out that the actors shared the national belief that the unification of the country was beyond ideological dispute. But this fact should not lead us to dismiss the balance-of-power model on the ground that the Chinese system represented a "terminal" system. It must be remembered that while national unification had long been a powerful political force throughout China's long history, there had also been prolonged periods of division. The "Six Dynasties" period, for example, lasted so long that it constituted a historical epoch by itself. Therefore, while it is true to say that Chinese political actors always had unification as a goal, it is more pertinent to examine how they tried to achieve that goal. Although the Chinese militarists of the early twentieth century all envisaged the end of the system, each of them envisaged this end on his own terms. The terms guided their political behavior, which in turn determined why the system lasted only as long as it did and how it became transformed.

In our application of the model to the Chinese system, the military factions are defined as the political actors. These actors are divided into the two categories—essential and nonessential actors—on the basis of their capabilities, as discussed in the previous chapters (organizational, military, and economic); the more powerful factions are treated as essential actors, and the less powerful as nonessential actors.

In the following sections, the Chinese militarist system has been divided into three phases: 1916–20, 1920–24, and 1924–28. Each phase exhibited a distinct behavioral pattern and was separated from the next phase by a major event that significantly altered that pattern. In dealing with each phase, we will first discuss how its behavioral pattern developed and then suggest certain points of general theoretical interest.

The First Phase: 1916–1920

The important political events of the period after the death of Yüan Shih-k'ai that led to the emergence of the military factions have already been described in Chapters 2 and 3 and need not be repeated. Here we shall discuss the important characteristics of this formative phase of the militarist system.

First, the atomization of the country almost immediately gave rise to a pattern of limited local reintegration. Although the small militarists cherished their newly acquired authority and autonomy, the more powerful militarists (especially the provincial military governors) were unhappy to see their territorial domains fragmented and their privileges infringed upon. They were determined to reclaim their authority and to consolidate their control over provincial internal affairs, even if they had to use force.

The task of internal consolidation was a formidable one, and in most cases consumed nearly all the militarists' energy. The few who were capable of making inroads into other provinces limited their activities to their most immediate neighbors. T'ang Chi-yao had some success in extending his control over Kweichow and part of Szechwan but was eventually driven back to Yunnan. Only Chang Tso-lin was able to entrench himself in a large area, the whole of Manchuria.

Second, most militarists possessed meager capabilities in this early phase of the system. An infantry division, roughly equal to about fifteen thousand men, was a highly respectable military instrument even in 1918–19. The whole fight at Hunan was dominated by Wu P'ei-fu's 3d Division. Other northern military units that boasted of divisional strength and that looked formidable also took part in the Hunan campaign, but their incompetence was exposed as soon as they came into contact with the shabbily clad, ill-fed, and poorly equipped Hunanese troops.

Thus, this was a phase of high intraregional but low interregional activities. The militarists generally lacked both the energy and the capabilities to interact with each other. Without interaction, there was no cause for conflict. Therefore, this period was marked by the absence of large-scale hostilities. The militarists were more concerned with their internal affairs than with affairs affecting the system (country) as a whole. Though they sometimes expressed opinions on national issues, they were seldom able to go any further.

The campaign launched by Tuan against Hunan might seem to contradict this analysis. Actually, however, Tuan's activities are best explained by these two factors. Tuan did not have a personal military machine even as late as the end of 1917; he was able to dominate politics on the national level precisely because no other militarists were powerful enough to intervene.

Furthermore, the Hunan campaign was not really a great exception to the absence of large-scale conflict that otherwise characterized the phase. In terms of both scale and intensity, the battles fought in Hunan were probably as limited as those within Szechwan and along the Kwangtung-Fukien borders. All of them demonstrated the meager resources of the participants. But the Hunan campaign did have political significance. It was the painful experience acquired through the execution of the campaign that prompted Tuan to seek outside assistance to establish an independent and personal military force.

Tuan's political ambition and the many manifestations of this ambition alarmed other militarists. It was the reaction to Tuan's aggressive policy that accelerated the formation of centers of counterforce. The Hunan campaign presented the militarists with a pressing need to organize themselves into more cohesive groups and ushered the militarist system into its second phase, in which several groups of militarists decided to act together over a fairly long period of time.

The Second Phase 1920–1924

When the system entered its second phase in 1920, the actors had already assumed definite shape. By the first half of 1920, the distribution of their power was approximately as follows:

Fengtien	Fengtien, Heilungkiang, Kirin
Anhwei	Northern Chihli (including Peking), Shantung, Jehol, Suiyuan, Shensi, Anhwei, Chekiang, Fukien
Chihli	Southern Chihli, Honan, Kiangsu, Hupeh
KMT	Kwangtung, Kwangsi, Yünnan, Kweichow
Szechwan	Szechwan
Hunan	Hunan
Shansi	Shansi

Of these factions, the first three, Fengtien, Anhwei, and Chihli, were definitely in the essential actor category. In terms of territorial size and aggregate strength, the KMT was surely on equal footing with any of the first three actors; however, its internal divisions had immobilized it during this period, and it did not yet belong in the essential actor category.

The Anhwei-Chihli war of 1920 marked the first large-scale con-

The Chinese Political System

flict. It also marked the first time that two actors (Chihli and Fengtien) had entered into an alliance to block what in their view was a hegemonial actor (Anhwei). Thus events with a system-wide dimension now took place. The various militarists had by now established themselves in their territories firmly enough to begin looking outward and to become concerned with the overall distribution of power within the system.

Although the scale of hostilities was limited, the defeat of Anhwei greatly reduced its capabilities. It lost control of the central government and with the dissolution of the Anfu Club it also lost control of the parliament. The Northwestern Frontier Army was totally destroyed. Anhwei also lost an enormous territory: of the eight provinces it had controlled or influenced at the peak of its power, only Chekiang and Fukien remained firmly in its camp. As an actor, Anhwei was greatly diminished and gradually began to play the role of a nonessential actor.

The two victors divided the spoils. A new cabinet was formed with a premier acceptable to both factions (Chin Yün-p'eng was related to Chang Tso-lin by marriage and was Wu P'ei-fu's most respected teacher and early patron). Fengtien acquired Jehol, Chahar, and Suiyuan, while Chihli gained Shantung, Shensi, Honan, and Anhwei.

By the end of 1921, the relationship between Chihli and Fengtien had gradually deteriorated. However, there was still one field, national politics, in which they had smooth cooperation. Up to this time the Chin Yün-p'eng cabinet had enjoyed the blessing of both factions. Since Chin's appointment reflected the desire of both actors to be conciliatory toward each other in dividing the spoils of the Peking government, he was careful to assume a neutral attitude and acted on important issues only after securing concurrence from both.

However, almost since its formation the cabinet had been in financial jeopardy. The finances of the government deteriorated, and in November 1921, clerks in the Ministry of Education and the Peking judiciary stopped working because the government had not paid their salaries.[12] The situation apparently called for some fundamental solution. Chang Tso-lin seized this opportunity and maneuvered to have his own choice, Liang Shih-i, named to form the new cabinet (December 1, 1921).

Fengtien's choice had never had Chihli's full support, but what

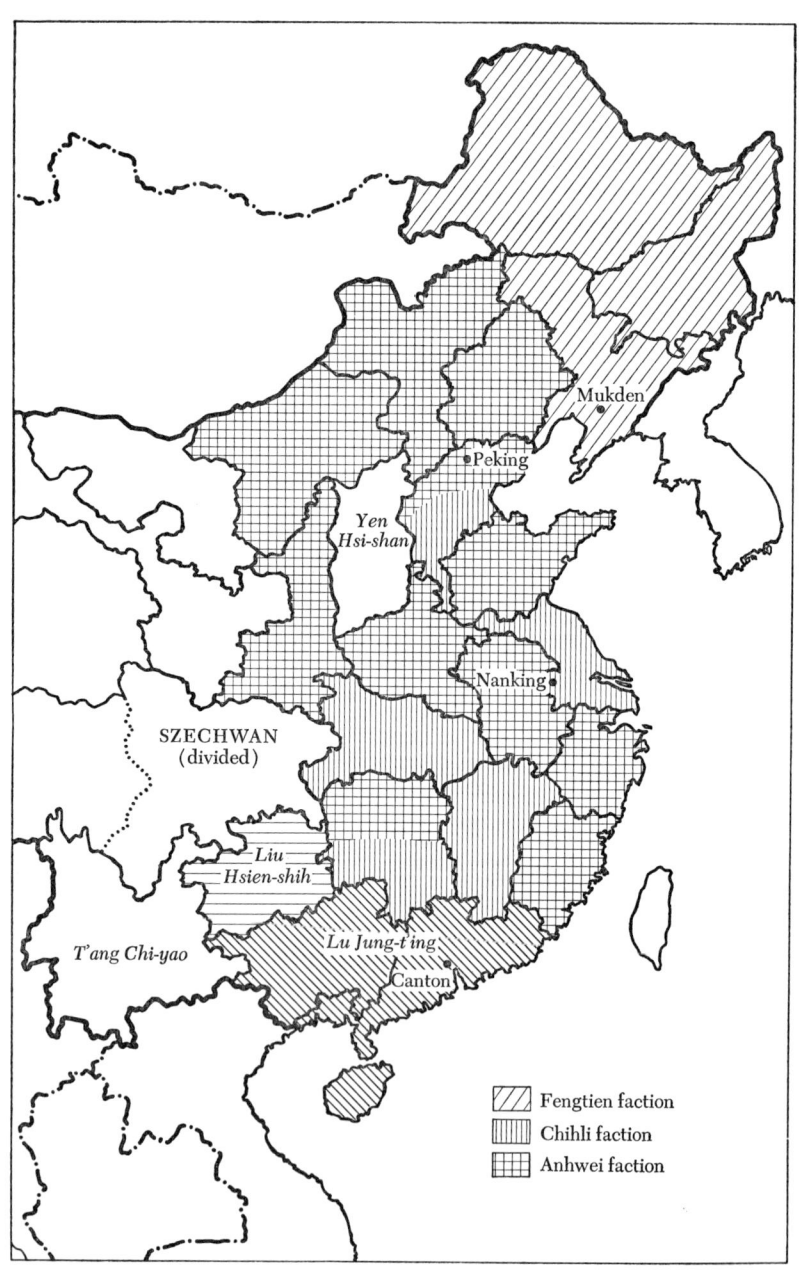

Distribution of factional power in China, 1920, prior to the Chihli-Anhwei War

angered Chihli most and drove it to challenge the new cabinet's authority was the government's failure to pay the military expenses previously promised to Wu.[13] Immediately, on January 5, 1922, Wu issued a circular telegram opposing the Liang cabinet and charging it with treason. A supporting chorus of protests came from the eight military governors in the Chihli camp. Faced with this stiff opposition, Liang took sick leave on the 25th, requesting his foreign minister to act in his absence.

But Wu was not satisfied with the removal of Liang; in February he again attacked the cabinet, charging the Minister of Finance with embezzlement. Chang Tso-lin now had no reason to doubt that Wu was trying to topple the entire cabinet supported by Fengtien. During the previous two years Wu had been very reticent about national politics. His sudden outburst, coming after his troops had undergone a long period of intensive training, could not but be an ominous sign. Considered in conjunction with Chihli's greatly increased power, Wu's recent behavior could easily be taken by Fengtien as a prelude to an attempt to pursue a hegemonial policy, to dominate national politics, and to carry out a policy of national unification by force.

In order to counter the threat from Chihli, Fengtien sent emissaries to Kwangtung in February 1922 to seek cooperation from Sun Yat-sen. The KMT agreed to launch its own drive against Kiangsi. Next, Fengtien attempted to induce the Anhwei remnants in Chekiang and Fukien to join it to make a tripartite alliance.[14] On the last day of March, Chang Tso-lin announced that his 27th Division would be transported from the Fengtien area to the vicinity of Peking to "bolster" the defense of the capital. He apparently felt strong because of the new allies he had won and was determined to exact some major concessions from Chihli. In the first half of April, Ts'ao Yin, the younger brother (both Ts'ao brothers were related to Chang by marriage), twice journeyed to Fengtien to seek a peaceful solution. But Chang would not budge unless the Liang cabinet was restored and Wu and other militarists stopped meddling in national politics. This was much more than Chihli was prepared to concede, and the negotiations soon broke off. On April 25, Chihli made a formal denunciation of Chang Tso-lin, and four days later war broke out.

In several respects, the first Chihli-Fengtien war of 1922 dif-

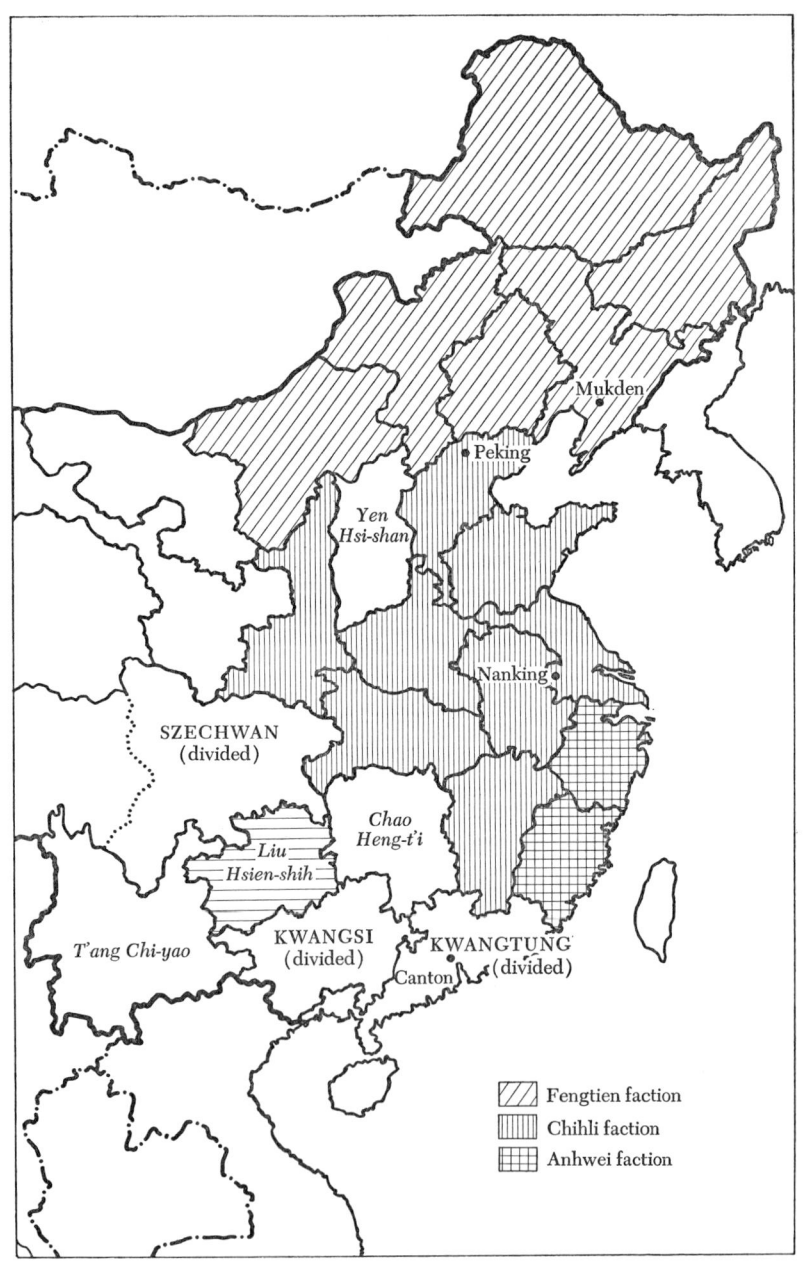

Distribution of factional power in China, 1922, on the eve of the First Chihli-Fengtien War

fered markedly from the Anhwei-Chihli war of 1920. Substantially larger numbers of troops engaged in actual combat. It was estimated that at least 100,000 soldiers from each side were involved in active fighting. Defections were less frequent and casualties were high.[15]

The combat zone was considerably enlarged too. Fighting spread to nearly the entire border area between the warring factions. The concentration of troops on such a grand scale and with such speed and orderliness could not have been accomplished in 1920.

After a week of fierce fighting, Fengtien was defeated and driven beyond the Great Wall. Although the inferiority of the Fengtien military establishment was the primary reason for its defeat, another reason was the failure of the tripartite alliance to materialize. Sun's inability to fulfill his promise, in turn, made it inadvisable for Chekiang to take unilateral action, since it was surrounded by Chihli militarists on three sides.

The victory was a boost for Chihli in general and for Wu in particular. The provinces of Jehol, Chahar, and Suiyuan were added to Chihli's territory. The revolt of Honan was quickly smashed, bringing that province closer to the faction than before. Now Chihli was the supreme military power in the system. Fengtien could do little for the time being except nurse its wounds. The KMT was as weak as ever; the Anhwei remnants were only too happy that they escaped unscathed from the war and did not dare to stir up any more trouble. The three other nonessential actors were all anxious for Chihli to leave them alone.

If the Chihli militarists had shown any caution before 1922 about interfering with national politics, they did not need to worry now. Ten days after the victory, several junior Chihli militarists proposed to restore Li Yüan-hung to the presidency and to reconvene the parliament of 1917 to elect a vice-president. After another four days Ts'ao, Wu, and a train of Chihli dignitaries sent a joint telegram to all the provinces requesting them to express their position on the proposal.[16] The message was too clear to miss. On June 2, President Hsü duly resigned and left the capital. In less than a week, Li was back in office under the aegis of Chihli power. Thereafter, the composition of the cabinets was dictated by Chihli, and their policies followed its orders closely.

By January 1923, however, Chihli was no longer satisfied with merely controlling the cabinet. Ts'ao K'un was now intent on taking the presidency for himself and spent a large sum of money to bribe the parliamentary members. In the next few months, Li's tenure suddenly became a point of heated debate. On June 6, several hundred army officers and policemen surrounded the presidential mansion to demand payment of their long overdue salaries. On the 9th, Peking policemen started a general strike. Three days later, the Inspector General of the Army, Feng Yü-hsiang, and the Commander of the Peking Garrison, Wang Huai-ch'ing, resigned and declared that they would no longer be responsible for maintaining order in the capital. Li, finally forced to conclude that he was no longer wanted, fled to Tientsin.[17] After a period of caretaker government, Ts'ao K'un was duly elected and inaugurated as president in October.

The whole episode aroused a great furor in the country, since this was the first time since Yüan Shih-k'ai's era that the members of parliament were openly paid for their votes. Fengtien, the KMT, and Anhwei issued separate statements opposing the illegally elected president. But the war between Chihli and its opponents that was so widely anticipated failed to materialize for almost another year. Several factors may have accounted for this delay.

First, since the end of the 1922 war there were indications that a rift was slowly developing between two rival cliques within Chihli. The Tientsin-Paoting clique was responsible for engineering Li's ouster and Ts'ao's election. The Loyang clique, centered around Wu P'ei-fu, was not opposed in principle to Ts'ao's seeking the presidency but was convinced that the first thing to do was to unify the country. Their differences on these priorities created a serious strain on the internal cohesion of the faction.[18] Therefore, after the election, Ts'ao handled Chihli's relations with other factions with great caution, probably to gain time to smooth over the internal division and to placate Wu in particular.

Second, Chihli was making some progress in Fukien and might not have wanted to push the pace of its expansion too fast. In March 1923, Sun Ch'uan-fang and Chou Yin-jen were sent to seize Fukien from Anhwei. They were met by strong resistance and had to fight their way into the province. Understandably, Chihli did not want to make enemies on more than one front.

Third, from Chihli's point of view, the most dangerous challenge to its power would come only from Fengtien. The steady improve-

The Chinese Political System

ment of the Fengtien army after 1922 obviously caused Chihli grave concern. Between August and October of 1923, Chihli sent several emissaries to try to persuade Fengtien to renounce its autonomy and to rejoin the government.[19] And when Fengtien issued a stern denunciation on October 31 against Ts'ao's presidency and threatened to form a separate government, Chihli conveniently ignored it. These events suggest that Chihli realized it had more urgent business to attend to and was extremely careful not to get into direct confrontation with Fengtien at that time.

Despite its bold words, Fengtien was equally cautious. Although its military program was geared to a final confrontation with Chihli, at the end of 1923 that program had been in execution for barely over a year. However much Fengtien would have liked to aid Anhwei in Fukien, its army had not been sufficiently overhauled to meet the test. Furthermore, if Fengtien moved against Chihli, it could not expect any help from the KMT, which was occupied throughout 1923 with fighting southern militarists on its own home ground. The party itself was also undergoing a thorough reorganization. These two trains of events made the KMT unable to turn its attention to its external relations with other actors. Thus, Fengtien, with no possibility of forging a second tripartite alliance with the same actors, decided to bide its time and delay the final showdown.

Although war did not break out immediately, the tension was at best only temporarily subdued. Chihli's policy of dominating the central government and seeking to expand its territorial domain was bound to lead to a collision with the other essential actors. A year after the inauguration of Ts'ao, the objective situation had changed substantially. Fengtien had gained one more year to train its troops. The KMT had founded its own military academy, and Sun Yat-sen was again planning for a northern expedition. Although the military academy had not produced a significant number of soldiers, and Sun's plan to march north was to prove yet another futile effort, his determination might have been a great encouragement to Fengtien. On the other hand, Chihli had now firmly established its control over Fukien and was in a much more comfortable position to deal with Fengtien. Therefore, all three actors were in an expectant mood. What was needed was an explosive issue.

Precisely such an issue was provided by Chekiang. When Sun

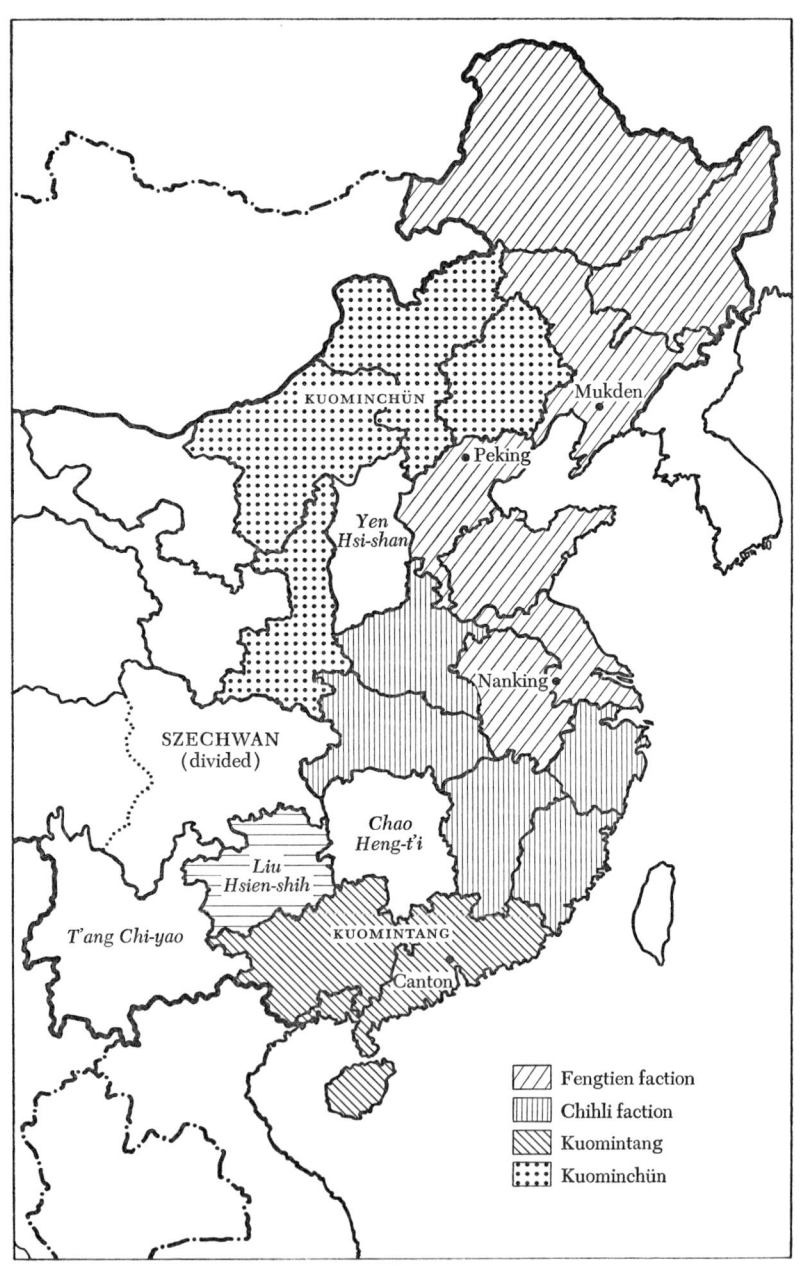

Distribution of factional power in China, 1924, at the conclusion of the Second Chihli-Fengtien War

The Chinese Political System

Ch'uan-fang invaded Fukien, the defeated Anhwei troops retreated into neighboring Chekiang and were incorporated into the latter's command system.[20] This move considerably strengthened its position against the southern provinces of the Chihli faction. In August 1924, Kiangsu, Kiangsi, Anhwei, and Fukien (now a member of the Chihli faction), delivered an ultimatum to Chekiang demanding the disbanding of these troops. Chekiang refused, and war broke out on September 1.

In retrospect, it is difficult to understand how Chekiang dared to defy the superior power of Chihli, unless it had secured Fengtien's pledge of assistance. In any event, on September 5, Chang Tso-lin announced that his army would support Chekiang. On the same day, Sun Yat-sen announced that he would lead a northern expedition in a matter of days. On September 17, Chihli set up the command structure to wage war against Fengtien. By October 13, the Chihli-Anhwei war had ended with the total defeat of Anhwei, and Chekiang was conquered by Sun Ch'uan-fang. In the north, Chihli and Fengtien were locked in fierce combat. Then suddenly, on October 23, news came that Feng Yü-hsiang of Chihli had clandestinely returned from the front, occupied the capital, and taken over the central government. This shattered the morale of the Chihli troops. Within days, their front was broken and the whole army was routed. Wu P'ei-fu made a desperate attempt to rescue the capital, but failed and fled to the south with a few thousand soldiers. On November 3, hostilities ceased on all fronts.[21] The period of Chihli's domination was formally ended, although the faction still retained a large territory in the Yangtze valley.

With the defeat of Chihli, the second phase of the system was brought to a conclusion. As we noted earlier, the beginning of this phase marked the move toward a balance-of-power system. A comparison of some of the characteristics of this phase with the rules of the Kaplan model will reveal the similarities between them.

The Chinese actors followed the first rule (Act to increase capabilities but negotiate rather than fight) very closely. The increase in the total number of soldiers, the intensification of the fighting, the mounting casualties, and the expansion of the conflict zones, as well as the ever larger number of troops marshaled by the chief antagonists, all pointed to the fact that the war-making machinery of the actors was being refined constantly. The training of the

War Participation Army of Anhwei, the training program of Chihli in Loyang, and the reform of the Fengtien army between 1922 and 1924 are specific examples of the great effort the factions put into their military establishment. The actors' primary interest in the competitive increase of capabilities was not to achieve parity with other actors, however, but to gain a margin of superiority.

Yet the Chinese militarists did not resort to war the moment the balance was disturbed. During a crisis, the actors involved always demonstrated a willingness to negotiate for a peaceful settlement. Thus all three major wars were preceded by a period of tension during which the main antagonists or some third party tried to resolve the points of conflict at a conference table. Only after negotiation failed did the parties go to war. In 1920, the refusal of Anhwei to relinquish its control over the War Participation Army was the direct cause of war. In 1922, Fengtien was determined to retain the Liang Shih-i cabinet because this appeared to be the only way to compensate for its relative disadvantage in territorial expansion in comparison with Chihli. When both actors stood their ground, war broke out. In 1924, Anhwei (Chekiang) was unwilling to disband a part of its army and Fengtien was unwilling to see another aggrandizement of Chihli's power at the expense of Anhwei. Again the consequence was war. In every one of these instances, the actors refused to forgo an opportunity to increase capabilities and chose to fight.

The actors apparently did not feel that they should stop fighting rather than eliminate an essential national actor, as shown by the diminution and eventual elimination of Anhwei as an essential actor. However, the weakening of Anhwei coincided with the gradual strengthening of the KMT, which helped maintain the flexibility of alignment among the essential actors.

In three specific instances, the Chinese actors proved their opposition to the hegemonial actor by the formation of coalitions: Anhwei in 1920 and Chihli in both 1922 and 1924. The status quo actors were able to enter into an alliance quickly and to oppose the hegemonial actor. In 1920 the alliance included Fengtien and Chihli, in 1922 and 1924 the alliance included Fengtien, Anhwei, and the KMT. These actors were individually weaker than, and more or less the intended victims of, the hegemonial actors. Therefore, in every instance there was a defensive alliance of the weak against the strong.

The Chinese Political System

Several factors made the observance of this rule possible in the Chinese system. First of all, the internal structure of the actors was conducive to action rather than inaction, which greatly simplified alignment policies. Since a faction's decision-making body was composed of a very small core of individuals of similar perspective, it was easy for it to recognize its common interests and to act accordingly.

Second, the existence of a special "subculture" with a network of intricate personal relationships and a set of commonly shared values greatly improved mutual understanding among them. Every militarist was an acceptable ally. Because the actors were concerned with the requirements of self-interest and not with persons, they were able to view the power developments within the system without passion and to make and unmake alliances in accordance with short-term interests to counter specific and immediate threats from hegemonial actors. Thus, although Anhwei had been Fengtien's enemy in 1920, neither of them found any difficulty in working together against Chihli in 1922 and 1924.

Still another factor that enhanced the flexibility of alignment was the absence of ideologically committed actors. The actors did not set out to regulate the activities of the system according to some preconceived blueprint, and, in fact, even the KMT's repeated efforts to portray itself as a distinct ideological actor aroused little alarm among the northern militarists. It must be remembered that the reorganization of the KMT came only after 1923–24; during a great part of this second phase, the KMT acted no differently than its northern counterparts. At one time or another, it had formed or attempted to form alliances with virtually every essential actor in the system, in spite of ideological opposition. The militarists were by instinct and by training pragmatic politicians. They themselves were masters at exploiting the propaganda value of whatever principles might benefit their personal cause, and they found it hard to believe that others might behave differently. This belief, which was periodically confirmed and encouraged by the KMT's alignment preferences, helped to maintain the atmosphere of mutual acceptability of all actors in matters of alignment.

Yet readiness to work with any actor in the system for short-term purposes was a necessary but not a sufficient condition. All actors needed adequate and quick information to help recognize a change in power distribution in the system, correctly interpret other actors' deeds and motives, identify the hegemonial actor, and take countervailing measures as quickly as possible.

In the Chinese system, information was improved by two factors. First, the makeup of the groups of militarists was quite stable and constant. As time went on, these men came to know more about each other's strengths and weaknesses, personal styles, and military strategies. As long as the same personalities continued to interact with each other, a certain degree of efficiency in information accumulation and retrieval and of policy consistency could be expected. Second, the actors made conscientious efforts to establish channels of communication among themselves as well as within their own domain. Exchanges of emissaries or special envoys, third parties, and occasional summit meetings were utilized to collect information. Consequently, the chance of misjudgment resulting from mistaken or unobtainable information about the other actors was minimized.*

Of course, the availability of information did not necessarily guarantee that accurate judgments would be made. It did mean that most militarists, especially the more important ones, were unlikely to feel constrained in the process of their decision making by lack of information and that they were then provided with a basis for assessing the situation realistically and taking responsive action. As the history of the second phase shows, none of the major wars was brought about by mutual misunderstanding or insufficient information; rather, the wars were the outcome of coolheaded deliberation and negotiation.

The fact that three major wars took place within five years bears testimony to how effective the balancing mechanism of the Chinese system was. The second phase was, therefore, actually a period of dynamic equilibrium.

The nonessential actors, on the other hand, demonstrated the

---

* The Chinese militarists seem to have been very poor at keeping secrets. Many subordinates were ready to leak top secrets for cash or for the sake of friendship. The telegraphic service was also notoriously ineffective in guarding information. Furthermore, there were newspaper reporters in large cities to observe troop movements, important visits, and other indications of tension. Consequently, most wars were preceded by days of forecasts and rumors in the papers. Even the supposedly ultrasecret plot of Feng Yü-hsiang to overthrow the Chihli government in Peking was reported in the papers several days before it was carried out.

The Chinese Political System

greatest reluctance to participate in the system's regulatory process during this phase. Because of the wide discrepancy in capabilities between the essential and the nonessential actors, the latter were always fearful that their active participation in the system might jeopardize their security. It was not accidental that the rise of Chihli's power coincided with the beginning of the "movement for provincial constitutionalism" or "federalism." In their desperate attempt to remain within the system, the nonessential actors turned to the exploitation of latent regional sentiments as a shield. This entire movement, however, was a hoax, a scheme adopted to meet temporary defense needs. The staunchest advocates of this movement, Hunan and Szechwan, did not hesitate to encroach upon other provinces' rights to self-government once they felt adequately strong to do so. Furthermore, this movement was the most convenient instrument for the ruling militarists in a faction to perpetuate their power. Without exception, the movement was sponsored by the militarists in power. After the installation of a constitutional government, the same people remained in power, now sanctioned by a fictitious "election." Provincial constitutionalism was thus exploited not only to protect the militarists from outside pressure but also to enhance their claim to legitimacy internally.

Behind this legalistic shield, many of the nonessential actors declined to take an active part in the regulatory process of the system and shifted the main burden to the shoulders of the essential actors. This undoubtedly constituted a strain on the system. But the strain was not yet serious in this particular phase because of the essential actors' awareness of their regulatory role.

The KMT was not opposed as an actor with supranational organizing principles because, as we noted earlier, the KMT could not yet be taken seriously in this role. In addition, the KMT's internal weakness made it unnecessary for the other actors to take immediate action against it. From the point of view of maintaining the militarist system, it would have been ideal had some preventive action been taken against the KMT's reorganization program, for in the long run that program was to have enormous repercussions on the system. However, at this time the task was not yet urgent, and the neglect of other actors to do so did not constitute an immediate threat to the balance of the system.

The actors partially failed to permit a defeated essential actor to revive its status by eliminating Anhwei. However, since the elimination of Anhwei came at the conclusion of this phase, it did not affect the operation of the system. The elimination of this one essential actor was accompanied at this time by the ascendency of two other actors to essential-actor status. The rise of the KMT and the Kuominchün resulted from a blending of chance with their own efforts rather than from any actions by the other actors. Nonetheless, their presence did much to mitigate the potential threat to the system posed by the violation of this rule.

The Third Phase: 1924–1928

The system entered a new phase with the conclusion of the 1924 war, which had drastically changed the scene in China. Chihli had lost a large army, as well as the presidency. Most important, it had lost a vast territory, including Suiyuan, Jehol, Chahar, Chihli, Shantung, Honan, Chekiang, and Fukien. The imprisonment of Ts'ao K'un and the near-total defeat of Wu P'ei-fu left the faction temporarily leaderless.

The Kuominchün emerged as a new actor. Feng Yü-hsiang and his co-conspirators of the 1924 coup all had previously been Chihli generals. The Kuominchün was given a free hand in the areas along the Peking–Hankow and Peking–Suiyuan railways. It occupied part of Chihli, Honan, Shensi, Kansu, Jehol, Suiyuan, and Chahar as a reward for its contribution in the war.

The lion's share of the spoils went to Fengtien. It acquired the areas along the Peking–Tientsin–Pukow railway as well as a part of Chihli (including the military governorship of the province), Shantung, and Anhwei to prepare for an eventual thrust into the Yangtze area. The defeat of Chihli made Fengtien the strongest actor in the system; its army of 200,000 men was the best equipped in the country.

Although the division of territories was intended to allow the victors to expand in different directions, trouble began almost immediately after the war ended. Despite the fact that Tientsin had been taken by Kuominchün, Fengtien troops marched into the city, pressured the pro-Kuominchün military governor to resign, and disbanded his troops.[22] On November 24, 1924, another 10,000 Fengtien soldiers were sent to occupy Peking jointly with the Kuominchün. On the same day, Feng Yü-hsiang announced his intention of resigning from the command of the Kuominchün to travel abroad, apparently because of mounting pressure from Fengtien. His resignation was refused by the regent government that had been formed after the war by mutual agreement between Fengtien and the Kuominchün and was headed by Tuan Ch'i-jui, now a powerless political figurehead. Thereupon, Feng went to Kalgan to assume his long-ignored office as the Tupan of Northwestern Defense.

There was little doubt that the Kuominchün had bent over backward to avoid conflict with Fengtien. Its army was still small in comparison with that of Fengtien, and it had suddenly acquired a territory larger than it could manage. Therefore, the Kuominchün needed time both to expand its army and to consolidate its territory. For the next year, Feng contented himself with developing the resources of the northwest and turning it into a powerful territorial base. During this period Feng's army swelled into a formidable force of over 100,000 men. He also began to receive Soviet military aid and to have closer contact with the KMT in the south. Other Kuominchün units were busy expanding too. Hu Chin-yi's force reached 250,000 men and Sun Yo's reached 30,000 men in a single year.[23]

Fengtien was occupied with more or less the same types of problems. It took time for the faction to establish itself in the newly acquired provinces. In addition, the provinces still under Chihli's control were stronger and richer than the Kuominchün territory at the beginning of 1925, and they were the logical target of Fengtien's next expansionist move. In December 1924, the regent government ordered the removal of the Chihli military governor from Kiangsu. In early January 1925, Fengtien troops took possession of Nanking. This precipitated a war between Fengtien and Chihli's Ch'i Hsieh-yüan. By the end of the month, Ch'i had been defeated and Kiangsu became a part of Fengtien's territorial domain.

The struggle between Fengtien and Chihli was far from concluded. In the peace treaty, both actors had pledged to respect Shanghai's status as a demilitarized zone. In June Fengtien took advantage of the labor strike in Shanghai to move its troops into the city, thus violating the treaty. In the next three months, Fengtien appointed three of its generals to be military governors— Chang Tsung-ch'ang in Shantung, Chiang Teng-hsüan in Anhwei, and Yang Yü-t'ing in Kiangsu. Since these three provinces lay on the main thoroughfare that connected the capital with the Yangtze valley, the Peking–Tientsin–Pukow railway, Chihli could not but view the Fengtien move as a prelude to further expansion policy in the south. On October 10, 1925, the Chihli militarist in Chekiang, Sun Ch'uan-fang, launched a surprise attack on the Fengtien force in Kiangsu, and in two weeks forced all Fengtien troops in Kiangsu and Anhwei to evacuate to Shantung, thus reclaiming the two provinces for Chihli.

In the meantime, Fengtien also got into trouble with the Kuominchün. Even as Fengtien troops were headed north, the Kuominchün started moving eastward toward Chihli. Although a new crisis was brewing, both sides appeared amenable to negotiation, and subsequently an agreement was reached whereby Paoting was returned to the Kuominchün in addition to the section of the Peking–Hankow railway in Chihli that had been lost to Fengtien not long before. The agreement was honored, and for a while it seemed that the crisis had subsided. Then suddenly on November 31, 1925, came news of the revolt of Kuo Sung-ling, a powerful Fengtien general. Evidence that later became accessible showed that Kuo had planned his revolt with Feng's full knowledge.[24] Therefore, Feng's willingness to talk peace was clearly a tactical move to deceive Fengtien. As soon as Kuo's army marched north to attack the Fengtien home base, the Kuominchün marched east to attack other Fengtien units in Chihli province. For the next two or three weeks the war went well for Kuo and the Kuominchün also gained some ground in Chihli. Then the tide turned against Kuo, and in a matter of days at the end of the year, Kuo's force was totally annihilated and he was killed. The Kuominchün was left alone in the field. As a gesture to soften Fengtien's anger and to pave the way toward peace, Feng again offered to retire from politics. Shortly afterward, he went to the Soviet Union.

At about this time, another unexpected turn of events was taking place in a different quarter. During the time of the Chihli-Fengtien war in the autumn of 1925, Wu P'ei-fu was making plans to march north from Hupeh to attack Fengtien's rear. In the early part of December, some Chihli units were actually sent to Shantung province and attacked the Fengtien force in coordination with the Kuominchün. But Feng's conspiracy with Kuo angered Wu P'ei-fu more than Fengtien's hegemonial policy. Announcing that he would "teach the traitors a lesson," Wu suddenly decided to switch sides. A rapprochement was quickly reached between Fengtien and Chihli in January 1926, by which they agreed to wage war jointly against the Kuominchün. From this point on, until the very end of the system in 1928, the Kuominchün was almost continuously at war with one or both of these actors.

At this point, the KMT leaders apparently felt strong enough to make another effort to unify the nation. On June 6, 1926, in the midst of heavy fighting in the north, the KMT formally appointed Chiang Kai-shek commander in chief of the Nationalist Revolutionary Army. The strategy of the KMT was to "attack Wu P'ei-fu, appease Sun Ch'uan-fang, and ignore Chang Tso-lin." Therefore, its first step was to attack Wu's stronghold in Wuhan. At this time, Wu was preoccupied with the offensive against the Kuominchün forces at the Nankow Pass and thought the KMT attack on his rear could easily be repulsed. The other Chihli militarist, Sun Ch'uan-fang, preferred observing and would not come to the rescue of his fellow Chihli militarists. By the time Wu took Nankow and returned to the south, the KMT forces had already penetrated deep into Wu's territory and laid siege to the city of Wuch'ang. Moreover, a new alliance was forged between the KMT and the Kuominchün, which received a KMT commission in September 1926.

As soon as Wu P'ei-fu's downfall was imminent, the KMT turned its strength against Sun Ch'uan-fang. In the provinces of Kiangsi, Chekiang, and Kiangsu, the KMT forces met stiff resistance from Sun's army. Furthermore, the party's internal schism in the summer of 1927 delayed progress on the battlefield. Thus, it was not until August 1927 that Sun's power was finally crushed.

In the north, the Kuominchün had never ceased fighting Fengtien. After a brief stay in the Soviet Union, Feng Yü-hsiang came back just in time to give his men the leadership they desperately needed after the Nankow campaign. After a brief period of regroupment and rest in the northwest, he started marching his troops eastward through Kansu and Shensi. In the summer of 1927, the Kuominchün was deep in Honan and was pushing Fengtien troops farther north.[25] In April 1927 Shansi formally joined the KMT and actively participated in the war against Fengtien. (The other two nonessential actors, Hunan and Szechwan, had joined the KMT much earlier.) This marked the first and only time that Shansi participated in the regulatory process of the system.

In the following year, the Fengtien army and some remnants from Chihli were locked in fierce battle with the allied forces of the KMT, Kuominchün, and Shansi on the plains of northern China. By the spring of 1928 the Fengtien defense perimeter in Chihli was showing signs of crumbling. On June 3, 1928, Chang Tso-lin decided to abandon North China and started back to Manchuria. On the following day, his special train was blown up by high explosives, and Chang was killed instantly. On June 8, Shansi contingents took possession of Peking. For practical purposes, the war was over. On December 7, 1928, the new leader of Fengtien, Chang Hsüeh-liang, announced that he was relinquishing the faction's autonomous status and was returning all administrative and military authority to the Nationalist government (now located in Nanking). After twelve tumultuous years, the Chinese militarist system thus came to an end.

During the third phase, the Chinese militarists continued to act to increase their capabilities. The dynamic equilibrium of the second phase had not created a sense of complacency among the participants; on the contrary, it reinforced their belief that only force would prevail. The phenomenal expansion of the Kuominchün between 1924 and 1925 serves as a good example. In the south, the KMT also spared no effort in expanding its army.

The utility of negotiation in resolving conflicts was undermined by the emergence of the KMT as an essential actor. Now, in the third phase of the system, the KMT developed a fixed policy, and it was capable of implementing that policy. This made the KMT less amenable to negotiate at the expense of its broader policy goals. However, the KMT used negotiation extensively in order to exploit the latent cleavages between northern militarists and their southern subordinates. Many timely defections and surrenders by provincial militarists in Hunan, Kiangsi, Fukien, and Chekiang were the results of hard bargaining with the KMT agents. Unlike northern militarists, who were more prepared to accept compromise and the status quo, the KMT tried to negotiate from a position of strength. Peaceful coexistence was not the objective of its negotiation—terms of surrender or collaboration were the objectives.

However, in the earlier part of the phase, when some conflicts still concerned the northern militarists only, such as the Fengtien-Chihli conflicts in the Yangtze valley and the Fengtien-Kuominchün conflicts in Chihli, negotiations were still used to prevent war, and they generally succeeded in at least delaying the outbreak of war for a considerable period of time.

During this phase, the inclination to fight rather than miss an opportunity to increase capabilities was obvious. The two Fengtien-Chihli wars, the Fengtien-Kuominchün war, and even the KMT-Fengtien war were all examples of this aspect of balance-of-power behavior.

However, there was less of an inclination to spare essential actors from elimination than there had been in the previous phase. In the north, Fengtien and Chihli waged war against the Kuominchün relentlessly, with the avowed purpose of eliminating that actor. In the south, the KMT launched its Northern Expedition with the determination that all other actors in the system, essential and nonessential, should be eliminated. There was no question of stopping short of the realization of this policy goal.

Opposition to coalitions or hegemonial actors was completely abandoned in this phase. In the two Fengtien-Chihli conflicts in 1925, Chihli had to face Fengtien alone, the main reason being that the Kuominchün, the actor most qualified to render assistance, was preoccupied with managing the vast territories it had just acquired. Thus, for a period of about one year, there occurred a phenomenon of parallel expansion: Fengtien along the Tientsin–Pukow railway to the Yangtze valley, and the Kuominchün along the Peking–Suiyuan railway into the northwestern part of China. Only minor incidents took place between these two actors; their relations on the whole remained cordial, both actors avoiding major clashes with each other because there was much to be done in their respective areas. In a sense, there was a race between them, each attempting to conquer as much territory as possible within its own sphere of influence while respecting the right of the other actor to do the same. To reciprocate for the Kuominchün's standoffishness in the Fengtien-Chihli conflicts, Fengtien adopted the same attitude with regard to the military campaigns conducted by the Kuominchün in Honan, Shensi, and Kansu. It is difficult to decide which of these two actors was hegemonial—it is likely that both tried to be. But the fact remains that the Kuominchün was

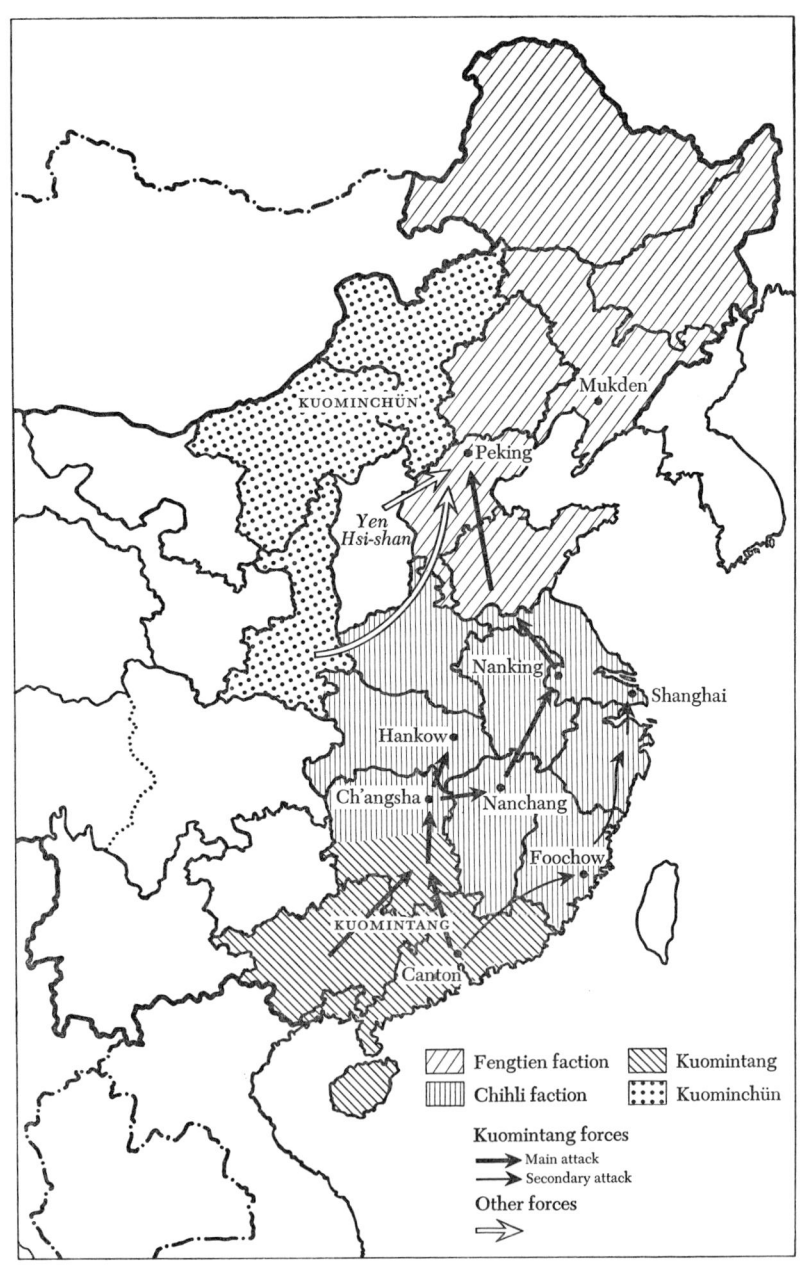

Northern Expedition, 1926–1928

The Chinese Political System

far weaker than Fengtien and had much to lose by neglecting the general trend toward imbalance in the system.

But the Kuominchün's neglect of its responsibility constituted only half of the problem. Equally important was the attitude of Chihli. Would Chihli have wanted to ally with the Kuominchün if the latter had offered to do so? The answer is no. The history of this phase shows that as soon as Fengtien and the Kuominchün reached a saturation point in their expansionist policies, they came into conflict with each other. At this time, Wu P'ei-fu's position was still to march north and attack Fengtien. Then came the revolt of Kuo Sung-lin and the outbreak of Fengtien-Kuominchün war in the north. At this juncture, Wu changed his position, reached an understanding with Chang Tso-lin and turned to attack the Kuominchün, which had attempted to win his cooperation. The Kuominchün released Ts'ao K'un from house arrest, deposed Tuan Ch'i-jui as regent, and invited Wu to express his opinion on how to form a new national government. Yet Wu was unmoved by these goodwill gestures. This incident bore special significance because it was the first time in the Chinese system that an aggressive alliance was concluded. The hegemonial actor no longer stood alone. On the contrary, the weaker actor was forced to stand alone and fight two enemies. This was a serious departure from the balance-of-power model and nearly brought about the decimation of the Kuominchün.

This incident also revealed the limited utility of information. As in the previous period, the flow of information (among the northern militarists at least) was not impaired, but the injection of personality factors into the operation of the system was new. Intense personal hatred of treachery and doubledealing had made some actors view others as unacceptable allies. The vindictiveness of Wu P'ei-fu finally drove the Kuominchün into the arms of the KMT and precipitated the evolution of two permanent alliances: the KMT and Kuominchün against Fengtien and Chihli. The gradual transition of the Kuominchün into an ideological actor made this alliance pattern all the more irrevocable. Flexibility of alignment, which was so essential to the balancing of the system, was now destroyed. At this point, the struggle for power had become more and more a struggle between different personalities and different kinds of sociopolitical orders. The KMT and the Kuominchün viewed "warlord" rule as fundamentally feudalistic, as an anachronism not to be tolerated in the age of nationalism and modernization. Fengtien and Chihli viewed the KMT and the Kuominchün as "reds" and destroyers of traditional values. They no longer desired to keep the system going, because they no longer had a common frame of reference within the system. A balance-of-power system thus became impossible.

The realization of the impossibility of coexistence with the KMT was perceived by the other militarists too late. Several factors contributed to the militarists' self-deception about the KMT, the first being the lateness of the KMT's rise to substantial power. The northern militarists ignored the KMT for quite some time, partly because it had been a weak actor. This record of weakness proved to be an asset to the KMT in the sense that it gave the northern factions a sense of false security. In addition, geographical barriers protected it from easy access from the north and, as a consequence, the northern militarists turned their attention to more urgent business, i.e. against each other. Their complacency caused them to fail to revise their estimation of KMT strength. Even after being furnished with information about the KMT's force-building efforts, they still refused to be alarmed. The fact that Wu P'ei-fu chose to stay in the northern battlefield against the Kuominchün while his home base was being attacked by the KMT was partly a reflection of Wu's low opinion of the KMT troops. While the KMT was fully engaged in Hupeh, Sun Ch'uan-fang simply stood on the sidelines and watched his fellow Chihlians being routed.

It can be argued that even while the KMT was making progress in its Northern Expedition, there was still much evidence to lend credence to the northern militarists' low opinion of its capabilities. For one thing, the KMT had within its ranks an assortment of local militarists who were a liability rather than an asset to the Expedition. In addition, although the party had been reorganized, it was not free of factional strife and the coalition between the KMT and the CCP proved to be less solid than it looked. Even in the midst of victory, the KMT revealed its internal weaknesses. The factional feud between Nanking and Wuhan nearly split the party asunder; for a while, it raised serious doubts that the KMT force was capable of holding the line of defense at all, not to mention advancing.

Another critical element that contributed to the northerners'

The Chinese Political System

misconceptions about the KMT was its previous record of flexible alignment policies. That record mitigated the militarists' suspicion about its ideological intransigence and led them to believe that the KMT was, after all, not fundamentally different from themselves.

Thus, the KMT's record of weakness succeeded in conditioning the northern militarists to entertain a highly distorted view of the KMT. That view remained unchanged even after the dominant power within the KMT had shifted from the local militarists to party functionaries and a new crop of military leaders. Therefore, when the northern militarists were finally compelled to confront the KMT, they failed to devise new approaches to cope with the new threat.

Even toward the close of the phase, the northern militarists could not escape the KMT trap of "divide and conquer." The KMT strategy of splitting the Chihli forces was rewarded because Sun Ch'uan-fang believed that either the KMT force would be defeated by Wu P'ei-fu or, if Wu was defeated, the KMT would be satisfied with territorial gains and would be willing to negotiate. And it was not until Sun Ch'uan-fang had been severely mauled that Fengtien began to be concerned with the growing KMT threat and to take steps toward military cooperation with Sun. By that time it was too late. In this sense, the fact that those actors subscribing to supranational organizing principles were not constrained was decisive in the destruction of the system.

In addition, the KMT's adherence to "supranational (suprafaction) organizing principles" not only made the actors' alignment pattern more rigid but also expanded the number of participants in the political process to an unprecedented extent. The KMT did this through playing the role of champion of Chinese nationalism and anti-imperialism. Both these themes had been present in Chinese politics for some time, but the nonideological militarists were never totally committed to them. In contrast, the KMT not only engaged more heavily in nationalistic and anti-imperialistic propaganda; it also was able to act more aggressively by virtue of its superior ideological and organizational weapons. Consequently, the KMT (with the CCP) quickly established its leadership position in the Nationalist movement. It helped organize labor unions, encouraged a militant attitude in bargaining with foreign capitalists, gave material assistance to workers on strike, and organized boycotts of foreign goods.

These concrete demonstrations of the KMT's dedication to nationalism enabled it to mobilize a large reserve of hitherto untapped human resources against both foreign enemies and militarists. The injection of the power of the people into the political system confused and threatened the rule of the militarists from within and below, and the militarists lacked both the intellectual sophistication to understand it and the physical force to subdue it. In time, the mounting popular support made a significant contribution to the KMT's political ambition. The most dramatic example occurred in Shanghai, where the people openly rebelled against the ruling militarist. In other areas, the people achieved valuable results by spreading rumors, obstructing communications, paralyzing the economy, or simply by passive noncooperation with the militarists. Hence, the rise of the KMT as an essential actor was significantly aided by the response of a hitherto apathetic people to its ideological agitation.

Little need be said about the question of permitting defeated national actors to reenter the system in this phase. Had the northern militarists won the war, the existing system might have been preserved a while longer. But this was not possible when the KMT was victorious. The KMT had set out to destroy the system not only to satisfy its ambition for power but also—and more important—to fulfill its ideological mission. The KMT's victory thus also spelled doom to the system.

Conclusion

It seems appropriate at the end of this work to try to explain why the Chinese militarist system lasted so short a time. In addition to the new factors introduced in the third phase, there were several other factors inherent in the very structure of the Chinese system that I believe hastened the end of the system.

Foremost was the common aspiration (and expectation) that the nation should eventually be unified. This national aspiration made the militarists acutely aware of the transient character of their regimes and made them feel an intrinsic insecurity. None of them had any illusions about the possibility of perpetuating the status quo; some form of unification would have to occur. Consequently,

The Chinese Political System

what concerned them most was to ensure that the form of unification that occurred was not inimical to their personal interests. Better still, they desired to unify the country under their own control. Thus, whenever one faction became stronger than the others, it was only natural for it to try to gain a position of predominance in the system as the logical first step toward national unification. Although the central government had long been defunct, the hegemonial actor was always anxious to control it, since this control would enormously enhance the actor's prestige and strengthen its claims to be the sole ruler of the nation.

Thus, it was quite logical for Tuan Ch'i-jui to become the first militarist to espouse the policy of unification by force, when his suddenly increased capabilities gave him a superior position in the system. He was defeated, but his aspiration was inherited by Chihli in 1922 and Fengtien in 1924. The role of the deviant essential actor became a constant feature of the Chinese system, although the holder of that role changed from time to time. It is true that occasional deviance in the behavior of one or more actors in a balance-of-power system is not entirely unexpected or inconsistent with equilibrium. If other actors are able to follow the rules suggested by the model, such deviance can be checked and the stability of the system maintained. But the Chinese system offered an extreme case, because it was never free from the threat of deviance by an essential actor, usually the most powerful one. This was especially true as the system moved into the third phase, in which the pace of activities among the actors in general accelerated, with one crisis following on the heels of another. Thus, the effects of continuous dysfunctional tension placed the Chinese system under more strain than a balance-of-power system can normally tolerate.

The common expectation of eventual national unification had the further consequence of removing the actors' incentive to keep other actors in the system. In fact, it would be more accurate to say that it enhanced the actors' desire to destroy the other actors and to monopolize the system.

The fact that every essential actor had this propensity to eliminate the other actors as soon as it felt capable of doing so directs our attention to the relationship between the number of actors and the general stability of the system. And here lies one of the most important causes of the system's instability. At no time were there more than three essential actors. In the first phase, the actors were gradually coming into being; they were still only loosely organized by the end of that phase. The essential actors of that phase were Anhwei, Chihli, and Fengtien. In the second phase, Chihli and Fengtien were unquestionably essential actors. Anhwei probably was still an essential actor, although it was greatly reduced in strength. In the third phase, Fengtien and Chihli still stood at the head of the list. The Kuominchün was strong for a while, but it was much weakened after the Nankow defeat. The KMT came fully into the picture only in 1925–26.

Thus the stability of the system was primarily predicated upon the ability and willingness of the two weaker essential actors to combine against the stronger one. Because of the fact that in a conflict situation an essential actor could expect to obtain support from only one other essential actor, any action that might be interpreted as leading to the increase of one actor's capabilities to the detriment of others was a cause for grave concern. Such a system placed a premium on promptness of counteractions; delay or moderation might be very costly or even disastrous to an actor because of the serious limitation on potential allies. If the actor did not move quickly enough to combine with the only other available essential actor to oppose the third, it might find itself opposed by an alliance of the other two. Given the roughly equal capabilities of the three actors in the Chinese system, the outcome of an alliance of two against one would be a foregone conclusion.

From a superficial, arithmetic point of view, it would seem that the system had a good prospect of enduring because at any time there were more actors interested in preserving the system than in destroying it. At a given time there was only one actor harboring hegemonial aspirations to upset the balance. The two weaker essential actors were, at least temporarily, in favor of the status quo, and nearly all nonessential actors strongly favored the status quo because they wanted to avoid being overrun by the hegemonial essential actor. But the numerical majority was an unreal one, for the nonessential actors were by no means anxious to assume their share of responsibility. In fact, the Chinese system can be divided into two subsystems. In one subsystem, composed of the essential actors, much interaction took place across the actors' boundaries. In the other subsystem, involving the nonessential actors, relatively

The Chinese Political System

little interaction took place. Whereas the essential actors were understandably eager to interact with the nonessential actors, either to conquer them or to obtain their assistance, the nonessential actors deliberately tried to give the others a wide berth. The low level of participation of the nonessential actors in the regulatory process meant that for practical purposes the Chinese system was built on the support of the small number of essential actors.

Within the subsystem of action among the three essential actors, one might have expected that in any conflict between two essential actors, the third uncommitted essential actor would play the role of the "balancer" in the system. In the Chinese system, however, the role of balancer was highly untenable. Hypothetically, a balancer should possess certain qualifications. Its territory should be geographically removed from the core area of potential hostilities and relatively immune from attack. It should not be subject to the direct and immediate impact of boundary changes of other actors, but should be primarily concerned with the overall balance among them. It should possess a highly mobile and compact military force capable of achieving quick offensive victory but unfit for long-term occupation of alien territory. Such an actor would always be an attractive potential ally for others, while its nonaggressive nature would allay their fear. In addition, it should have easy access to the area of potential danger and have secure supply lines. The desirability of these qualifications was shown by Great Britain in the nineteenth century.

In the Chinese system, however, all essential actors were land-based, and they often had intermingled territories. Geographical deachment was impossible. Contiguity created border problems that drew actors into disputes, sometimes against their own wishes. Although nearly all essential actors possessed a portion of China's coastline, none of them successfully developed a naval force that would allow it to intervene in a noncontiguous area. In addition, the three-actor system itself placed a heavy burden on the method of "balancing." Since the number of potential allies was restricted, a decision had to be made prior to attack. If one actor played the observer, the other two would be left in suspense. Such an act would be viewed as opportunistic and dangerous by both antagonists and hence intolerable. Both antagonists had an active interest in pressuring the third actor to clarify its position.

Furthermore, it is doubtful that any actor would have been willing to play the role of "balancer" consistently even if it had been possible. Voluntary retreat after balance had been restored was difficult in several ways. First, the balancer would be confronted with a continuous need for balancing, which required never-failing vigilance in a system with so few actors. Second, the balancer had to forgo any chance to augment its own capabilities at the expense of the defeated actor. In contrast, the possible gains from joining an alliance with another essential actor were more concrete and substantial, since such an alliance stood a very good chance of winning. Under these circumstances, the chances were that an actor would rather be a partner than a balancer.

A still further factor that discouraged any actor from playing the role of the balancer in a three-actor system was that the balancer had a very short life span. The only force that could conceivably stop the winner of a conflict from eliminating the defeated actor was the active intervention of the balancer. To do so, however, was only to fight for a losing cause. An attempt to revive a defeated actor would only drag the balancer into a new war against the winner. While the outcome of the new war might go either way, one thing was certain—the balancer had failed in its balancing.

These factors caused the actors to prefer compensation (in territory or other resources) as the formula of settlement between victorious actors after a war. The merit of this formula was that it enabled the actors to base their security on increases in their own capabilities rather than to depend on a balancer's impartiality. The defect was that it entailed almost insuperable difficultes in objectively assessing the value of the capabilities of the defeated actor and agreeing on a fair distribution to the victors. The wars of 1920 and 1924 both ended in the partitioning of the defeated territories by the actors in the winning alliance. Despite the effort to split the spoils as evenly as possible, sharp clashes of interest immediately followed, which led to new antagonism between the victors.

In the Chinese system, the sole foundation of an actor's power and legitimacy was the physical force it commanded. If that force was destroyed, the territory previously under the actor's influence would suddenly become a power vacuum. This phenomenon both restricted the policy alternatives available to the victors and encouraged their ambitions. The defeated essential actor could not regain its previous status without active assistance from the victors. The victors thus could either show self-restraint and rely for security on the highly unstable three-actor balance-of-power system or follow a policy of self-expansion by compensation, which promised sizable immediate gains, and rely for their security on their own capabilities. The militarists' choice was obvious.

Our examination of these factors has shed some light on the brief duration of the Chinese system. Although at one time or another the system exhibited certain characteristics analogous to a balance-of-power system, the system was always under pressure to deviate from this and move toward a unified nation-state system. As long as the actors' capabilities were generally low and as long as the hegemonial actor or actors were in the minority, the militarist system might have survived. But increases in all the actors' capabilities, the rise of ideological actors, the widening of the gulf between information and reality, and finally the superiority of the hegemonial actors over the status quo actors (when all the nonessential actors joined the hegemonial drive) converged to create strains greater than the Chinese system was capable of sustaining. The system then quickly broke down.

A final word should be said about the aftermath of the system. The fact that this study stops at 1928 in no way implies that the politics of militarism terminated in that year. In fact, militarism remained a dominant feature of Chinese politics for a long time afterward. As the Northern Expedition proceeded, the KMT was compelled to absorb en bloc many militarists into its organization. Because of negotiations involved with their joining the KMT, they managed quite successfully to retain their own military power. Consequently, militarism continued as an important aspect of the Nationalist government between 1928 and 1949. And yet it would be an error to view militarism under Nationalist rule as a mere extension of early Republican militarism. While it is true that Nationalist militarism cannot be adequately understood without prior knowledge of early Republican militarism, it is doubtful to this author whether these two types of militarism can be profitably analyzed within the same theoretical construct. This is the case because the power relationships and operational code that guided militarist politics before 1928 were significantly altered after that date. While it is out of the scope of the present study to discuss the political system of the Nationalist era, some crucial differences can be suggested.

First, the composition of the military elite and the geographical distribution of power had shifted dramatically. During the early Republican period, the Peiyang group reigned supreme. The Northern Expedition effectively demolished the forces under Chihli and Anhwei commands. Although the Fengtien forces were successfully withdrawn to Manchuria with only minor losses, they were dealt a shattering blow by the surprise Japanese invasion in 1931. Of all northern militarists, only Yen Hsi-shan and Feng Yü-hsiang remained politically active.

In contrast, the Northern Expedition actually aided many southern militarists in expanding their geographical control and political power. Not only did the Kwangsi and Kwangtung groups become major political actors; even Hunan and Szechwan militarists made significant political gains. Thus, in rough terms, the political center stage had shifted from the northern plains to the Yangtze valley. This is shown by the fact that all major politico-military struggles between 1928 and 1937, with the exception of the 1930–31 war of the central plains, had their main battlegrounds south of the Yangtze River. The emergence of a Communist movement of armed struggle only further increased the strategic importance of South China.

Second, the pattern of confrontation during the early Republican period was quite flexible. Any of the essential actors could be, and in fact were, challenged militarily whenever pursuing a hegemonial policy. The dynamics of the balance-of-power system created a musical-chairs effect whereby the essential actors took turns being the target of a coalition of militarists. After 1928, the pattern of confrontation became virtually fixed. Each military crisis pitted the party army of Chiang Kai-shek against a coalition of militarists. To meet these chronic challenges, Chiang Kai-shek devoted more effort than had any previous Peiyang militarist to training his forces to perfection. Durng this process, military modernization proceeded far more quickly than it had in the previous period.

Third, during the early Republican period, the militarist groups remained fairly stable structurally over time. It was analytically possible to identify the hard core of the various military factions.

Contrary to popular belief, the main threat to the organizational viability of these military factions was not frequent defections by leading members. Defections were certainly a recurrent problem during the formative stage of the factions (1916–20), when most militarists were engaged in a search for their factional identifies. Once factional lines were drawn, however, they remained quite firm. After 1920, the only major case of defection occurred in 1924 when Feng Yü-hsiang turned against Chihli. Rather, the major threat to the military factions was the failure to impose strict discipline and to implement serious training programs, both failures being the direct result of the leading militarists' own professional inadequacies. Therefore, as we discussed in the main body of this book, while defections by minor subordinates certainly occurred throughout the entire period, crucial military tests were failed because the main units exhibited little propensity to fight hard. Characteristically, the commanders of these units lost power with their faction; they were not rewarded by the victor, as should have been the case with defection.

The complexion of military confrontation changed drastically during the Nationalist era, and this was nowhere more visible than in the number of defections by leading militarists that occurred during the midst of fighting. There was not a single civil war between 1928 and 1937 that did not produce a defection of major proportions. This leads us to the conclusion that the sources of solidarity of militarist groups and their operational norms had changed.

This new "game" was further convoluted by the intrusion of the Japanese army in China after 1931, and particularly after 1937, when a full-scale national war was initiated. For most militarists, the strategic calculations were rendered infinitely more complicated by the need to cope with two exacting tasks simultaneously: to work for the preservation of one's politico-military power within China vis-à-vis other contenders in the context of waging a successful war of national resistance against a foreign enemy.

The above observations are offered as possible lines along which one might extend the inquiry into militarism in modern Chinese politics into another time frame. Further research to explore in depth these suggested connections and contrasts would be a challenging and inviting task.

Appendixes

APPENDIX A

Political and Military Leaders, 1916-1928

Heads of State

Official title	Name	Tenure in office
President	Yüan Shih-k'ai	March 1912–June 1916
President	Li Yüan-hung	June 1916–July 1917
Acting President	Feng Kuo-chang	July 1917–Oct. 1918
President	Hsü Shih-ch'ang	Oct. 1918–June 1922
President	Li Yüan-hung	June 1922–June 1923
President	Ts'ao K'un	Oct. 1923–Nov. 1924
Regent (chief executive)	Tuan Ch'i-jui	Nov. 1924–April 1926
Ta-yüan-shuai	Chang Tso-lin	June 1927–June 1928

Prime Ministers and the Tenure of Their Cabinets

Name	Tenure	Name	Tenure
Tuan Ch'i-jui	April 22, 1916–June 29, 1916	Wang Ch'ung-hui	Sept. 19, 1922–Nov. 29, 1922
Tuan Ch'i-jui	June 29, 1916–May 22, 1917	Wang Ta-hsieh	Nov. 29, 1922–Dec. 11, 1922
Li Ching-hsi	June 24, 1917–July 1, 1917	Chang Shao-tseng	Jan. 4, 1923–June 6, 1923
Tuan Ch'i-jui	July 14, 1917–Nov. 22, 1917	Sun Pao-ch'i	Jan. 10, 1924–July 2, 1924
Wang Shih-chen	Nov. 30, 1917–Feb. 20, 1918	Yen Hui-ch'ing	Sept. 14, 1924–Oct. 30, 1924
Tuan Ch'i-jui	March 23, 1918–Oct. 10, 1918	Huang Fu	Oct. 30, 1924–Nov. 24, 1924
Ts'ien Nun-hsün	Dec. 20, 1918–June 13, 1919	Tuan Ch'i-jui	Nov. 24, 1924–Dec. 31, 1925
Chin Yün-p'eng	Nov. 5, 1919–July 2, 1920	Hsü Shih-yin	Dec. 26, 1925–March 4, 1926
Chin Yün-p'eng	Aug. 9, 1920–May 10, 1921	Chia Teh-yao	March 4, 1926–April 20, 1926
Chin Yün-p'eng	May 10, 1921–Dec. 18, 1921	Yen Hui-ch'ing	May 13, 1926–June 22, 1926
Liang Shih-i	Dec. 24, 1921–May 5, 1922	Ku Wei-chün	Jan. 11, 1927–June 16, 1927
Yen Hui-ch'ing	June 11, 1922–Aug. 5, 1922	P'an Fu	June 20, 1927–June 3, 1928
T'ang Shao-i	Aug. 5, 1922–Sept. 19, 1922		

Highest Military Authorities in the Provinces
1916–1927

Province	1916	1917	1918	1919	1920	1921
Fengtien	Chang Tso-lin	—	—	—	—	—
Kirin	Meng En-yüan	T'ien Chung-yü	Meng En-yüan	Pao Kuei-ch'ing	—	Sun Lieh-ch'eng
Heilungkiang	Pi Kuei-fang	Hsü Lan-chou / Pao Kuei-ch'ing	Pao Kuei-ch'ing	Sun Lieh-ch'eng	—	Wu Chün-sheng
Chihli	Ts'ao K'un	—	—	—	—	—
Honan	Chao T'i	—	—	—	—	—
Shantung	Chang Huai-chih	—	Chang Shu-yüan	T'ien Chung-yü	—	—
Shansi	Yen Hsi-shan	—	—	—	—	—
Shensi	Ch'en Shu-fan	—	—	—	—	Yen Hsiang-wen / Feng Yü-hsiang
Kansu	Chang Kuang-chien	—	—	—	Ts'ai Ch'eng-hsün	—
Sinkiang	Yang Tseng-hsin	—	—	—	—	—
Kiangsi	Li Shun	Ch'en Kuang-yüan	—	—	—	—
Fukien	Li Hou-chi	—	—	—	—	Ch'i Hsieh-yüan
Kiangsu	Feng Kuo-chang	Li Shun	—	—	—	Chang Wen-sheng
Anhwei	Chang Hsün	Ni Tz'u-ch'ung	—	—	—	—
Chekiang	Lü Kung-wang	Yang Shan-te	—	Lu Yung-hsiang	—	—
Kwangtung	Lu Jung-t'ing	Ch'en Ping-k'un	—	Mo Jung-hsin	—	Ch'en Chiung-ming
Kwangsi	Ch'en Ping-k'un	T'an Hao-min	—	—	—	—
Szechwan	Tai K'an	Liu Ts'un-hou	None	None	Hsiung K'o-wu	Liu Hsiang
Kweichow	Liu Hsien-shih	—	—	—	—	Lu T'ao
Yunnan	T'ang Chi-yao	—	—	—	—	Ku P'ing-cheng
Hunan	T'an Yen-k'ai	Fu Liang-tso / Ch'en Chien	Chang Ching-yao	—	T'an Yen-k'ai / Chao Heng-t'i	Chao Heng-t'i
Hupeh	Wang Chan-yüan	—	—	—	—	Hsiao Yao-nan
Jehol	Chiang Kuei-t'i	—	—	—	—	Chi Chin-shun
Chahar	T'ien Chung-yü	Chang Ching-yao	—	—	Chang Ching-hui	Chou Teng-hui
Suiyuan	Chiang Yen-hsing	Ts'ai Ch'eng-hsün	—	—	Ma Fu-hsiang	

Province						
Fengtien	—	—	—	—	—	Wu Chün-sheng
Kirin	—	—	—	—	—	Wan Fu-lin
Heilungkiang	—	—	Chang Tso-hsiang	—	—	—
Chihli	—	Wang Ch'eng-ping	Lu Yung-hsiang	Li Ching-lin / Sun Yao	Chu Yü-p'u	None
Honan	Feng Yü-hsiang / Chang Fu-lai	Chang Fu-lai	Hu Ching-yi	Yao Wei-chün	K'ou Ying-chieh	None
Shantung	—	Cheng Shih-ch'i	—	Chang Tsung-ch'ang	—	—
Shansi	Liu Cheng-hua	—	—	—	Li Yün-lung	—
Shensi	—	—	—	Sun Yao / Li Yün-lung / Feng Yü-hsiang / Liu Yü-fen	Li Ming-chung / Liu Yü-fen	Liu Yü-fen
Kansu	Lu Hung-t'ao	—	—	—	—	—
Sinkiang	—	—	—	—	—	None
Kiangsi	Ts'ai Ch'eng-hsün	—	Fang Pen-jen / Chou Ying-jen / Han Kuo-chün	—	Teng Ju-cho	None
Fukien	—	Sun Ch'uan-fang	—	—	—	—
Kiangsu	—	—	—	Lu Yung-hsiang / Yang Yü-t'ing	Sun Ch'uan-fang (from 1925)	—
Anhwei	Ma Lien-chia	—	Wang I-t'ang	Chiang Teng-hsüan / Teng Ju-cho	Ch'en T'iao-yüan	—
Chekiang	—	—	Sun Ch'uan-fang	Lu Hsiang-t'ing	Ch'en Yi / Meng Chao-yüeh	—
Kwangtung	Hsü Ch'ung-chih / Ch'en Chiung-ming	Hsü Ch'ung-chih	KMT	KMT	KMT	KMT
Kwangsi	Liu Cheng-huan	None	None	Li Tsung-jen / Huang Shao-hung	Huang Shao-hung	—
Szechwan	Liu Ch'eng-hsün	Teng Hsi-hou / Liu Hsiang	Liu Ts'un-hou / Yang Sheng	Liu Hsiang	None	None
Kweichow	Liu Hsien-shih	—	—	Yüan Tsu-ming / Chou Hsi-ch'eng	Chou Hsi-ch'eng	None
Yunnan	T'ang Chi-yao	—	—	—	None	None
Hunan	—	—	—	—	None	None
Hupeh	—	—	Kan Ch'ao-hsi	Sung Che-yüan	Ch'en Chia-mu	None
Jehol	Wang Huai-ch'ing / T'an Ch'ing-lin	Chang Hsi-yüan	Chang Chih-chiang	—	T'ang Yü-lin / Lu Chung-lin / Kao Wei-yü	—
Chahar	Chang Hsi-yüan	—	—	—	—	—
Suiyuan	Ma Fu-hsiang	—	—	Li Ming-chung	Liu Yü-fen / Chiang Hung-yü	Shang Cheng (from 1926)

APPENDIX B

Chronology

1916

June	6	Yüan Shih-k'ai died. Li Yüan-hung succeeded as president
Sept.	21	Chang Hsün called conference of provincial leaders at Hsüchow
Oct.	30	Feng Kuo-chang elected vice-president

1917

Jan.	11	Chang Hsün called conference of provincial leaders at Hsüchow
March	10	Parliament voted to break relations with Germany
May	23	Premier Tuan Ch'i-jui dismissed from office
May	29	Military governors severed relations with Peking government
June	2	Rebellious military governors set up headquarters at Tientsin
June	12	Parliament dissolved
July	1	Chang Hsün restored monarchy
July	6	Restoration failed. Feng Kuo-chang became president
July	14	Tuan Ch'i-jui appointed premier
Aug.	14	Peking government declared war against Germany and Austria
Sept.	18	Hunan generals declared independence from Peking government. Premier Tuan ordered a punitive expedition
Nov.	15	Chihli militarists favored peaceful solution in Hunan. Tuan resigned premiership
Dec.	18	Tuan Ch'i-jui became director of War Participation Bureau

1918

Jan.	30	Peking government renewed offensive in Hunan
Feb.	25	Fengtien moved troops into Chihli
March	23	Tuan appointed premier
May	16	Sino-Japanese Mutual Defense Pact signed
May	30	Ts'ao K'un terminated his involvement in the Hunan war
June	14	Lu Chien-chang assassinated
Aug.	21	Wu P'ei-fu demanded cessation of civil war
Oct.	10	Hsü Shih-ch'ang elected president of Peking government

Appendix B   247

1919

Feb.   20   North-South Peace Conference convened in Shanghai
May   13   Northern and southern delegates to the Peace Conference resigned
June   24   Hsü Shu-cheng appointed commander in chief of Northwestern Frontier Defense Army

1920

March   18   Chihli troops began evacuation from Hunan
April   23   Military governor of Chekiang, Lu Yung-hsiang, proposed abolition of the *tuchün* system
May   26   Hunan troops mounted offensive against northern troops
June   11   Chang Ching-yao dismissed as military governor of Hunan
July   3   Ts'ao K'un and Chang Tso-lin denounced Hsü Shu-cheng's crimes
July   6   Anhwei troops mobilized for war
July   14   Chihli-Anhwei war began
July   19   Chihli-Anhwei war ended with Anhwei's defeat
Nov.   1   Hunan declared self-rule

1921

April   25   Tientsin conference among Ts'ao K'un, Chang Tso-lin, and Wang Chan-yüan
May   30   Chang Tso-lin acquired control over Jehol, Chahar, and Suiyuan.
June   29   Mutiny in Wuhan brought Hunan and Chihli to war
July   7   Wang Chan-yüan resigned as military governor of Hupeh; was succeeded by Hsiao Yao-nan
Sept.   1   Truce between Hunan and Chihli troops in Hupeh
Sept.   20   Szechwan attack against Hupeh repulsed by Chihli troops

1922

Jan.   1   Hunan promulgated provincial constitution
Jan.   6   Wu P'ei-fu declared opposition to the Liang Shih-i cabinet
Jan.   19   Chihli militarists demanded ouster of Liang Shih-i as premier
March   31   Chang Tso-lin sent troops to the vicinity of Peking
April   8   Fengtien and Chihli forces began mobilizing
April   29   Chihli-Fengtien war began
May   5   Chihli-Fengtien war ended with Fengtien's defeat
May   15   Chihli generals petitioned Li Yüan-hung to resume presidency
June   3   Chang Tso-lin declared autonomy for Manchuria
June   11   Li Yüan-hung resumed presidency

1923

Jan.   23   Sun-Joffe Declaration issued in Shanghai
Feb.   21   Sun Yat-sen returned to Canton and assumed the post of ta-yüan-shuai of the military government

March 6 Sun Ch'uan-fang of Chihli invaded Fukien
June 13 President Li ousted from office
Oct. 5 Ts'ao K'un elected president
Oct. 13 Sun Yat-sen declared an expedition against Ts'ao K'un. Fengtien and Anhwei declared opposition to Ts'ao's presidency

1924

Jan. 21 Kuomintang held congress and announced plan for party reorganization
Feb. 23 Peking government bought $4 million's worth of Italian arms
Aug. 25 Canton Chamber of Commerce challenged KMT
Sept. 1 War broke out between Kiangsu and Chekiang
Sept. 4 Chang Tso-lin and Sun Yat-sen declared support for Chekiang
Sept. 17 Chihli declared war against Chang Tso-lin
Oct. 13 Chekiang defeated
Oct. 15 Canton Chamber of Commerce uprising suppressed
Oct. 23 Feng Yü-hsiang seized government in Peking
Nov. 2 Ts'ao K'un resigned presidency
Nov. 8 Chihli-Fengtien war ended with total defeat of Wu P'ei-fu
Nov. 24 Tuan Ch'i-jui became chief executive
Dec. 31 Sun Yat-sen arrived at Peking to confer with northern leaders

1925

Jan. 7 Fengtien troops occupied Anhwei and Kiangsu
Feb. 1 Rehabilitation conference began
March 12 Sun Yat-sen died in Peking
April 20 Rehabilitation conference ended
Oct. 15 Sun Ch'uan-fang attacked and forced Fengtien troops to withdraw from Yangtze valley
Oct. 21 Wu P'ei-fu assumed post as commander in chief of allied forces from 14 provinces, and declared war against Chang Tso-lin
Nov. 22 Kuo Sung-lin revolt
Nov. 23 KMT's western-hill faction met in Peking
Dec. 5 Feng Yü-hsiang's Kuominchün began operations against Fengtien
Dec. 24 Kuo Sung-lin's revolt crushed
Dec. 30 Hsü Shu-cheng murdered near Peking

1926

Jan. 4 Feng Yü-hsiang relinquished command over Kuominchün. Wu P'ei-fu directed troops to attack the Kuominchün.
March 20 KMT moved against the Communists after the Chung-shan Incident
April 9 Tuan Ch'i-jui ousted as chief executive by Kuominchün generals
April 15 Kuominchün relinquished control over Peking government and withdrew to the northwest

Appendix B

May	17	KMT imposed new restrictions on Communists
June	6	KMT designated Chiang Kai-shek as commander in chief of entire National Revolutionary Army for a Northern Expedition
July	11	KMT forces occupied Changsha
Aug.	23	Feng Yü-hsiang joined the National Revolutionary Army
Sept.	7	KMT forces took Hankow
Sept.	20	KMT forces took Nanchang
Oct.	10	KMT forces took Wuchang
Dec.	1	Chang Tso-lin assumed office as commander in chief of Ankuochün
Dec.	31	KMT completed occupation of Fukien and Chekiang

1927

March	7	KMT CEC plenum held in Hankow
March	22	KMT forces occupied Shanghai
March	24	KMT forces occupied Nanking and created the Nanking Incident
April	12	Shanghai Labor Union disarmed. KMT purged Communists. Yen Hsi-shan declared allegiance to Sun Yat-senism
April	17	Wuhan and Nanking set up rival regimes
June	2	KMT forces occupied Hsüchow
June	18	Chang Tso-lin assumed post as ta-yüan-shuai of a new military government in Peking
June	19	Feng Yü-hsiang declared support for Nanking regime
July	23	Wuhan KMT repudiated Communists
Aug.	1	Communist-inspired uprising in Nanchang
Aug.	6	KMT forces lost Hsüchow to Chang Tsung-ch'ang
Aug.	12	Chiang Kai-shek resigned to promote party unity
Aug.	24	Sun Ch'uan-fang mounted offensive against Nanking-Shanghai area
Sept.	1	Sun's offensive repelled
Sept.	10	KMT Nanking and Wuhan factions reconciled
Sept.	29	Yen Hsi-shan declared war against Chang Tso-lin
Dec.	16	KMT forces retook Hsüchow

1928

Jan.	9	Chiang Kai-shek resumed post as commander in chief of National Revolutionary Army
April	30	KMT forces occupied Chinan
May	3	Chinese and Japanese troops clashed over Chinan
May	19	Japan advised Chang Tso-lin to withdraw to Manchuria
May	25	Chang Tso-lin rejected Japanese advice
June	3	Chang Tso-lin left Peking for Manchuria, killed in explosion
June	8	Yen Hsi-shan's forces entered Peking. Northern Expedition concluded

Notes

Complete authors' names, titles, and publication
data are given in the Bibliography, pp. 267–75.

Biographical Dictionary	Biographical Dictionary of Republican China	HSCTK	Hsü Shu-cheng tien kao
CWR	China Weekly Review	KMWH	Ko ming wen hsien
CYB	China Year Book	NCH	North-China Herald
CCWH	Chuan chi wen hsüeh	TFTC	Tung fang tsa chih
CHMKKKWSN	Chung-hua min ko k'ai kuo wu shih nien shih lun chi		

Chapter 1

1. William Tung has analyzed a total of 72 documents of the 1911–18 period, including constitutions, constitutional drafts, laws, and regulations governing the organization of national, provincial, and local governments. He concludes that these rules and laws were seldom obeyed or implemented (pp. 380–85).
2. Ch'en Hsi-chang, *Pei-yang ts'ang shuang shih hua*, 2: 503–8.
3. For example, see Chen Kung-fu, *Chung-kuo ko ming shih*, and Li Fang-ch'en, *Chung-kuo chin tai shih*.
4. Ralph L. Powell was the first to emphasize the importance of the military in Republican China; his *Rise of the Chinese Military Power* gives a detailed account of the origin of the Peiyang Army. F. F. Liu's *Military History of Modern China* focuses mostly on the Nationalist military machine and its political impact.
5. Sheridan, *Chinese Warlord*, and Gillin, *Warlord*.
6. Pye's *Warlord Politics* does aspire to present "warlord politics" in a theoretical framework. However, although it was published as recently as 1971, the book's basic research was done two decades ago and drew primarily upon English language materials and a few Chinese works then available. It has not incorporated the considerable amount of relevant primary and secondary work that has since appeared. This unfortunate defect is shown throughout the descriptive parts of the book and inevitably affects the theoretical analysis.
7. Some of the theoretical problems involved in making a choice between microscopic and macroscopic studies of politics are ably discussed in J. David Singer, "The Level-of-Analysis Problems in International Relations," in Klaus Knorr and Sidney Verba, eds., *The International System: Theoretical Essays* (Princeton, N.J., 1961), pp. 77–92.

Chapter 2

1. Ralph L. Powell, pp. 17–18.
2. Kuhn, Part IV.

3. Franz Michael, "Military Organization and Power Structure of China During the Taiping Rebellion," *Pacific Historical Review*, 18 (Nov. 1940): 478–83.

4. The agenda included such items as (1) reaffirmation of respect for the terms of the Manchu abdication; (2) the inviolability of Yüan Shih-k'ai's family and property; (3) convocation of the parliament to carry out constitutional government; (4) a demand that the southwest renounce its independence or face punitive action; (5) opposition to the participation of "extremists" in politics; (6) discussion on strengthening local defense and reducing taxes; and (7) the holding of future consultations among members to coordinate their policies. See T'ien Pu'i, 6 (1967): 32–41.

5. *Ibid.*
6. T'ao Chü-yin, *Tu chün t'uan chuan*, pp. 18–19.
7. T'ien Pu-i, 6: 32–41.
8. T'ao Chü-yin, *Tu chün t'uan chuan*, pp. 140–41.
9. Ts'ao Ju-lin, pp. 172–73.
10. Li Chien-nung, 2: 509.
11. *NCH*, Jan. 26, 1918.
12. *NCH*, Nov. 24, 1917.
13. *HSCTK*, nos. 1–4.
14. *NCH*, Jan. 5, 1918.
15. *Ibid.*
16. Pan-li, pp. 184–85.
17. *HSCTK*, nos. 19–64.
18. *NCH*, March 16, 1918.
19. *HSCTK*, no. 103.
20. *NCH*, March 23, 30, 1918.
21. Li Chien-nung, II, 515.
22. For a discussion of how the Tuan party perceived Ts'ao's alienation, see *HSCTK*, nos. 120, 125, 136, 139, 140, 148, 159, 223.
23. *HSCTK*, no. 293.
24. Ts'ao Ju-lin, pp. 173–74.
25. *NCH*, June 2, 1918.
26. Reinsch, pp. 292–94.
27. *NCH*, April 20, 1918.
28. Li Chien-nung, 2: 516.
29. *Ibid.*, p. 517.
30. *NCH*, April 27, May 11, 1918.
31. *Ibid.*, June 8, 1918.
32. Ts'ao Ju-lin, pp. 174–75.
33. Li Chien-nung, 2: 528–29.
34. T'ao Chü-yin, *Wu P'ei-fu chiang chün chuan*, p. 20.
35. *NCH*, April 6, 1918.
36. These included the Japanese arms, and Ch. $1,200,000 for the initial mobilization of the Fengtien forces. *NCH*, April 13, 1918. When Hsü Shu-cheng was invited to serve as the deputy commander of the Fengtien forces inside the Great Wall, he also became responsible for their provisions and training expenses.
37. *NCH*, April 3, 1920.
38. *Ibid.*, Feb. 21, Feb. 28, March 6, 1920.
39. "Chih-wan chan cheng shih mo chi," *Chin tai shih tzu liao*, no. 2, 1962, pp. 80–88.
40. For instance, Odoric Wou, who has done some quite exciting pioneer work in the analysis of militarism, explained Ts'ao K'un's behavior prior to mid-1918 by saying, "Ts'ao K'un, though a Chihli militarist, sided with the Anfu Clique in favor of war" (p. 268).
41. *HSCTK*, nos. 120, 125, 136, 140.

Chapter 3

1. For a theoretical treatment of father-son and brother-to-brother relationships, see Francis Hsü, especially pp. 59–63.
2. *Biographical Dictionary*, 1: 62.
3. For instance, Lu Jung-t'ing, the leader of the Kwangsi military group, was the brother-in-law of T'an Hou-min, military governor of Kwangsi from 1917 to 1921. T'an's brothers also held important military posts in the Kwangsi army. Huang Shao-hung, 1: 87.
4. T'ao Chü-yin, *Pei-yang chün fa t'ung chih shih ch'i shih hua*, 1: 14.
5. *Biographical Dictionary*, 3: 445.
6. *NCH*, Nov. 11, 1922.
7. Jung Meng-yüan, "Pei-yang chün fa ti lai yüan," *Li shih chiao hsüeh* (April 1957), pp. 22–24. Wen Kung-chih, 1: 15.
8. Huang Shao-hung, 1: 59–62, 107–9. Kao Tung, "Li Tsung-jen, Huang Shao-hung ch'i chia chen shih," *Ch'un ch'iu*, no. 74 (Aug. 1, 1960, pp. 9–10.
9. Wu-ch'iu-chung-tzu, 1: 88; *Biographical Dictionary*, 1: 62–63.
10. *Biographical Dictionary*, 3: 330–31.
11. *Biographical Dictionary*, 2: 24–26.
12. Apter, pp. 270n, 319–21.
13. Sheridan, pp. 78–83, 170, 210.
14. *Wu P'ei-fu hsien sheng nien p'u*, pp. 1–9.
15. Krech et al., pp. 438–42.
16. *Ibid.*, p. 434.
17. Richard H. Solomon, "Mao's Effort to Reintegrate the Chinese Polity: Problems of Authority and Conflict in Chinese Social Process," in A. Doak Barnett, ed., *Chinese Communist Politics in Action* (Seattle, 1969), pp. 271–351.
18. Wen Kung-chih, 2: 12.
19. *NCH*, Jan. 31, 1920.
20. Odoric Wou, for example, divides the membership of the Chihli clique into six different categories—*ta-yüan-lao*, *ti-hsi*, branches, adopted sons, *chun Chih-hsi*, and *ch'in Chih-hsi*. Based on this elaborate typology, he proceeds to draw up a "genealogy" for the Chihli clique during 1918–24. Odoric Wou, "A Chinese Warlord Faction: The Chihli Clique, 1918–1924," in *Columbia Essays in International Affairs*, pp. 249–73.
21. For a discussion of how this term was used in the traditional context, see Francis Hsü, pp. 122, 273; and Hsiao Kung-ch'uan, pp. 342–43.
22. For instance, Wen Kung-chih, the most authoritative military historian, lists the following as constituting the *ti-hsi* of Chihli under the leadership of Ts'ao K'un in August 1920: Feng Yü-hsiang, Hsiao Yao-nan, Ko Shu-p'in, Lu Chin, Peng Shou-hsin, Sun Yao, Tung Chen-kuo, Ts'ao Yin, Wang Ch'eng-pin, Wu P'ei-fu. On the other hand, Odoric Wou lists Feng Yü-hsiang, Sun Yao, and Lu Chin as adopted sons. Neither spells out the basis for making such classifications. Furthermore, the scheme becomes further confused when one tries to differentiate qualitatively be-

tween the "adopted sons" and the "quasi-Chihli faction"; the categories are not logically exhaustive and mutually exclusive. Wen Kung-chih, 2: 12; Odoric Wou, "A Chinese Warlord Faction," in *Columbia Essays in International Affairs*.

Chapter 4

1. Ralph L. Powell, *The Rise of the Chinese Military Power*, pp. 317–18.
2. Morton H. Fried, "Military Status in Chinese Society," *American Journal of Sociology*, 57, 4 (1952): 349–50.
3. T'ao Meng-ho, "I ko chün tui ping shih ti tiao ch'a," *She hui k'o hsüeh tsa chih*, 1, 2 (June 1930): 92–115.
4. Chiang Fang-cheng, *Ts'ai ping chi hua shu* (Shanghai, 1922), 1: 3–4.
5. *NCH*, Sept. 4, 1920. For a vivid description of how the 21st Division in Hupeh staged a mutiny in defiance of the order to disband, see *NCH*, June 18, 1921.
6. It was a consistent pattern for northern militarists to take northern troops with them even when they went to a southern province. For examples of Hupeh, Chekiang, Kiangsu, Fukien, Kiangsi, etc., see Wen Kung-chih, 2: 190–91, 208–9, 232–34, 269–70, 273, 284.
7. For comparisons of the levels of living conditions, agricultural productivity, and income between the north and the south, see Tawney, pp. 49, 70; Buck, *Land Utilization*, p. 281; Perkins, pp. 89–96; and Buck, *Chinese Farm Economy*, pp. 82–89.
8. *CYB*, 1921–22, pp. 820–21.
9. Perkins, p. 92; Teng Yün-t'e, pp. 130–32.
10. Sonoda, pp. 476–77.
11. Gillin, p. 25; Wen Kung-chih, 1, chap. 2.
12. Sheridan, p. 75.
13. Liu Ju-ming, "I ko hang wu chün jen ti hui i," *CCWH*, 2, 4 (Oct. 1942): 18–22.
14. Sonoda, pp. 418–26.
15. *Ko ming wen hsien*, ed. Lo Chia-lun (henceforth referred to as *KMWH*), 7: 19.
16. *KMWH*, 10: 27–36.
17. "Even the common soldiers ... shared in the good fortune, flaunting gold rings and gold watches, and ... earning more in a day than ordinary people spent in a month." Sutton, p. 256.
18. *Sheridan*, p. 161.

Chapter 5

1. Chang Tso-lin once lost one million dollars in a single night's gambling. Ts'ao Ju-lin, p. 145. Chang Tsung-ch'ang was another reckless gambler. When he was a brigade commander in the Fengtien army, he once lost in one night of gambling $100,000 of the $300,000 he had just received as payment for his troops. Chou Chun-shih, "Chang Tsung-ch'ang ti fa chi chi ch'ü wen," *CCWH*, 7, 3 (Sept. 1965): 42–47.
2. For instance, Ts'ao K'un reportedly embezzled $20 million during

his stint as military governor of Chihli. Kung Kan, Shou K'ang, "Erh shih erh sheng ti hsien chuan," *Ku chün*, 1, 2 (Oct. 1922). For a list of leading militarists' personal wealth, see Lai Hsin-hsia, "Pei-yang chün fa tui nei sou kua ti chi chung fang shih," *Shih hsüeh yüeh k'an* (March 1957), pp. 8–11.

3. One report said that the 70-mile stretch between Changsha and Pingkiang was totally desolate after being visited by northern troops in 1918. The situation was the same in other parts of Hunan. *NCH*, April 1918. By August 1919, the northern troops had been without pay for five months and were on the verge of another breakdown of discipline. The various chambers of commerce, acting with the local magistrates, hastily decided that the local gentry and merchants must "stump up" for public safety. As a result, the Changsha chamber of commerce paid $100,000, and Hsiangt'an paid $70,000 to the soldiers. *NCH*, Oct. 4, 1919.

4. Huang Shao-hung, 1: 41–42.
5. *NCH*, Oct. 5, 1918.
6. Sutton, pp. 210–12; *Ting chi T'ien Ch'uan chün tou chi lu*.
7. T'ao Chü-yin, *Wu P'ei-fu*, pp. 44–46; Sun To, "Wu P'ei-fu yü Kuomin-tang," *Hsiang tao*, no. 24 (May 9, 1923).
8. Wen Kung-chih, 2: 128; Gillin, p. 27.
9. Sheridan, pp. 121, 210, 213.
10. Sheridan, pp. 93–94.
11. Feng Yü-hsiang, *Wo ti sheng ho*, 3: 101–28.
12. Garthoff, pp. 47–48.
13. Mao Ssu-ch'eng, pp. 335–39.
14. Wilbur and How, p. 200.
15. The commander was to direct all military operations, and the political commissar was to undertake political administrative chores and to supervise the sanitation conditions. See Chiang Kai-shek's speech (April 8, 1926), quoted in Mao Ssu-ch'eng, pp. 643–45.
16. Ch'en Hsün-cheng, 1: 95–96.
17. F. F. Liu, pp. 19–20. During the Eastern Campaign of 1925, Whampoa's propaganda department prepared 500,000 pamphlets for the soldiers, 100,000 leaflets for the peasants, and 50,000 texts containing revolutionary songs. The political workers then distributed this large quantity of written propaganda materials, and they also organized labor and peasant unions and conducted mass meetings to complement military activities.
18. Liu Chih, p. 16.
19. Mao Ssu-ch'eng, pp. 245–46; F. F. Liu, p. 13.
20. Mao Ssu-ch'eng, p. 396.
21. *Pei fa chan shih*, 1: 183–84.
22. A most celebrated case involved Kuei Yung-ch'ing, a Whampoa cadet who later became the Nationalist commander in chief of the Navy and chairman of the Joint Chiefs of Staff. Kuei had confiscated some "enemy" property without authorization, for which he was sentenced to death. The Whampoa cadets filed a joint petition for clemency, and it

took the KMT Central Executive Committee to pass a special resolution for the death sentence to be commuted. Mao Ssu-ch'eng, p. 412.

23. She-ling-wai-shih, "Pao-ting chün kuan hsüeh hsiao ts'ang shang shih," *Ch'un ch'iu*, no. 63 (Feb. 16, 1960), p. 203.

24. Ch'in Te-shun, pp. 128–29. In practice, however, its applicants were not always graduates of Paoting or even the other preparatory schools. For instance, Huang Hsü-ch'u was graduated from the Kwangsi Army Short-Course School, which was actually comparable to a primary school, and went on to attend the Military College in 1913. Huang Hsü-ch'u, "Pa Kuei i wang lu," *Ch'un ch'iu*, no. 153 (Nov. 1963), p. 11.

25. Ralph L. Powell, pp. 338–39.

26. Jerome Ch'en, "Defining Chinese Warlords and Their Factions," *Bulletin of the School of Oriental and African Studies* (London, 1968), 31, part 3: 568. These figures must be treated with caution. In the first place, "brigadier" denotes a military rank rather than a command position. At times, it was purely honorific with no substance; or the holders might occupy administrative positions. If we are interested in those who actually command troops, say the commander of a brigade or a larger unit, the total number would be drastically reduced, which in turn might alter the percentage in favor of the educated militarists. Second, there is some problem with the accuracy of the statistics. For instance, Ch'en listed 29 brigadiers as having graduated from the military school in Tientsin. This is a curiously small number, since it is well known that this was the most important military educational institution of the Peiyang Army. My spot check revealed that among those whose surnames began with C (English transliteration) alone, Ch'en omitted nine graduates of Tientsin—Chang Chiu-ch'in, Chang Huai-chih, Chang Fu-lai, Chao Yü-k'o, Ch'en Kuang-yüan, Ch'i Hsieh-yüan, Chiang Yen-hsin, Chin Yün-ao, and Ch'en T'iao-yüan. All of these men held actual command positions, of brigade commander or higher.

27. Hu Shih, *Ting Wen-chiang ti chuan chi*, pp. 61–62.

28. Ts'ao Chü-jen, pp. 7–8.

29. Huang Shao-hung, 1: 15–16.

30. Ch'in Te-shun, pp. 109–17.

31. There was no comprehensive, standardized plan from the Ministry of War for this internship. The lower-echelon officers in the units had little education themselves and did not know how to teach the students. They were also unwilling to treat these temporary guests seriously. Huang Shao-hung, 1: 26–27.

32. Huang Shao-hung, 1: 29–30.

33. One school, the Shantung Army Survey School, which had produced 35 graduates in the previous four years, had only one instructor. Another, the Metropolitan Army School (*pu chün t'ung lin ya men chiang hsiao yen chiu so*), which produced 221 officers and 879 noncommissioned officers during the same period, had only four instructors altogether. *Lu chün t'ung chi*, 5, part 2, chap. 1.

34. *Lu chün t'ung-chi*, charts nos. 19, 20, 22; Wen Kung-chih, 1: 90–139.
35. *Lu chün t'ung chi*.
36. Sun To, "Wu P'ei-fu yü Kuo-ming-tang," *Hsiang tao*, no. 24 (May 9, 1923); *CYB*, 1923, p. 573; T'ao Chü-yin, *Wu P'ei-fu*, pp. 95–96.
37. Gillin, p. 26; Wen Kung-chih, 2: 128.
38. Soviet Advisers' report on the first Kuominchün officers, written shortly after April 1926, in Wilbur and How, p. 365. Shyu Nae-lih estimated that only two of Feng's 25 top commanders in 1925 had graduated from military schools before they began service. See his "Feng Yü-hsiang and the Kuominchün" (M.A. thesis, University of Washington, 1960), pp. 11–13.
39. Sheridan, pp. 76–87, 121.
40. The number of Soviet advisers in Feng's army in 1925 is a matter of disagreement among several sources. There were at least 36 Russians, but there may have been as many as 200. See the minutes of meeting held in the Soviet Embassy in Peking, Dec. 2, 1925, in Wilbur and How, pp. 344–48; the Soviet adviser Ya-en's report on the Kalgan Soviet Group, in Wilbur and How, pp. 355–59; Sheridan, pp. 166–67, 167n.
41. Mao Ssu-ch'eng, p. 275; *Pei fa chan shih*, 1: 102.
42. My preliminary survey of entries in the *Biographical Dictionary* turned up 25 persons who had served on the faculty of Whampoa. Of these, five had attended the Shikan Gakko or its preparatory school in Japan, seven had studied in colleges and universities in Japan, two had studied in the United States, two had studied in France, and nine had graduated from Paoting Military Academy.
43. F. F. Liu, p.14.
44. The chief of the Soviet Group was General Galen (or Galin), whose real name was Vasil Konstantinovich Blücher (1889–1938), a hero of the Russian civil war who later became one of the Soviet Union's most outstanding military leaders. Other distinguished members of the Group included A. I. Yegorov, Victor Rogacheff, and possibly G. K. Zhukov. F. F. Liu, p. 6; Jan J. Solecki, trans., "Blücher's 'Grand Plan' of 1926," *China Quarterly*, no. 35 (July–Sept. 1968), p. 18.
45. Garthoff, pp. 46–47.
46. Mao Ssu-ch'eng, p. 595.
47. Len Hsi, "Hsüeh sa Hui-chou ch'eng," *CCWH*, 3, 4 (Oct. 1963): 13.
48. She-ling-wai-she, *Ch'un ch'iu*, no. 64 (March 1, 1960), pp. 4–5.
49. Mao Ssu-ch'eng, p. 675.
50. *Pei fa chan shih*, 1: 104–8, 114; Mao Ssu-ch'eng, p. 382. It should be further pointed out that before the Northern Expedition, officers' training had already extended to other KMT armies with some Soviet assistance. Kisanko reported that "there are officers' schools in the First, Second, Third, and Fourth Armies." The Second Army had 750 students in the officers' school and 550 in the enlisted men's school. In the Third

Army, there were 800 in officers' school and 600 in supplementary school. Wilbur and How, pp. 191–97.

Chapter 6

1. In 1916 the survey conducted by the Ministry of War indicated that the following varieties of rifles were in use in different armies: by countries of origin—German, Russian, Italian, British, Austrian, French, Belgian, Japanese, American, and Chinese; by models or calibers—65, 68, 70, 79, 80 mm rifles; old-styled mausers, single-barrel mausers, double-barrel mausers, and "miscellaneous types." *Lu chün t'ung-chi*, 1–2.
2. *CYB*, 1921–22, p. 516.
3. The 1916 survey of the Ministry of War listed 24 kinds of artillery, from Germany, Japan, France, Britain, and China's own arsenals. *Lu chün-t'ung chi*, 1–2.
4. *TFTC*, 15, 5 (May 1918): 181–86.
5. In 1916 there were at least six different models and five calibers. *Lu chün-t'ung chi*, 1–2.
6. *CYB*, 1921–22, p. 516.
7. *NCH*, July 21, 1923.
8. Hu Shih, *Ting Wen-chiang ti chuan chi*, p. 86.
9. T'ien Pu-i, 4: 98.
10. *CYB*, 1924, p. 954.
11. *CYB*, 1928, p. 1285.
12. *Lu chün t'ung chi*, 1–28.
13. *CYB*, 1921–22, p. 532.
14. *CWR*, Feb. 9, 1924.
15. For example, the Techow arsenal in Shantung was completely dismantled in 1926 by Chang Tsung-ch'ang. The Chengtu arsenal of Szechwan was burned in 1925. When Mo Jung-hsin was forced out of Canton in 1920, he tried to destroy the Canton arsenal, causing considerable damage. *CYB*, 1929–30, pp. 751–53.
16. For instance, in two separate battles at Mi-lo in Hunan and Ho-sheng-ch'iao in Hupeh in July 1926, the KMT forces on the offensive expended more than 630,000 rounds of rifle and machine-gun ammunition. *KMWH*, 12: 149–52.
17. For a discussion of the sums of money involved, see Li Chien-nung, 2: 516.
18. The original signers were Britain, Spain, Portugal, the United States, Russia, Brazil, France, and Japan. The Netherlands, Denmark, Belgium, and Italy later endorsed the document. *CYB*, 1923, pp. 598–99.
19. "Mr. Strawn and the Gun-running Business in China," *CWR*, Dec. 11, 1926.
20. *CYB*, 1924, p. 957.
21. *CYB*, 1924, p. 957.
22. The crucial role played by foreign arms in China's civil wars is discussed in Jowe.
23. "The Japanese and Recent Chinese Arms Deals," *CWR*, Feb. 4, 1928.
24. Jowe, "Who Sells the Guns to China's War Leaders?"

25. For instance, in the summer and fall of 1922, the Chinese Maritime Customs authorities at Shanghai and Tientsin discovered that large shipments of Italian, Japanese, German, and Russian arms and ammunition were making their way to Canton from other Chinese ports. Peter S. Jowe, "Who Sells the Guns to China's War Leaders?" *CWR*, April 18, 1925.

26. See Kisanko's report, in Wilbur and How, pp. 191–97.

27. The first shipment of Soviet arms arrived in Canton on October 8, 1924, with some 8,000 rifles and 4 million rounds of ammunition. It is estimated that the Soviets provided a total of 3 million rubles for the initial expenses of the Whampoa Academy alone. Garthoff, p. 46. For other estimates of Soviet assistance during this stage, see Chiang Kai-shek, *Soviet Russia in China*, p. 272; *KMWH*, 10: 4.

28. *CYB*, 1928, p. 802. For an eyewitness account of Soviet shipment to China in 1926, see Abend, pp. 18–19.

29. F. F. Liu, pp. 26–27.

30. *CYB*, 1928, p. 802.

31. Mao Ssu-ch'eng, pp. 663, 686. In fact, the *China Weekly Review* estimated that the Soviets sold some $10 million worth of arms to the KMT during 1926–27. "The Japanese and Recent Chinese Arms Deal," *CWR*, Feb. 4, 1928.

32. For instance, the KMT 7th Army from Kwangsi does not seem to have benefited from Soviet assistance at all throughout the Northern Expedition. Huang Hsü-ch'u, "Kuo min ko ming chün ti ch'i chü shih shih," *Ch'un ch'iu*, no. 247 (Oct. 16, 1967), p. 19; no. 250 (Dec. 1, 1967), p. 21.

33. *CYB*, 1928, p. 818.

34. One estimate put the Soviet aid in 1926 to Feng at 24 guns, 10 trench mortars, 90 maxim guns, 25,970 rifles, 24 million cartridges, 22,000 artillery shells, 10,000 hand grenades, and 1,000 French mortar shells. J.A.J., "The Futility of the Arms Embargo," *CWR*, Feb. 11, 1928.

35. In Szechwan, for example, the sulfuric acid used by the provincial armories to make white gunpowder had to be carried from K'un-ming through Kweichow on ponies, each carrying only two jars. The transportation cost was very high, and there were considerable losses on the rocky, mountainous trails. Yang Chao-jung, "Hsin-hai hou chih Ssu-ch'uan chan chi," *Chin tai shih tzu liao*, 23 (1958): 57.

36. Ch'en Hsün-cheng, 3: 364–88.

37. For instance, during the height of the 1924 war, planes of the Fengtien faction made 24 sorties in eight days to the Shan-hai-kuan area, where large Chihli forces were concentrated. The bombs killed five soldiers, felled two trees, and partially damaged one hotel. And Fengtien even managed to lose two planes. *Feng Chih chan shih*, pp. 41–42.

38. For instance, one eyewitness reported that during the 1924 Chihli-Fengtien war, the soldiers regarded the planes more as a curiosity than a threat, and scrambled for bomb fragments as souvenirs. Impey, "Chinese Progress in the Art of War."

39. Chang Chün-ku, 2: 360–93; *Feng Chih chan shih*, pp. 65–82.
40. *Pei fa chan shih*, 4: 1065–66.
41. Of the nine main "national highways" in existence in 1916, seven radiated from Peking, and all but one traversed the northern plains of China. No major roads existed between other cities, and even these "highways" were no more than "tracks or mere footpaths" which could accommodate a very small amount of traffic. *CYB*, 1916, pp. 240–41.
42. *CYB*, 1923, pp. 403–13.
43. "Silas Strawn Describes China Conditions," *CWR*, Dec. 4, 1926.
44. Feuerwerker, *The Chinese Economy, 1912–1949*, pp. 40–44.
45. *CYB*, 1925, pp. 347–77.
46. For more detailed illustrations, let us look at the Peking–Hankow railway, which had a distance of 892 miles. In 1916 this line had 129 locomotives and 2,867 cars in operation, and carried 2,690,000 persons and 3,520 million tons of goods. "Min kuo wu nien kuo yu t'ieh lu ko lu tsung k'uang," *TFTC*, 15, 1 (Jan. 1918): 165–66. Thus, if the militarists fully controlled the line, they could transport about a quarter of a million soldiers with nearly 300 million tons of war matériel from Hankow to Peking within any month of the year. By 1924, this line had 229 locomotives and 4,200 cars, a substantial increase from 1916. *CYB*, 1925, pp. 347–77. Though we have no figures on this point, it is natural to assume that its transportation capacity also increased substantially.

The Peking–Mukden railway played a crucial role in many civil wars. After the conclusion of the first Chihli-Fengtien war of 1922, the press reported that 1,500 railway cars had been concentrated at Ch'ing-huang-tao by Wu P'ei-fu to move his troops back to their bases at the rate of 5,000 men per day. *NCH*, July 8, 1922. During the second Chihli-Fengtien war of 1924, more than 600 trains were mobilized by Chihli to move troops and equipment. To facilitate this operation, thousands of cars were borrowed from other lines. Chien Pei-yu, "Chinese Railways Recovering from War Effects in North," *CWR*, Jan. 17, 1925.

47. Huang Shao-hung, 1: 157–58.
48. During 1913, the water level in Wu-chow recorded a difference of 73 feet. *Ibid.*
49. Ch'en Hui, p. 38.
50. *NCH*, July–Aug., 1923.
51. *NCH*, May 1918; Huang Hsü-ch'u, "Pa Kuei i wang lu," *Ch'un ch'iu*, no. 160 (March 1, 1964), pp. 15–16.
52. Wen Kung-chih, 2: 9–10; Lai-chiang-chu-wu, "Chih Wan chan cheng shih mo chi," *Chin tai shih tzu liao*, no. 2 (Aug. 1962), pp. 93–96.
53. Close, p. 57; Gale, pp. 110–11; T'ao Chü-yin, *Tu chün t'uan chuan*, p. 128.
54. Sheridan, pp. 22–23.
55. T'ien Pu-i, *Pei yang chün fa*, 4: 98–104; Reinsch, pp. 270–85.
56. Lai-chiang-chu-wu, *Chin tai shih tzu liao*, no. 2 (1962), pp. 99–101; *NCH*, Aug. 7, 1920.

57. *CYB*, 1923, pp. 573–76.
58. Wen Kung-chih, 3: 119–31.
59. *Feng Chih-chan shih*, pp. 44–57, 94.
60. *Pei fa chan shih*, 5, "Kuo min ko ming chün pei fa cheng wang chiang shih t'i min lu."
61. Wen Kung-chih, 3: 274–81.
62. T'ao Chü-yin, *Wu P'ei-fu*, pp. 159–60, 163.
63. *KMWH*, 15: 692–702.

Chapter 7

1. Peng Yu-hsin, "Ch'ing mo chung yang yü ko sheng ts'ai cheng kuan hsi," *She hui k'o hsüeh tsa chih*, 9, 1 (June 1947): 83–110; Ralph L. Powell, pp. 23–26.
2. "China's Finances under the Republican Regime," *CWR*, Nov. 1, 1925. Supplement.
3. Hsieh Keng-min, "Ti fang shui chüan t'i chih chih shan pien chi ch'i shih shi," *CHMKKKWSN*, 1: 621.
4. Perkins, pp. 176–77.
5. Chou K'ai-ch'ing, *Min-kuo Ssu-ch'uan shih shih*, pp. 225–37.
6. Feuerwerker, *Chinese Economy, 1912–1949*, p. 49.
7. Chou Te-wei, T'ao Yü-ch'i, "Kuan shui yü kuan cheng," *CHMKKKWSN*, 1: 540.
8. For cases of local confiscation in Yunnan, Szechwan, and Kwangtung in 1916–18, see Adshead, pp. 199–200. For cases in Kwangtung and Kwangsi in 1918, see *NCH*, March 16, 23, 1918. For cases in Manchuria in 1919, see *NCH*, Oct. 11, 1919.
9. *CYB*, 1926–27, pp. 507–10.
10. Adshead, p. 197; *CYB*, 1926–27, pp. 507–10.
11. For a good example in Fukien in 1926, see C. Martin Wilbur, in Ho and Tang, *China in Crisis*, 1, Book 1, p. 211.
12. At the beginning of the twentieth century, there were at least 23 regional and provincial likin bureaus, 790 local stations, and 1,446 substations, staffed by some 25,000 people. (Figures for Hupeh, Kiangsi, Kwangtung, Shansi, Kweichow, and Chihli were incomplete.) Peng Yü-hsin, "Ch'ing mo chung yang yu ko sheng ts'ai cheng kuan hsi," *She hui k'o hsüeh tsa chih*, 9, 1 (June 1947): 83–110.
13. For instance, although Kiangsu had only 58 likin stations, it had another 511 substations. Kan Lee, "Likin and Its Abolition," *CWR*, Aug. 20, 1927. Moser estimates that the number of likin substations and barriers for the whole country ran into the thousands. Moser, *CWR*, Aug. 7, 1926. Ma Yin-ch'u, the foremost Chinese economist of his time, estimated that these likin offices employed some 1.5 million people. Ma Yin-ch'u, 3: 292–93.
14. Feuerwerker, *Chinese Economy, 1870–1911*, Table 21, p. 65.
15. Moser, *CWR*, Aug. 7, 1926.
16. *CWR*, Nov. 15, 1924; Liu Yen, 2: 121–37.

17. One study suggests that between 1911 and 1927, Japan provided nearly 40 percent of China's foreign loans. The Western capitalist countries were left far behind: 15.45 percent for France, 14.66 percent for Great Britain, and 5.03 percent for the United States. Hsü I-sheng, p. 244. Also see *Ts'ai-cheng-pu chin kuan wu chüeh shih tan pao wai chai piao*.

18. Hsü I-sheng, pp. 148–97, 240–41.

19. *CYB*, 1923, pp. 703–12; *CYB*, 1929–30, pp. 657–60. For other years, see Woodhead, *The Truth about the Chinese Republic*, pp. 130–31; A. G. Coons, *The Foreign Public Debt of China* cited in Liu Ping-lin, pp. 194–97.

20. Hsü I-sheng, pp. 148–97. For a case in Kwangtung in 1916, see *TFTC*, "Chung-kuo ta shih chi," 14, 2 (Feb. 1917): 211; for Fukien, see *NCH*, May 3, 1919; for Hunan in 1921 see *TFTS*, "Chung-kuo ta shih chi," 18, 5 (March 1921): 133.

21. Hsü Ts'ang-shui, charts between pp. 22 and 23.

22. Ch'ien Chia-chü, "Chiu chung-kuo fa hsin kung chai shih ti yen chiu," *Li shih yen chiu*, no. 2 (April 1955), pp. 112, 118.

23. Ch'ien Chia-chü, *Chiu chung-kuo kung chai shih tzu liao*, Preface, p. 10.

24. Lai Hsin-hsia, "Pei yang chün fa tui nei sou kua ti chi chung fang shih," *Shih hsüeh yüeh k'an*, no. 3 (March 1957), pp. 8–11; Ch'ien Chia-chü, *Li shih yen chiu*, no. 2 (April 1955), p. 112.

25. Ch'ien Chia-chü, *Li shih yen chiu*, pp. 113–15.

26. To cite a few examples: in 1918 the Finance Commissioner of Kiangsu province floated a short-term provincial bond issue in the amount of Ch. $1,500,000, bearing interest at 7 percent per annum. *NCH*, July 13, 1918. Then in 1921 Kiangsu issued two more bonds totaling nearly Ch. $9 million. Hsü Ts'ang-shui, Appendix, pp. 3–6. For cases in Hunan in 1918–21, see Hsü Ts'ang-shui, *ibid*. For cases in Manchuria and Shantung in 1926, see *TFTC*, 23, 12 (June 25, 1926): 142; and 23, 13 (July 10, 1926): 138.

27. *NCH*, Oct. 6, 1917.

28. Ch'ien Chia-chü, *Chiu chung-kuo kung chai shih tzu liao*, pp. 369–70.

29. Shang Hsi-ch'ing, "Ti fang yin hang," *Chung hua min kuo k'ai kuo wu shih nien shih lun chu*, 1: 685; T'ao Chü-yin, *Tu chün t'uan chuan*, p. 29; *CYB*, 1928, p. 658. There are minor disagreements among scholars about how many banks issued their own currency in significant amounts. For instance, Chin Kuo-pao lists 38 large banks, both public and private, as having issued currency. Chin Kuo-pao, pp. 126–29.

30. For cases in Kwangtung and Kwangsi, see Huang Shao-hung, 1: 80–90; for Chihli and Shantung, see *TFTC*, 23, 16 (Aug. 25, 1926): 142.

31. T'ao Chü-yin, *Tu chün t'uan chuan*, p. 29.

32. C. Martin Wilbur, in Ho and Tang, *China in Crisis*, 1, Book 1, p. 210.

33. Feng Yü-hsiang, *Wo ti sheng ho*, 3: 164–65.
34. *Ibid.*
35. Charles Dailey, "Chinese Militarists on Road to Bankruptcy," *CWR*, May 28, 1927.
36. For a description of how Feng Kuo-chang and other high Peking officials were involved in an opium scandal, see Woodhead, *Adventures in Far Eastern Journalism*, pp. 75–76; *NCH*, Sept. 14, 1918; Jan. 11, 1919.
37. *CYB*, 1923, pp. 886–93; *CYB*, 1928, pp. 528–35.
38. Chou Hsien-wen, "Chung-kuo chih yen ho chi ch'i ts'e," *TFTC*, 23, 20 (Oct. 25, 1926): 33–34.
39. *Chung-kuo ching chi lun wen chi*, 2: 34–37. For some provincial figures see *CYB*, 1923, pp. 886–93; *CYB*, 1924, p. 572; Ma Yin-ch'u, 3: 136; *CYB*, 1928, pp. 528–35.
40. As a result, in 1924, for example, the transit taxes collected by Hupeh militarists amounted to about $15 million. Chou Hsien-wen, "Chung kuo chih yen ho chi ch'i chiu chi ts'e," *TFTC*, 23, 20 (Oct. 25, 1926): 33–34.
41. Huang Shao-hung, 1: 154–55; also Huang Hsü-ch'u, "Pa Kuei i wang lu," *Ch'un ch'iu*, no. 177 (Jan. 16, 1964), pp. 14–17.
42. *CYB*, 1928, pp. 528–35.
43. *CWR*, July 26, 1924.
44. Silas H. Strawn, "China Today," *Annual Report, 1926–1927* (London), pp. 13–14, as quoted by C. Martin Wilbur, in Ho and Tang, *China in Crisis*, 1, Book 1, p. 210.
45. *NCH*, Feb. 10, 1917.
46. *NCH*, April 23, 1923.
47. Ts'ao Ju-lin, p. 171.
48. Ch'ien Chia-chü, *Li shih yen chiu*, no. 2 (April 1955), p. 118.
49. Ts'ao Ju-lin, pp. 169–71, 175–76; *NCH*, May 11, 1918.
50. Kung-kan, Shou-k'ang, *Ku chün*, 1, 2 (Oct. 1922); Wu-liao-tzu, pp. 33–34, chap. 3.
51. Sung-kao, "Feng Chang ju kuan yü Pei-ching cheng chü," *TFTC*, 22, no. 13 (July 10, 1925): 3.
52. *Shan hou hui i kung pao*, no. 2, "Resolutions," p. 27.
53. *CYB*, 1929–30, p. 635.
54. *NCH*, Feb. 5, 1921.
55. Chen Han-sheng, of Academia Sinica, quoted in Nieh, p. 38. For other years see *NCH*, Feb. 5, 1921; Kung-nu, "Lu chün yü ts'ai cheng," *Ku chün*, 1, nos. 4–5 (Jan. 1, 1923).
56. *Shan hou hui i kung pao* contains information to show that in province after province military expenditures exceeded regular income, sometimes by over twice as much.

57. Myers, pp. 276–77.
58. *Ibid.*, p. 277.
59. Ma Yin-ch'u, 2: 16–17.
60. *KMWH*, 20: 1572–82.
61. *CYB*, 1928, pp. 1338–39.
62. *KMWH*, 20: 1616–22.
63. *Ibid.*, pp. 1677–82.
64. *Ibid.*

65. Tsou Lu, *Chung-kuo kuo-min-tang shih kao* (Chungking, 1944), 2d ed., pp. 290, 299n22.

Chapter 8

1. For example, Jerome Ch'en points out that many militarists were stout defenders of the Confucian tradition, and some of them even went so far as to write expositions on Confucian virtues and political doctrines. Jerome Ch'en, "Defining Chinese Warlords and Their Factions," *Bulletin of the School of Oriental and African Studies*, 31, part 3 (1968): 569–70.

2. Redfield, pp. 42–43.

3. For a more detailed discussion of this trait, see Robert Ruhlmann, "Traditional Heroes in Chinese Popular Fiction," in *Confucian Persuasion*, ed. Arthur F. Wright (Stanford, Calif., 1960), pp. 141–76.

4. Pearl Buck, "Chinese War Lords," *The Saturday Evening Post*, 205, 43 (April 22, 1933): 77. As quoted in Sheridan, p. 20.

5. Lucian Pye's content analysis of some 300 circular telegrams, public addresses, proclamations, and interviews by the militarists shows that the references to "personal associations," "attacks on personalities," and "appeal for moral virtues" outnumbered other themes (such as republicanism and anti-imperialism) by a considerable margin. See his *Warlord Politics*, Table 7.1, p. 116.

6. Mao Ssu-ch'eng, pp. 954, 966–67; Ch'en Hsi-chang, p. 310.

7. Wen Kung-chih, 1: 444.

8. Wang Gungwu, "Comments," in Ho Ping-ti and Tsou Tang, *China in Crisis*, 1, Book 1, p. 269.

Chapter 9

1. Mao Ssu-ch'eng, pp. 384–85, 878, 726–29, 736.

2. The battle plan for the KMT's first eastern expedition in January 1925 was drawn largely by General Blücher, the chief Soviet adviser. Garthoff, p. 49.

3. A. I. Cherepanov, *Zapiski voennogo sovetnika v Kitae* (Memoirs of a Soviet Military Adviser in China; Moscow, 1964), quoted in Garthoff, p. 50.

4. Garthoff, p. 50.

5. MacNair, *China in Revolution*, p. 108.

6. For a theoretical discussion of the peculiar features of an international system as distinct from a national system, see Morton A. Kaplan, "Problems of Theory Building and Theory Confirmation in International Politics," in *The International System*, ed. by Klaus Knorr and Sidney Verba (Princeton, N.J., 1961), pp. 13–17. For a different set of reasons why international political theory can be used to study national politics, see Fred W. Riggs, "International Relations as a Prismatic System," *ibid.*, pp. 144–81.

7. For an incisive discussion on the different shades of meaning of the

term "balance of power," see Ernest B. Haas, "The Balance of Power: Prescription, Concept, or Propaganda?" in *World Politics*, 5 (July 1953): 442–47.

8. For different interpretations of this common theme, consult Toynbee, p. 233; Taylor, p. xx.

9. Claude, pp. 43–51. For a discussion of why such uses of the term should be rejected, see Organski, chap. 2.

10. Kaplan, p. 23.
11. *Ibid.*, pp. 25–28.
12. Pan-li, p. 237.
13. Li Chien-nung, 2: 559.
14. *Ibid.*, pp. 562–63.
15. Wen Kung-chih, 2: 119–232.
16. Pan-li, p. 259; Li Chien-nung, 2: 576.
17. Li Chien-nung, 2: 574–98.
18. *Ibid.*, pp. 591–96.
19. Pan-li, pp. 319–27.
20. Li Chien-nung, 2: 648–49.
21. Wen Kung-chih, 2: 181–96.
22. Pan-li, p. 375.
23. Sheridan, pp. 160–69.
24. *Ibid.*, pp. 180–85.
25. *Ibid.*, pp. 221–23.

Bibliography

Abend, Hallett. *My Years in China, 1926–1941.* London, 1944.
Adshead, S. A. M. *The Modernization of the Chinese Salt Administration, 1900–1920.* Cambridge, Mass., 1970.
Andrzejewski, Stanislaw. *Military Organization and Society.* London, 1954.
Apter, David E. *Politics of Modernization.* Chicago, 1967.
Arnold, Julean. *Commercial Handbook of China.* Washington, D.C., 1924.
———. *China Through the American Window.* Shanghai, 1932.
Barker, John Earl. *Explaining China.* London, 1927.
Barnett, A. Doak, ed. *Chinese Communist Politics in Action.* Seattle, 1969.
Bienen, Henry, ed. *The Military Intervenes: Case Studies in Political Development.* New York, 1968.
———. *The Military and Modernization.* Chicago, 1971.
Biographical Dictionary of Republican China. New York, 1967–71, 4 vols.
Borg, Dorothy. *American Policy and the Chinese Revolution.* New York, 1947.
Browder, Earl Russell. *Civil War in Nationalist China.* Chicago, 1927.
Buck, John Lossing. *Chinese Farm Economy.* Shanghai, 1930.
———. *Agricultural Survey of Szechwan Province, China.* New York, 1943.
———. *Land Utilization in China.* New York, 1964.
Bulletin of the School of Oriental and African Studies (University of London, 1968), Vol. XXXI, Part 3.
Carlson, E. F. *The Chinese Army, Its Organization and Military Efficiency.* New York, 1940.
Chang Ch'i-yün. *Chung-kuo chün shih shih lüeh.* Shanghai, 1946.
———. *Tang shih kai yao.* Taipei, 1950. 3 vols.
———. *Chung-hua min-kuo shih kang.* Taipei, 1954.
———. *Chung-hua min-kuo k'ai kuo wu shih nien shih lun chi.* Taipei, 1964. 2 vols.

Chang Chung-fu. *Chung-hua min-kuo wai chiao shih*. Peiping, 1936.
Chang Chung-li. *The Chinese Gentry*. Seattle, 1955.
———. *The Income of the Chinese Gentry*. Seattle, 1962.
Chang Chün-ku. *Wu P'ei-fu chuan*. Taipei, 1968. 2 vols.
Chang Chün-mai. *Six Lectures on the Civil War*. Shanghai, 1924.
Chang Hsiao-mei. *Ssu-ch'uan ching chi ts'an k'ao tzu liao*. Shanghai, 1939.
Chang Hsiung. *Chung-hua min-kuo ti nei ko*. Peiping, 1928.
Chang Kuo-p'ing. *Pai Ch'ung-hsi chiang chün chuan*. N.p., 1938.
Chang ta yüan shuai ai wan lu. N.p., n.d.
Chang Tzu-sheng. *Feng Chih chan cheng chi shih*. Taipei, 1967.
———. *Jen hsü cheng pien chi*. Shanghai, 1924.
Chang Yün-chia. *Yü Yu-jen chuan*. Taipei, 1958.
Chapman, H. O. *The Chinese Revolution, 1926–1927*. London, 1928.
Chen Kung-fu. *Chung-kuo ko ming shih*. Shanghai, 1930.
Ch'en Chin-ts'un hsien sheng nien p'u. N.p., n.d.
Ch'en Hsi-chang. *Pei-yang ts'ang shuang shih hua*. Tainan, 1967. 2 vols.
Ch'en Hsün-cheng. *Kuo-min ko-ming chün chan shih ch'u kao*. Nanking?, 1936. 6 vols.
Ch'en Hui. *Kuang-hsi chiao t'ung wen t'i*. Changsha, 1938.
Ch'en, Jerome. *Yüan Shih-k'ai: 1859–1916*. London, 1961.
Ch'en Kao-yung. *Chung-kuo li tai t'ien tsai jen ho piao*. Shanghai, 1939.
Ch'en K'o-hua. *Chung-kuo hsien tai ko ming shih*. Hong Kong, 1965. 3 vols.
Ch'en Kung-lu. *Chung-kuo chin tai shih*. Shanghai, 1935.
Ch'en Lieh-fu *Chung-kuo chin tai shih*. Hong Kong, 1964.
Ch'en Shao-hsiao. *Chün fa pieh chuan*. Hong Kong, 1966.
Cheng Fang. *A General Course on Chinese District (Hsien) Government*. Changsha, 1939. 2 vols.
Cheng Sih-gung. *Modern China: A Political Study*. London, 1919.
Chia I-chün. *Chung-hua min-kuo shih*. Peiping, 1930.
———. *Chung-kuo ming jen chuan*. Peiping, 1932–33. 2 vols.
Chia Shih-i. *Min-kuo ts'ai cheng shih*. Shanghai, 1927. 2 vols.
———. *Min-kuo hsü ts'ai cheng shih*. Shanghai, 1932.
Chia Tsung-fu. *Chung-ku chih hsien chien shih*. Taipei, 1953.
Chiang Che chan shih. Shanghai, 1924.
Chiang-hsi sheng yün shu kai k'uang. N.p., 1941.
Chiang Kai-shek. *Soviet Russia in China*. New York, 1958.
———. *Su-o tsai chung-kuo*. Taipei, 1958.
Chiang Pai-li. *Ts'ai p'ing chi hua shu*. Shanghai, 1922.
———. *Kuo fang lun*. Taipei, 1965.
Ch'ien Chia-chü. *Kuang-hsi sheng ching chi kai k'uang*. Shanghai, 1926.
———. *Chung-kuo nung ts'un ching chi lun wen chi*. Peiping, 1935.
———. *Chiu chung-kuo kung chai shih tzu liao*. Peking, 1955.
Ch'ien Tuan-sheng. *Min-kuo cheng chih shih*. Shanghai, 1946. 2 vols.
———. *The Government and Politics of China*. Cambridge, Mass., 1950.
Chih Feng ta chan shih. Shanghai, 1922.

Ch'ih-sung-tzu. *Min-kuo ch'un ch'iu.* Hong Kong, 1961.
Chin Kuo-pao. *Chung-kuo pei chih wen t'i.* Shanghai, 1927.
Ch'in Te-shun. *Ch'in Te-shun hui i lu.* Taipei, 1967.
Ching chi chien she. Shanghai, 1929.
Chou K'ai-ch'ing, ed. *Min-kuo Ssu-ch'uan jen wu chuan chi.* Taipei, 1966.
———. *Min-kuo Ssu-ch'uan shih shih.* Taipei, 1969.
Chou Ku-ch'eng. *Chung-kuo she hui chih pien hua.* Shanghai, 1931.
Chow Tse-tsung. *The May Fourth Movement.* Stanford, Calif. 1960.
Chu Ch'i-hua. *Chung-kuo she hui ti ching chi chieh kou.* Shanghai, 1931.
Chu Chung-yü. *Pei-yang chün fa ti t'ung chih.* Peking, 1956.
Chu Ssu-huang. *Min-kuo ching chi shih.* Shanghai, 1948.
Ch'uan T'ien chan cheng pao kao shu. Chungking, 1920.
Chung-kuo ching chi lun wen chi. Shanghai, 1934. 2 vols.
Chung-kuo hsien tai ko ming yün tung shih. Hong Kong, 1949.
Ch'ü T'ung-tsu. *Law and Society in Traditional China.* The Hague, 1961.
———. *Local Government in China under the Ch'ing.* Stanford, Calif., 1962.
Claude, Inis L. *Power and International Relations.* New York, 1962.
Close, Upton. *In the Land of the Laughing Buddha.* New York, 1924.
Clubb, Edmund. *Twentieth Century China.* New York, 1964.
Columbia Essays in International Affairs: The Dean's Papers, 1967. Edited by A. W. Cordier. New York, 1968.
Daalder, Hans. *The Role of the Military in the Emerging Countries.* The Hague, 1962.
Durkheim, Emile. *The Division of Labor in Society.* New York, 1964.
Earle, Edward Mead, ed. *Makers of Modern Strategy.* Princeton, N.J., 1941.
Fan Wen-lan. *Chung-kuo chin tai shih.* Peking, 1952–.
Fan Yin-nan. *Tang tai Chung-kuo min jen-lu.* Shanghai, 1937.
Fang Hsien-ting. *Chung-kuo ching chi yen chiu.* Changsha, 1938.
The Federalist (Papers). New York, 1961.
Fei Hsiao-t'ung. *Peasant Life in China.* New York, 1939.
———. *Earthbound China.* Chicago, 1945.
Fei Pao-yen. *Shan hou hui i shih.* Peking, 1925.
Feng Chih chan shih. Shanghai, 1924.
Feng Yü-hsiang. *Feng Yü-hsiang chün shih yao tien hui pien.* N.p., n.d.
———. *Feng Yü-hsiang jih chi.* Peiping, 1932.
———. *Wo ti sheng huo.* Shanghai, 1947. 3 vols.
Feng Yü-hsiang ti tsung chien ch'a. Peking, 1922.
Feuerwerker, Albert. *The Chinese Economy, 1912–1949.* Ann Arbor, Mich., 1968.
———. *The Chinese Economy, 1870–1911.* Ann Arbor, Mich., 1969.
Fong, H. D. *China's Industrialization: A Statistical Survey.* N.p., n.d.
Freedman, Maurice. *Lineage Organization in Southeastern China.* London, 1958.
Fu Ch'i-hsüeh. *Kuo-fu Chung-shan hsien sheng chuan.* Taipei, 1965.

Gale, Esson M. *Salt for the Dragon: A Personal History of China, 1908–1945.* East Lansing, Mich., 1953.
Gamble, Sidney D. *Peking: A Social Survey.* New York, 1921.
———. *Ting Hsien: A North China Rural Community.* New York, 1954.
———. *North China Villages.* Berkeley, Calif., 1963.
Garthoff, Raymond L., ed. *Sino-Soviet Military Relations.* New York, 1966.
Gendai chuka minkoku, manshu teikoku jinmei roku. Tokyo, 1927.
Gendai shina jinmei kan. Tokyo, 1928.
Gilbert, Rodney. *What's Wrong with China?* London, 1926.
Gillin, Donald G. *Warlord: Yen Hsi-shan in Shansi Province, 1911–1949.* Princeton, N.J., 1967.
Ho Ping-ti. *Studies on the Population of China, 1368–1953.* Cambridge, Mass., 1959.
———. *The Ladder of Success in Imperial China: Aspects of Social Mobility, 1368–1911.* New York, 1962.
———. *Chung-kuo hui kuan shih lun.* Taipei, 1966.
Ho Ping-ti and Tsou Tang, eds., *China in Crisis.* Chicago, 1968. 2 vols.
Houn, Franklin. *Central Government of China, 1912–1928.* Madison, Wis., 1959.
Hsiao Hsiao. *Tang tai chung-kuo min jen chih.* Shanghai, 1939.
Hsiao Kung-chuan. *Rural China: Imperial Control in the Nineteenth Century.* Seattle, 1960.
Hsin chien lu chün ping lüeh lu ts'un. Peking, 1898.
Hsü, Francis. *Under the Ancestors' Shadow.* New York, 1948.
Hsü I-sheng. *Chung-kuo chin tai wai chai shih t'ung chi tzu liao, 1853–1927.* Peking, 1962.
Hsü Shu-cheng. *Hsü Shu-cheng tien kao.* Peking, 1964.
Hsü Tao-lin. *Hsu Shu-cheng hsien sheng wen chi nien p'u ho k'an.* Taipei, 1962.
Hsü Ts'ang-shui. *Nei kuo kung chai shih.* Shanghai, 1932.
Hsü Yung-ch'ang hsien sheng chi nien chi. Taipei, 1962.
Hu Kuang-piao. *Po chu liu shih nien.* Hong Kong, 1964.
Hu Shih. *Ting Wen-chiang ti chuan chi.* Taipei, 1956.
———. *Ting Wen-chiang che kuo jen.* Taipei, 1967.
Huang-p'u chien chün shih hua. N.p., n.d.
Huang Shao-hung. *Wu shih hui i.* Hangchow, 1945. 2 vols.
Huang Yüan-yung. *Yüan-sheng i chu.* Taipei, 1962.
I chiu i chiu nien nan pei ho hui tzu liao. Peking, 1962.
I Kuo-kan. *Li fu tsung t'ung cheng shu.* Taipei, 1962.
Impey, Lawrence. "Chinese Progress in the Art of War," *China Weekly Review,* Dec. 27, 1924.
———. *The Chinese Army as a Military Force.* Tientsin, 1926.
Isaacs, Harold. *The Tragedy of the Chinese Revolution.* Stanford, Calif., 1961, 2d rev. ed.
Janowitz, Morris. *The Professional Soldier.* New York, 1960.

———. *The New Military.* New York, 1964.
Janowitz, Morris, ed. *The Military in the Political Development of New Nations.* Chicago, 1964.
Johnson, John J., ed. *The Role of the Military in Underdeveloped Countries.* Princeton, N.J., 1962.
Jowe, Peter S. "Who Sells the Guns to China's War Leaders?" *China Weekly Review,* April 18, 1925.
(Kaitei) Gendai shina jinmei roku. Tokyo, 1928.
Kann, Eduard. *The Currencies of China.* Shanghai, 1926.
Kao Pai-shih. *Ku ch'un feng lou su chi.* Taipei, 1960. 2 vols.
Kao Yin-tsu. *Chung-hua min-kuo ta shih chi.* Taipei, 1957.
Kaplan, Morton A. *System and Process in International Politics.* New York, 1957.
Ko ming wen hsien. Ed. Lo Chia-lun. Taipei, 1953–74. Vols. 1–67.
Kotenev, Anatol. *The Chinese Soldier.* Shanghai, 1933.
Krech, David, Richard S. Crutchfield, and Egerton L. Ballachey. *Individual in Society: A Textbook of Social Psychology.* New York, 1962.
Kuhn, Philip A. *Rebellion and Its Enemies in Late Imperial China.* Cambridge, Mass., 1970.
Kung Te-po. *Kung Te-po hui i lu.* Hong Kong, 1964.
———. *Yeh shih yü hua.* Taipei, 1964.
Lai Hsin-hsia. *Pei-yang chün fa shih lüeh.* Wuhan, 1957.
Li Chien-nung. *Chung-kuo chin pai nien cheng chih shih.* Taipei, 1959. 2 vols.
Li Fang-ch'en. *Chung-kuo chin tai shih.* Taipei, 1960.
Li Lieh-chün. *Li Lieh-chün chiang chün tzu chuan.* N.p., 1944.
Li Shou-k'ung. *Chung-kuo hsien tai shih.* Taipei, 1958.
Li Tsung-jen. *Li tsung ssu ling tsui chin yen chiang chi.* N.p., 1935.
Liu Chien-ch'ün. *Yin ho i wang.* Taipei, 1966.
Liu Chih. *Huang-p'u chün hsiao yü kuo-min ko ming chün.* Nanking, 1947.
Liu, F. F. *A Military History of Modern China, 1924–1949.* Princeton, N.J., 1956.
Liu Feng-han. *Hsin chien lu chün.* Taipei, 1967.
———. *Yü Yu-jen nien p'u.* Taipei, 1967.
Liu Ping-lin. *Chin tai Chung-kuo wai chai shih kao.* Peking, 1962.
Liu Shih-jen. *Chung-kuo t'ien fu wen t'i.* Shanghai, 1925.
Liu Ta-chung. *Chung-kuo kung yeh tiao ch'a pao kao.* Nanking, 1937.
Liu Yen. *Ti kuo chu i ya p'o chung-kuo shih.* Shanghai, 1927. 2 vols.
Lo Yü-t'ien. *Chün fa i wen.* Taipei, 1967.
Lo Yü-tung. *Chung-kuo li chin shih.* Shanghai, 1936.
Lu chün t'ung chi chien ming pao kao shu. Peking, 1926. 28 vols.
Lunt, Carroll. *The China Who's Who, 1925.* Shanghai, 1925.
Ma Wu. *Wo ti sheng huo shih.* Taipei, 1965.
Ma Yin-ch'u. *Ma Yin-ch'u yen chiang chi.* Shanghai, 1925. 4 vols.
Machiavelli, Niccolo. *The History of Florence.* Gloucester, Mass.

———. *The Prince*. New York, 1904.
MacNair, Harley F. *Modern Chinese History: Selected Readings*. Shanghai, 1927.
———. *China in Revolution: An Analysis of Politics and Militarism under the Republic*. Chicago, 1931.
———. *China*. Berkeley, Calif., 1951.
Mallory, Walter H. *China, A Land of Famine*. New York, 1926.
Malone, C. B., and J. B. Taylor. *The Study of Chinese Rural Economy*. N.p., 1924.
Mao Ssu-ch'eng. *Min-kuo shih wu nien i ch'ien chih Chiang Chieh-shih hsien sheng*. Hong Kong, 1965.
March, James G., ed. *Handbook of Organization*. Chicago, 1970.
Matsumoto Collection of the Press Cuttings Relating to China, The Early Twentieth Century. Microfilm, University of Michigan, Ann Arbor.
Millard, Thomas F. *China: Where It Is Today and Why*. New York, 1928.
Murphey, Rhoads. *Shanghai: Key to Modern China*. Cambridge, Mass., 1953.
Myers, Ramon H. *The Chinese Peasant Economy*. Cambridge, Mass., 1970.
Nan-hai-ying-tzu. *An-fu t'ung shih*. Peking, 1926.
Nieh, C. L. *China's Industrial Development: Its Problems and Prospect*. China Institute of Pacific Relations, 1933.
Nivison, David S., and Arthur F. Wright. *Confucianism in Action*. Stanford, Calif., 1959.
North, Robert C. *Moscow and Chinese Communism*. Stanford, Calif., 1953.
Oman, Sir Charles. *A History of the Arts of War in the Middle Ages*. London, 1924.
Organski, A. F. K. *World Politics*. New York, 1968. 2d ed.
Ou Cheng-hua. *Pei-fa hsing chün chi*. N.p., 1931.
Pai-chiao. *Yüan shih-k'ai yü Chung-hua min-kuo*. Shanghai, 1936.
Pan-ch'ih-sheng. *Feng Yü-hsiang ch'üan shu*. Shanghai, 1922.
Pan-li. *Chung-shan ch'u shih hou Chung-kuo liu shih nien ta shih chi*. Shanghai, 1928.
Pearl, Cyril. *Morris of Peking*. Sydney, Australia, 1967.
Pei-fa chan shih. Taipei, 1967. 5 vols.
Perkins, Dwight H. *Agricultural Development in China, 1368–1968*. Chicago, 1969.
Powell, John B. *My Twenty-Five Years in China*, New York, 1945.
Powell, M. C., and H. K. Tong. *Who's Who in China*. Shanghai, n.d.
Powell, Ralph L. *The Rise of the Chinese Military Power, 1895–1912*. Princeton, N.J., 1955.
The Present Condition of China. N.p., 1932.
Pye, Lucian W. *Warlord Politics*. New York, 1971.
Quigley, Harold Scott. *Chinese Politics and Foreign Powers*. New York, 1927.
Records of the Department of State Relating to Internal Affairs of China,

1910–1929. National Archives Microfilm Publications, Microfilm no. 329.
Redfield, Robert. *The Little Community* and *Peasant Society and Culture*. In one volume. Chicago, 1963.
Reinsch, Paul S. *An American Diplomat in China*. New York, 1922.
Sa Meng-wu. *Shui-hu-chuan yü Chung-kuo she hui*. Macao, 1966.
Saishin shina kanshin roku. Tokyo, 1918.
Schwartz, Benjamin I. *Chinese Communism and the Rise of Mao*. Cambridge, Mass., 1951.
Shan hou hui i kung pao. Peking, 1925. 9 vols.
Shen I-yün. *I-yün hui i*. Taipei, 1968.
Shen Yün-lung. *Li Yüan-hung p'ing chuan*. Taipei, 1963.
Sheridan, James E. *Chinese Warlord: The Career of Feng Yü-hsiang*. Stanford, Calif., 1966.
Shih nien lai ti Chung-kuo. Shanghai, 1937. 2 vols.
Shih Yang-cheng. *The Chinese Provincial Administrative System*. Shanghai, 1947.
Sonoda, Kazuki. *Hsin Chung-kuo fen sheng jen wu shih*. Shanghai, 1930.
Spanier, John. *Games Nations Play*. New York, 1972.
Su-lien yin mou wen cheng hui pien. Peiping, 1928.
Sun Huai-jen. *Chung-kuo nung ts'un hsien chuang*. Shanghai, 1933.
Sutton, Donald Sinclair. "The Rise and Decline of the Yünnan Army, 1909–1925." Ph.D. dissertation, University of Cambridge, 1970.
T'ang Leang-li. *The Inner History of the Chinese Revolution*. London, 1930.
T'ang Tsu-p'ei. *Min-kuo ming jen hsiao chuan*. Hong Kong, 1953.
T'ao Chü-yin. *Chin tai i wen*. Shanghai, 1940.
———. *Wu P'ei-fu chiang chün chuan*. Shanghai, 1941.
———. *Liu chün tzu chuan*. Shanghai, 1946.
———. *Chiang Pei-li hsien sheng chuan*. Shanghai, 1948.
———. *Tu chün t'uan chuan*. Shanghai, 1948.
———. *Pei-yang chün fa t'ung chih shih ch'i shih hua*. Peking, 1957–.
T'ao Hsi-sheng. *Chung-kuo she hui chih tu fen hsi*. Shanghai, 1929.
Tawara Teijiro, ed. *Shinmatsu minsho chugoku kanshin jinmei roku*. Tokyo, 1918.
Tawney, R. H. *Land and Labor in China*. Boston, 1966.
Taylor, A. J. P. *The Struggle for Mastery in Europe, 1848–1918*. Oxford, 1954.
Te-i-chai-chu-jen, ed. *Wu P'ei-fu chan shih*. Tokyo: Toyo Bunko Microfilm, 1960.
Teng Yün-t'e. *Chung-kuo chiu huang shih*. Shanghai, 1937.
T'ien Pu-i. *Pei-yang chün fa shih hua*. Taipei, 1964–.
Ting chi T'ien Ch'uan chün tou chi lu. N.p., n.d.
Ting Wen-chiang. *Min-kuo chün shih chin chi*. Shanghai, 1926.
To-huang. *Wu P'ei-fu chiang chün chuan*. N.p., 1935.
Tosan-sho kanshin roku, ed. by Tanabe Shujiro. University of Michigan Library, Ann Arbor.

Toynbee, Arnold J. *A Study of History.* Abridgement of vols. 1–6 by D. C. Somervell. New York, 1947.
Ts'ai-cheng-pu chin kuan wu ch'üeh shih tan pao wai chai piao. Peking, 1925.
Ts'ai P'ing-fan. *Shan-hsi ko ming chi yao.* Taipei, 1962.
Ts'ai T'ing-k'ai. *Ts'ai T'ing-k'ai tzu chuan.* Hong Kong, 1946.
Ts'ao Chü-jen. *Chiang Pai-li p'ing chuan.* Hong Kong, 1963.
Ts'ao Ju-lin. *I sheng chih hui i.* Hong Kong, 1966.
Ts'ao K'un li shih. Tientsin, 1924.
Tso Shun-sheng. *Chung-kuo hsien tai ming jen i shih.* Taipei, 1952.
Tsou Lu. *Hui ku lu.* Nanking, 1946, 2 vols.
———. *Chung-kuo kuo-min-tang shih lüeh.* Taipei, 1951.
Tung, William L. *The Political Institutions of Modern China.* The Hague, 1964.
Wang, Y. C. *Chinese Intellectuals and the West, 1872–1949.* Chapel Hill, N.C., 1966.
Wang Yün-wu. *Wo ti sheng huo p'ien tuan.* Taipei, 1952.
Weber, Max. *The Theory of Social and Economic Organization.* New York, 1966.
Wen Kung-chih. *Tsui chin san shih nien Chung-kuo chün shih shih.* Taipei, 1962. 3 vols.
Wilbur, C. Martin, and Julie Lien-ying How, eds. *Documents on Communism, Nationalism, and Soviet Advisers in China, 1918–1927.* New York, 1956.
Willoughby, Westel Woodbury. *Constitutional Government in China: Present Conditions and Prospects.* Washington, D.C., 1922.
Woodhead, H. G. W. *The Truth about the Chinese Republic.* London, 1925.
———. *Adventures in Far Eastern Journalism.* Tokyo, 1935.
Wou, Odoric Ying-kwang. "Militarism in Modern China as Exemplified in the Career of Wu P'ei-fu, 1916–1928." Ph.D. dissertation, Columbia University, 1970.
Wright, Arthur F., and Denis Twitchett, eds. *Confucian Personalities.* Stanford, Calif., 1962.
Wright, Arthur F., ed. *Confucian Persuasion.* Stanford, Calif., 1960.
Wright, Mary Clabaugh, ed. *China in Revolution: The First Phase, 1900–1913.* New Haven, 1968.
Wu Ch'iu. *Pei-yang p'ai chih ch'i yüan chi ch'i peng k'uei.* Shanghai, 1937.
Wu-ch'iu-chung-tzu. *Tang tai ming jen hsiao chuan.* N.p., n.d. 2 vols.
———. *Tuan Ch'i-jui.* Shanghai, 1921.
Wu-liao-tzu. *Ti erh tz'u Chih Feng ta chan chi.* Shanghai, 1924.
Wu P'ei-fu. Peiping, 1940.
Wu P'ei-fu chuan. Taipei, 1957.
Wu P'ei-fu hsien sheng chi. Taipei, 1960.
Wu P'ei-fu hsien sheng nien p'u. N.p., n.d.

Wu T'ieh-ch'eng. *Ssu shih nien lai chih Chung-kuo yü wo.* Taipei, 1957.
Wu T'ing-hsieh. *Ho-fei chih cheng nien p'u.* Taipei, 1962.
Yang Chia-lo. *Min-kuo ming jen t'u chien.* Nanking, 1937.
Yang Ju-mei. *Min-kuo ts'ai cheng lun.* Shanghai, 1927.
Yen Chung-p'ing et al., eds. *Chung-kuo chin tai ching chi shih t'ung chi tzu liao hsüan chi.* Peking, 1955.
Yen Hsi-shan. *Chih Chin cheng wu ch'üan shu ch'u pien.* N.p., n.d.
———. *Yen ku tzu cheng Hsi-shan shih lüeh.* Taipei, n.d.
———. *Yen tu chün cheng shu.* Shanghai, 1920.
———. *Shih hsing ping nung ho i chih shang ch'üeh.* T'aiyüan, 1947.
Yu-ming. *Chang Tso-lin wai chuan.* Hong Kong, 1965. 2 vols.
Yüan Shih-k'ai ch'ieh kuo chi. Taipei, 1954.

Index

Anfu Club, 27–28, 29, 33, 156, 160; dissolution of, 209
Anhwei-Chihli war, *see* Chihli-Anhwei war
Anhwei faction, 34, 69, 71ff, 114, 147, 214, 217; and Tuan Ch'i-jui, 32, 45, 69, 71–72, 73; and Chihli faction, 34, 136, 138, 145–48 *passim*, 209, 214; and Northwestern Frontier Army, 34, 81; members of, 45, 70, 74; and balance-of-power system, 208, 234; and Fengtien faction, 211, 215ff, 219; and KMT, 218. *See also* Chihli-Anhwei war
Anhwei province, 23, 45, 130, 164
Anti-Restoration campaign, 137f
Arms Embargo Agreement, 121ff, 124, 258n18
Association of the Provincial (Military) Governors, 16–17. *See also* Hsüchow conferences

Balance-of-power system. *See* Kaplan's balance-of-power system model
Banner armies, 11f
Boxer Rebellion, 116
Braves, 12–13
Bureau of War Participation, 21, 30

Canton, 29, 113, 124, 160
Chang Chih-tung, 13
Chang Ching-hui, 71
Chang Ching-yao, 23, 25, 69, 73, 94
Chang Fu-lai, 70
Chang Hsüeh-liang, 71, 226

Chang Hsün, 17, 52, 54, 88, 127; and Anti-Restoration campaign, 137f
Chang Huai-chih, 22ff, 28, 42
Chang Tso-hsiang, 71
Chang Tso-lin, 25f, 37, 75, 88, 115, 123, 142, 177, 226; and Fengtien faction, 24, 71, 75, 197, 211; and Tuan Ch'i-jui, 24, 24n, 31; and Manchuria, 51, 207; and foreign arms, 123n; and Chihli faction, 162; and Chekiang province, 217
Chang Tsung-ch'ang, 88, 103, 161, 166n, 223
Chao Chieh, 70
Chao T'i, 31–32, 70
Chekiang province, 23, 50, 130, 136, 138, 143; and balance-of-power system, 215, 217f
Ch'en Chia-mu, 70
Ch'en Chiung-ming, 54, 200
Ch'en Kuang-yüan, 20f, 23f, 42; and Chihli faction, 65, 70, 73
Ch'en Shu-fan, 69
Ch'en Wen-yün, 69, 73
Cheng Shih-ch'i, 69, 73
Chi Chin-shun, 71
Ch'i Hsieh-yüan, 42, 70, 223
Chia Te-yao, 69
Chiang Fang-cheng, 80, 106n
Chiang Kai-shek, 40, 43, 100f, 190, 197; and Chinese Communist party, 200; and National Revolutionary Army, 225, 238
Chiang Teng-hsüan, 223
Chiang Yen-hsin, 42

Chihli-Anhwei war, 32, 34, 136f, 138–39, 145, 147; and balance-of-power system, 208–9
Chihli faction, 32f, 49, 64n, 69, 73, 214, 217; and Ts'ao K'un, 30–31, 34, 65, 70–72; and Fengtien faction, 32, 136, 138, 148, 209, 211, 214–15, 216ff, 223f; and Anhwei faction, 34, 136, 138, 145ff, 148, 209, 214; geographical distribution of members, 45, 74, 86; organization of, 70, 72, 73, 143; finances of, 167, 169; and Kuominchün, 225f, 229f; and KMT, 226, 230f; and balance-of-power system, 227, 234
Chihli-Fengtien wars, *see* First Chihli-Fengtien war; Second Chihli-Fengtien war
Chihli province, 129f
Chin Yün-ao, 70
Chin Yün-p'eng, 42, 69, 209
Chinese Communist party (CCP), 200, 230f
Ch'ing government, 10ff, 78, 116
Chou Yin-jen, 70, 214
Ch'u-chün, 12. *See also* Hsiang-chün
Ch'ü T'ung-feng, 60, 69, 73
Communications Faction, 28
Confucianism, 96, 180, 264n1
Currency, 161ff, 171, 262n29

Eastern Expedition, 101
Emperor Kuang-hsü, 102

Feng Kuo-chang, 20, 23f, 52–53, 104; and Tuan Ch'i-jui, 11, 20f, 20n, 24, 29, 33; views on local autonomy, 20, 29, 33; peace policy, 22–23, 24; and Yüan Shih-k'ai, 38
Feng Yü-hsiang, 4, 26, 49, 88f, 142, 162, 177f, 200; and troops, 44n, 59n, 63n, 85, 95ff, 109n, 111f; and Chihli faction, 49, 70, 239; ideology of, 56; and Soviet Union, 97, 110n, 112, 125, 223ff, 259n34; and Kuominchün, 98, 125, 222–23, 239; and KMT, 223
Fengtien faction, 24, 69, 75, 122f, 145f, 148, 169, 177; and Chihli faction, 32, 136, 138, 148, 211, 215, 217f, 223f; members of, 45, 71, 74f, 104f, 143; organization of, 71, 75, 143, 145; and Japan, 123; and KMT, 147ff, 211, 215, 218, 225f, 230f; and Anhwei faction, 209, 211, 215, 218f; and balance-of-power system, 222, 229, 234; Kuominchün, 222–23, 224ff, 230
Fengtien-Kuominchün war, 137, 140, 224, 227, 229
Fengtien province, 23
First Chihli-Fengtien war, 127, 137ff, 145, 147, 211, 217; cost of, 168; number of troops, 213; balance-of-power system and, 227
France, 121
Fu Liang-tso, 19, 21
Fukien province, 94f, 164, 214

Great Britain, 122, 157
Green Standards, 11–12

Han Fu-ch'ü, 98, 103
Hanyang arsenal, 118, 120
Ho Feng-lin, 42, 69, 143
Honan province, 31f, 118, 125, 129f, 136, 164, 193; revolt of, 213
Hsiang-chün, 12, 151
Hsiao-chan, 13, 14
Hsiao Yao-nan, 70
Hsü Lan-chou, 51
Hsü Shih-ch'ang, 29
Hsü Shu-cheng, 25, 31, 64, 69; and Anfu Club, 27; and Northwestern Frontier Army, 31
Hsüchow conferences, 17, 252n4
Hu Ching-i, 70, 223
Huai-chün, 12, 45
Huang Shao-hung, 47–48
Hunan campaign, 18–19, 20, 21, 135, 137f, 168; and Wu P'ei-fu, 207–8
Hunan province, 25, 28, 32, 125, 130, 161; fighting in, 18–19, 22, 25, 94f, 138; neutrality of, 50, 54; and provincial constitutionalism, 102n; and balance-of-power system, 208; and KMT, 226
Hupeh province, 21f, 32, 130, 136, 164; and Hanyang arsenal, 118, 120

Japan, 30, 107, 113, 116, 121, 123; and loans, 27, 156, 262n17; and Sino-

Index

Japanese Mutual Defense Pact, 27, 30, 121; and Tuan Ch'i-jui, 27, 30, 33, 121, 123, 156, 168; and first Sino-Japanese War, 116; as arms supplier, 120–21, 122f

Kan Ch'ao-hsi, 71
Kansu province, 23, 164
Kaplan's balance-of-power system model, 204, 214f, 264n6; behavioral rules of, 204–5; equilibrium of, 204, 220, 226, 238; actors in, 206, 208, 217–22 *passim*, 228f, 230–36 *passim*; stability and, 206, 233f; information and, 220, 229; "balancing," 235f
Kiangsi province, 21, 24, 32, 130, 164, 217
Kiangsu province, 21, 32, 50–51, 53, 130, 136, 138, 153; arsenal in, 24, 118; Chekiang province and, 217
KMT (Kuomintang), 2, 3, 9n, 43, 86, 101, 112, 142, 146, 148, 178; role in south, 4, 53f, 146, 177; ideology of, 56, 58–59, 99, 102, 115, 231, 255n17; military training of, 98–99, 100, 112ff, 198, 201, 257n50; organization of, 99f, 102, 174f, 190, 219, 231, 255n15; and Soviet Union, 112, 124f, 175f, 198f, 257n44, 259n32; finances of, 160–61, 169, 174n, 175–76, 197; and Chinese Communist party, 200; and balance-of-power system, 208, 218, 221f, 226, 230ff, 234, 237; and Fengtien faction, 211, 215, 218, 225, 228; and Anhwei faction, 218; and Kuominchün, 223, 225; and Chihli faction, 225f, 230; and nationalism, 231–32; *See also* Northern Expedition; Sun Yat-sen; Whampoa Military Academy
Kuan yü, 153f
Kung Pang-to, 70
Kuo Sung-lin, 163, 224, 227, 229
Kuominchün, 98, 115, 125, 169; and Fengtien faction, 137, 140, 222–23, 225ff; and KMT, 223, 225; and Chihli faction, 225f; and Soviet Union, 125, 257n38, 257n40, 259n34; and balance-of-power system, 222, 229, 234
Kwangsi province, 47f, 94, 125, 130– 31, 132, 193; opium and, 164–65; gambling and, 165–66
Kwangtung province, 118, 125, 130, 132, 164ff; attacks on, 48, 94f
Kweichow province, 125, 131f, 193

Li Ch'ang-t'ai, 42
Li Chi-ch'en, 201
Li Chin-ts'ai, 69
Li Ching-lin, 71, 74
Li Hou-chi, 42, 69, 73
Li Hung-chang, 12, 14
Li Shun, 16f, 20, 23, 42; and Chihli faction, 64, 70, 73; and Tuan Ch'i-jui, 21, 24
Li Tsung-jen, 48, 55, 166n1, 201
Li Yüan-hung, 16f, 213f
Liang Shih-i, 28, 209f
Liu Cheng-huan, 200
Liu En-ko, 27
Liu Hsün, 69, 73
Liu Yü-ch'un, 70, 140
Loyang clique, 214
Loyang military training program, 111, 218
Lu Chien-chang, 26, 188n
Lu Chin, 70
Lu Ching-shan, 70
Lu Hsiang-t'ing, 70
Lu Jung-t'ing, 48, 53, 88
Lu Yung-hsiang, 42, 69, 73, 143

Ma Liang, 69, 73
Manchuria, 51–52, 105, 130, 158, 183n, 193f; Japan and, 119, 123; currency in, 162f, 171
Maritime Customs, 153f, 259n25
Meng En-yüan, 51
Militarists: definition of, 1n; national unity and, 18, 191f, 206, 233; marriage-family ties between, 36ff, 39, 182, 253n3; teacher-student ties between, 39f; school ties between, 40ff, 43; friendship ties between, 41–42, 46, 59–60, 63–64, 68; loyalty and, 41, 61, 63, 183; geographic ties between, 44, 44n, 44–46, 85–86; mercenary mentality of, 87, 93, 114f; upward mobility and, 87, 88–89, 89n, 90; corruption among, 92f, 92n, 184, 255n2; sources of incomes of,

151n, 151–56 *passim*, 163–66 *passim*, 170–71, 254n1, 261n12; domestic borrowing and, 159f, 262n26; economic policies of, 172–73, 164, 177; values and, 180–81. *See also individual militarists by name*
Military factions: structure of, 61–64; organization of, 65, 67; ties between members of, 67–71 *passim*; geographic structure of, 143–47 *passim*; and balance-of-power system, 208–32 *passim*. *See also individual factions by name*
Military recruiting, 77ff, 80, 83f, 85–86; relationship to poverty, 78–79, 80, 82, 87; "average" recruit, 79–80
Military training, 41–42, 91, 102ff, 105f, 109ff; and Japan, 30, 107, 113; schools of, 41–42, 89, 102–7 *passim*, 111, 190, 218, 256n33; and officers, 89, 103f, 108–9, 110, 256n13, 256n31; discipline of, 91, 95, 254n17; indoctrination and, 96f; KMT and, 98–99, 112–13. *See also* Loyang military training program; Paoting Military Academy; Peiyang Military Academy

Nanking conference, 186
National Defense Army, 30. *See also* Northwestern Frontier Army
Nationalist Revolutionary Army, 225, 238
Nanyang Army, 13
Newly Established Army. *See* Peiyang Army
Ni Tz'u-ch'ung, 22, 25, 69, 73
Northern Expedition, 9n, 56, 75, 122, 125, 137–46 *passim*, 201, 227f, 238; and troops, 115, 200; cost of, 169; and KMT finances; 197–98; and Soviet advisers, 199n
Northwestern Frontier Army, 31f, 34, 81, 209; and Tuan Ch'i-jui, 30, 32, 52; and Hsü Shu-cheng, 31
Northwestern Frontier Bureau, 32

Opium, 92, 92n, 163; as source of military revenue, 151, 163ff

Pao Kuei-ch'ing, 42, 71

Paoting conference, 32
Paoting Military Academy, 43, 102, 105–6, 106n, 109, 256n24
Peiyang Army, 13, 16, 22, 42, 44, 82, 106, 115; Yüan Shih-k'ai and, 10–11, 13ff, 67; organization of, 11, 14, 16, 19, 66; Tuan Ch'i-jui and, 18, 34f, 52, 64, 67
Peiyang Military Academy, 42–43. *See also* Paoting Military Academy
Peking government, 3, 7, 13–18 *passim*, 31, 52, 191, 217; finances of, 151f, 153–54, 155ff, 159f, 167f, 209; and Japan, 156
Peking–Hankow Railway, 18, 21f, 130, 165; Kuominchün and, 222, 224, 260n46
Peking-Tientsin "Pivot," 147, 148
P'eng Shou-hsin, 70
Pi Kuei-fang, 51
Ping ch'ai, 166
Poverty, 82, 87, 254n7; military recruiting and, 78ff
Provincial constitutionalism, 192n, 221
Provincial military structure, 48–50

Railways, 128ff, 224, 260n46; use of, by militarists, 128, 165, 171. *See also* Peking–Hankow Railway
Recruiting, *see* Military recruiting
Research faction, 28

Second Chihli-Fengtien war, 118, 137ff, 140, 147, 227
Second Revolution, 15, 78, 151
Self-Strengthening Army, 13
Shanghai conference, 29
Shansi province, 23, 50, 84, 115, 120, 129f, 177, 193f; and Yen Hsi-shan, 56, 95f, 111; balance-of-power system and, 208; and KMT, 225
Shantung province, 23, 83, 118, 129, 143, 162, 193, number of soldiers, 83, 83n; railways in, 130
Shen Hung-ying, 48
Shensi province, 23, 125, 132, 164
Shih Yu-san, 98
Sino-Japanese Mutual Defense Pact, 27, 30, 121. *See also* Japan
Soviet Union, 97, 112, 121, 124f; and

Index

Feng Yü-hsiang, 97, 110n, 112, 125, 223, 259n34; and KMT, 112f, 124f, 175f, 198, 199n, 259n27, 259n32
Suiyuan, 130, 213
Sun Ch'uan-fang, 70, 123, 142, 197, 200, 214, 217; and KMT, 114, 138, 190, 225, 230f; and Chihli faction, 224
Sun Lieh-ch'eng, 71
Sun Yao, 70, 223
Sun Yat-sen, 124, 154, 166; KMT organization and, 56, 98; and Three People's Principles, 96, 98; and Fengtien faction, 211; and Northern Expedition, 215, 217
Systems theory, 6f. See also Kaplan's balance-of-power system model
Szechwan, 54, 94–95, 118, 125, 131f, 133n, 135, 193; recruiting in, 83–84; number of wars in, 134n; finances of, 153, 164, 169, 169n; provincial constitutionalism and, 221; and KMT, 226

T'ai-p'ing Rebellion, 12
T'an k'uan, 166
T'an Yen-k'ai, 19
Tang Yu-lin, 71
T'ang Chi-yao, 37, 207
T'ang Shao-yi, 17
Third Division (Chihli faction), 25, 28, 38, 41, 95. See also Hunan campaign; Wu P'ei-fu
T'ien Chung-yü, 43, 65, 70
Tientsin conference, 22, 86
Tientsin-Paoting clique, 214
Transportation system, 128ff, 131; number of railways, 128ff; number of roads, 129, 260n41; number of boats, 131n. See also Peking–Hankow Railway; Railways
Ts'ai Ch'eng-hsün, 43, 70
Ts'ao Ju-lin, 28
Ts'ao Jui, 70
Ts'ao K'un, 3, 22f, 26, 41, 60, 64, 88; and Hunan campaign, 21, 25, 28, 145; and Tuan Ch'i-jui, 29–30; and Chihli faction, 30–31, 34, 42, 65, 70, 72, 214, 229
Ts'ao Shih-chieh, 70
Ts'ao Yin, 70, 211

Tseng Kuo-fang, 12
Tseng Yun-p'ei, 27
Tso Tsung-t'ang, 12
Tuan Chieh-kuei, 43, 69
Tuan Ch'i-jui, 20–32 *passim*, 38, 52, 73, 104, 106, 138, 143, 168; and Feng Kuo-chang, 11, 20, 20n, 24, 29, 33; and Li Shun, 16f, 24; and Hunan campaign, 18–19, 135, 168, 207–8; and Peiyang Army, 18–19, 34f, 52, 64, 67; and Japan, 27, 30, 33, 121, 123, 156, 168; and Anhwei faction, 32, 45, 69, 71–72, 73; and national unity, 233
Tung Cheng-kuo, 70

Wang Chan-yüan, 20f, 23n, 43, 88; and Chihli faction, 33, 65, 70, 73
Wang Ch'eng-ping, 70
Wang Chin-ching, 43
Wang Huai-ch'ing, 43, 70, 214
Wang I-t'ang, 27f
Wang Ju-ch'in, 70
Wang Ju-hsien, 21, 43
Wang Shih-chen, 24f, 43
Wang T'ing-cheng, 43
Wang Wei-ch'eng, 70
Wang Yung-ch'üan, 69
Warlord. See Militarists
War Participation Army, see Northwestern Frontier Army
War Participation Bureau, 21, 30
War statistics: number of troops mobilized, 137; size of war zones, 137; casualties, 138, 140–41; cost of wars, 168–69
Weapons, 116–17, 118ff, 126f, 141–42; number of, 117, 119; arsenals, 118ff, 122f, 125, 258n15; foreign arms, 120n, 120–26 *passim*; and coastal provinces, 125f; and inner provinces, 131–32, 133; arms race and, 135–36
Wei Tsung-han, 69, 73
Whampoa Military Academy, 40, 43f, 98ff, 101, 114, 174; recruiting in, 86; training, 98n, 112–13
Wu Chün-sheng, 71
Wu Kuang-hsin, 19, 21, 69
Wu P'ei-fu, 55, 60, 89, 104, 111, 115, 140, 142, 165, 182n; and Hunan

campaign, 25, 28, 32, 95, 207; and Ts'ao K'un, 26, 41, 60; and Tuan Ch'i-jui, 30f, 47n; and Chihli faction, 32, 34, 70, 210, 217; and Fengtien, 229; and Kuominchün, 229. *See also* Hunan campaign; Third Division
Wu Ping-hsiang, 69
Wu-wei-chün, 14

Yang Ch'ing-ch'eng, 70
Yang Hsi-min, 200
Yang Shan-teh, 43
Yang Sheng, 135
Yang Yü-t'ing, 71, 224
Yen Chih-t'ang, 70
Yen Hsi-shan, 4, 55f, 177, 201; and military training, 95, 97, 111
Yen Hsiang-wen, 70
Yunnan province, 21, 48, 94–95, 125, 132, 193; opium in, 92, 164
Yüan Shih-k'ai, 14, 38, 40, 92, 151, 163; and Peiyang Army, 10–11, 13ff, 67, 151; and national unity, 15, 33